THE APOSTOLIC-PROPHETIC MANDATE

Bringing the Kingdom of God to Your Sphere of Influence.

DR. VOLKER KRÜGER
DORINE M. KRÜGER

Copyright © 2025 Volker Krüger and Dorine M. Krüger
All Rights Reserved
No part of this publication may be reproduced or distributed in any form or by any means without the prior permission of the author and/or publisher.

Kemp House
152 -160 City Road
London, EC1V 2NX
United Kingdom

ISBN: 978-1-917451-60-4

Published by Action Wealth Publishing and Volker & Dorine M. Krüger

Printed in the United Kingdom

Scripture quotations taken from The Holy Bible, New International Version® NIV® Copyright © 1973, 1978, 1984, 2011 by Biblica, Inc.® Used with permission. All rights reserved worldwide.

Scripture taken from the New King James Version®. Copyright © 1982 by Thomas Nelson. Used by permission. All rights reserved.

Scripture quotations are from the ESV® Bible (The Holy Bible, English Standard Version®), copyright © 2001 by Crossway Bibles, a publishing ministry of Good News Publishers. Used by permission. All rights reserved.

Although the author and publisher have made every effort to ensure the accuracy and completeness of information contained in this book, we assume no responsibility for errors, inaccuracies, omissions, or any inconsistency herein. Any slights on people, places, or organisations are unintentional. The material in this book is provided for educational purposes only. No responsibility for loss occasioned to any person or corporate body acting or refraining to act as a result of reading material in this book can be accepted by the author or publisher.

God is good. Always.

TABLE OF CONTENTS

PROLOGUE _____ 13
ACKNOWLEDGMENTS _____ 15
CHAPTER ONE: SALVATION FOUND US LOST AND IN NEED _____ 17
    Salvation Found Us _____ 20
    Background–The Core of Christian Faith in Short and Sweet _____ 22
    How Do You NOT Become a Born-Again Christian? 27
    The Typological Framework: The Bronze Serpent (Numbers 21:4-9) _____ 27
    The Lifting Up of the Son of Man _____ 28
    The Offer and the Condition: "Whoever Believes" __ 28
    Rejection of Universal Reconciliation _____ 29
    Belief is Essential, Not Optional _____ 30
    Perishing is a Real Possibility _____ 30
    The Typological Precedent _____ 31
    The Heart of the Gospel _____ 31
    Discipleship and Purpose _____ 32
    Transformed and Renewed _____ 34
    Living Out Salvation _____ 36
    Salvation For All and the Role of Evangelism _____ 42

Conclusion _____ 45
CHAPTER TWO: FOUNDATIONAL THEOLOGY IN CHURCH HISTORY _____ 47
The Early Church Fathers and Theological Foundations _____ 49
The Ecumenical Councils and Doctrinal Formulation 51
The Enlightenment and Challenges to Foundational Theology _____ 53
Modern Theological Movements and Their Impact _ 54
Contemporary Issues in Foundational Theology ____ 57
The Importance of Studying Foundational Theology 59
Conclusion _____ 61
CHAPTER THREE: HOMILETICS: BIBLE EXEGESIS AND APPLICATION _____ 63
Principles of Bible Exegesis _____ 64
Principles of Applying Biblical Truths _____ 67
Overemphasising Certain Doctrines or Cherry-Picking Verses _____ 69
Balancing the Tension Between Context and Application _____ 71
The Role of the Holy Spirit in Bible Study and Understanding _____ 73
Continuing Growth in Biblical Understanding _____ 76
Conclusion _____ 78
CHAPTER FOUR: HERMENEUTICS - BIBLE INTERPRETATION AND APPLICATION _____ 79
Contextual Interpretation _____ 80

Tools For Biblical Interpretation _____ 81
Approaches to Biblical Interpretation _____ 83
Applying Hermeneutical Principles _____ 85
Challenges in Biblical Interpretation _____ 87
Hermeneutics and the Community of Believers ____ 89
CHAPTER FIVE: ECCLESIOLOGY: THE 5-FOLD
MINISTRY _____ 92
Fold 1: Apostles _____ 93
Biblical Foundation of Apostleship _____ 93
The Apostolic Anointing and Gifting _____ 95
Relationship Between the Apostolic And Prophetic _ 98
New Apostolic Movement Terminology _____ 102
Apostleship and Missions _____ 104
Apostles' Relationship with Pastors, Teachers,
    Prophets, and Evangelists _____ 107
Conclusion _____ 108
Fold 2: Prophets _____ 109
Prophetic Ministry in the Life of the Church _____ 109
Prophetic Books and Major Prophets _____ 111
Functions and Responsibilities of Prophets _____ 116
Gifts of the Spirit in Prophetic Ministry _____ 118
Prophetic Ministry in the Modern Church _____ 120
Challenges and Controversies in Prophetic Ministry 122
Conclusion _____ 124
Fold 3: Evangelists _____ 125
Characteristics and Qualities of an Evangelist _____ 125

The Supernatural Nature of the Gospel _____ 128
Outreach and Evangelism Practicum _____ 130
The Impact of Evangelism _____ 132
Training and Equipping Evangelists _____ 135
Support and Collaboration Within the 5-Fold Ministry _____ 137
Fold 4: Pastors _____ 139
Shepherd's Heart and Love for the Flock _____ 139
The Ministry of a Pastor _____ 142
Challenges and Opportunities for Pastoral Ministry 145
Opportunities in Pastoral Ministry _____ 150
Synergy Between Pastors and Other Ministry Gifts 153
The Significance of Pastors in Church and Community _____ 156
Mentoring and Apprenticeship for Aspiring Pastors 158
Fold 5: Teachers _____ 161
Teaching as a Spiritual Gift _____ 161
Preparing and Delivering Teachings _____ 163
Teaching Methods and Approaches _____ 165
Teachers As Life-long Learners _____ 168
The Hub Model: A Proposal _____ 170
The Five-Fold Coordinated Efforts to Edify the Church _____ 174
Purpose and Function of the Five-Fold Ministry ___ 178
The Maturity and Character Required to Operate in the Five-Fold Offices _____ 180

Summary Table: A Practical Reference for the Five-Fold Ministry ___ 188
CHAPTER SIX: WOMEN CALLED AND COMMISSIONED ___ 191
The Biblical Perspective ___ 192
Historical Perspectives on Women in Ministry ___ 193
Women in Theological Education ___ 196
Women's Contemporary Expressions of Apostolic Ministry ___ 198
Addressing Barriers Faced by Women Apostles ___ 200
Partnering in Apostolic Ministry: Men and Women Together ___ 203
Advancing Women in Apostolic Ministry ___ 205
Women in Missions and Global Outreach ___ 208
Celebrating Women's Apostles ___ 210
Conclusion ___ 211
CHAPTER SEVEN: PNEUMATOLOGY: THE HOLY SPIRIT ___ 214
The Personhood of the Holy Spirit ___ 215
The Nature, Role, and Work of the Holy Spirit ___ 216
The Holy Spirit and the Church ___ 224
The Promise of the Holy Spirit: Baptism Into The Spirit ___ 227
Primary Indicators of the Holy Spirit Infilling ___ 229
The Holy Spirit and Spiritual Transformation ___ 232
Worship And Prayer in the Holy Spirit ___ 235

- Gifts and Fruit of the Spirit 237
- Global Perspectives on the Work of the Holy Spirit 241
- Conclusion 244

CHAPTER EIGHT: PRACTICAL THEOLOGY 246
- Laying On of Hands 246
- Ordination and Commission 248
- Healing and Prayer Ministry 250
- Impartation of Spiritual Gifts 252
- Worship and Community through the Laying on of Hands 254
- Ethical Considerations and Pastoral Guidelines in the Laying on of Hands 256
- Understanding Demonic Oppression 262
- Conclusion 273

CHAPTER NINE: LEADERSHIP 275
- Pastoral Leadership 278
- Servant Leadership 280
- Organizational Leadership 282
- Women in Leadership and Church Governance 285
- Spiritual Leadership 287
- The Apostolic Leadership Pattern of Christian Initiation 289
- Ethical Leadership 292
- Missional Leadership 294
- Conclusion 297

CHAPTER TEN: KINGDOM THEOLOGY IDENTITY 299
- Understanding the Kingdom of God 300

Kingdom Mission and Purpose 301
Kingdom Witness and Evangelism 303
The Identity of Kingdom Citizens 304
Kingdom Community and Unity 308
Kingdom Authority and Power 309
Living Kingdom Values 311
Kingdom Ethics and Social Justice 314
Kingdom Living in Everyday Life 315
Kingdom Hope and Future 317
Kingdom Discipleship 318
Conclusion 320

CHAPTER ELEVEN: IS CHRISTIANITY MOVING TOWARDS A NEW ERA? 322
Historical Perspectives 323
Contemporary Cultural Context 324
Emerging Theology and Doctrine 326
Worship and Spirituality 328
Ecumenical and Interfaith Relations 329
Faith and Technology 331
Conclusion 334

APOSTOLIC BENEDICTION 337
ABOUT THE AUTHORS 339

LIST OF FIGURES

Figure 01: The Apostolic–Prophetic Hub Model ___ 172

Table No.1: Five-Fold Ministry Summary _____ 189

Figure 02: The Top-Down Leadership Hierarchy Approach _____ 276

Figure 03: The Reverse Leadership Hierarchy Approach _____ 278

PROLOGUE

THERE IS A NEW UNDERSTANDING within the Pentecostal charismatic tradition of the apostolic prophetic role as a concept for deploying effective leadership. The so-called New Apostolic Reformation movement presents an alternative approach within contemporary Christianity, one that is noticeably distinct from the traditional leadership models in Protestantism, Roman Catholicism, and the evangelical traditions.

The leadership model of this movement is a church governance concept distinct from Episcopal, Presbyterian, and Congregational polity, representing a genuine approach that is arguably suitable for practical use.

This book argues that churches and Christian ministries need effective leadership models which are theologically grounded in the doctrine of the offices of apostle and prophet, as described in the New Testament. Its fundamental concept is the understanding that the offices of church governance, which have fallen into disuse, as well as the offices of the apostle and the five-fold ministry, are being restored in the church today.

The dominant Christian church polities and denominations are being challenged by a revised 'Apostolic–Prophetic Hub' model, which contrasts the traditional denominational landscape with a radical reconstruction.

Dr. Volker Krüger, M.A. in Theology

ACKNOWLEDGMENTS

IN ACKNOWLEDGMENT, I, Dorine Krüger, would like to accord much respect, heartfelt thanks, and honour to my wonderful husband, Dr Volker Krüger, for allowing me the freedom to contribute my flavour of thoughts to this spiritually inspired life transformational document.

Not only is he the vision bearer of the Apostolic Hub, but he has also invested much effort, time and knowledge, as witnessed, in his researched and published works over the years, out of which our very own book, *The Apostolic Mandate - Bringing the Kingdom of God to Your Sphere of Influence,* has been born.

Without all of his remarkable input, this would have been impossible. Nevertheless, we give the overall honour and glory to our dear Father Almighty God.

I, Volker Krüger, wish to sincerely acknowledge the great deal of excellent writing that my wonderful wife, Dorine, has done. I admire your profound spiritual understanding of the Kingdom of God, your prophetic perspective, and your ability to craft words, form sentences, and convey passion through effective communication.

This joint journey in writing this book has been awesome, and your inspiration and wisdom have been outstanding. Your unique insights and expertise have enormously assisted in this theological endeavour.

CHAPTER ONE

SALVATION FOUND US LOST

AND IN NEED

THE CHRISTIAN FAITH IS far more than a set of doctrines. It is a divine call to a life that is radically transformed, one that reflects the very heart of God. This transformation is not private or passive. It is active and visible, radiating outward into our homes, communities, workplaces, and every space we occupy.

We have come to understand that one of the core expressions of this life in Christ is what Scripture and history reveal as the Apostolic Mandate. It is not a man-made concept; it is a divine commission anchored in the very heartbeat of the Gospel. As a couple, we have walked with this mandate, not just as a theological theory, but as a living truth. It compels us to bring the influence of God's Kingdom into every sphere we touch.

In this book, *The Apostolic-Prophetic Mandate: Bringing the Kingdom of God to Your Sphere of Influence*, we unveil what the Lord has revealed to us through His Word, our lives, and the faithful examples set before us. This message is deeply personal. It is the story of how salvation found us when we were lost, broken, and in desperate need. Furthermore, it is also a teaching and a call to those who have received grace to now carry the presence, power, and purpose of the Kingdom into the world around them.

The Apostolic Mandate began not with us, but with the Lord Jesus Christ Himself. Before ascending into heaven, He commissioned His apostles with a clear instruction:

"Therefore, go and make disciples of all nations, baptising them in the name of the Father and of the Son and the Holy Spirit, and teaching them to obey everything I have commanded you..." (Matthew 28:19-20, NIV)

This command was not limited to preaching sermons or planting churches. It included confronting darkness, as we see in 1 John 3:8:

"The reason the Son of God appeared was to destroy the devil's work." (1 John 3:8, NIV)

Jesus called His followers to heal the sick, raise the broken, love the outcast, and bring justice to the oppressed. These are not optional acts of kindness; they are evidence of the Kingdom breaking in.

As we reflected on this mandate in our own lives, we began asking serious questions:

- ⌘ What does it mean to bring the Kingdom of God into our marriage? Into our parenting? Into the boardroom, the marketplace, and the streets of our communities?

- ⌘ How do we love with conviction, lead with humility, and serve with power?

- ⌘ How do we make our faith visible not only in pulpits and pews, but in policies, products, and relationships?

These questions led us deep into the New Testament, into the writings of the early Church fathers, and the counsel of modern theologians. However, more than that, they led us into the presence of God, where He began to show us that every believer has a sphere of influence and is called to steward that sphere with Kingdom authority.

Throughout this book, we will share stories of individuals and communities who have done just that. We will explore how the Apostolic Mandate is not reserved for pastors or prophets; it is the inheritance of every child of God.

We write this not from a distance, but from experience. We have lived through seasons of loss, redemption, realignment, and radical obedience. Our testimony is not one of perfection, but of grace that found us, changed us, and commissioned us.

This is not just a book to be read; it is a book to be experienced. It is a call to be answered. It is our prayer that as you read, the Holy Spirit will stir something deep within you: a hunger to see the Kingdom of God break into every part of your life.

Whether you are standing behind a pulpit or a shop counter, whether your influence is global or centred around your household, you are called. You are chosen and you are sent.

Welcome to this sacred conversation.

Salvation Found Us

We open up our hearts to share the personal encounters that led us to salvation through Jesus Christ. Though we come from different parts of the world and our upbringings were worlds apart, the same life-altering reality unites us. Jesus Christ found us when we were lost and in need of Him.

I, Volker Krüger, was born and raised in Germany in a warm and devout Christian home. My parents were faithful and committed believers who passed down their love for the Kingdom of God and the church to me. I grew up actively involved in church life and had a strong grasp of how ministry operated. Yet, despite the rich environment, I later realised that something vital was missing. We had reverence for God, but we lacked a personal relationship with the Holy Spirit.

On the other hand, I, Dorine Kruger, grew up in Uganda in a household that identified as Christian. We attended church services regularly, especially on Sundays, but our spiritual life did not extend beyond routine attendance. Deep within me, I felt a longing, a persistent hunger to know the One we sang about and prayed to. At the age of twelve, that longing led me to a Pentecostal church where I encountered Jesus for the first time. That moment awakened something in me. It filled my heart with clarity and purpose, igniting a desire to know God deeply and walk with Him daily.

We both look back on those teenage years as the sacred time when salvation found us. I, Volker, vividly recall attending a rally organised by Canadian missionaries. It was there that the conviction of the Holy Spirit rested on me, and I knew it was time to surrender my life to Christ.

For me, Dorine, it was during a church service led by my older sister. In that atmosphere of worship and the Word, I felt the joy and assurance of embracing Jesus as Lord over my life.

Our decision to be baptised followed soon after. Baptism became our public testimony of what had taken place within. For me, Volker, the opportunity to be baptised by full immersion was both logical and spiritual. It was a declaration that I had entered into a new life. My desire to follow Christ found meaning in that act of obedience. For me, Dorine, the moment came when my parents also gave their lives to Christ. Being baptised then felt like a seal of my earlier commitment, not just to Jesus, but to the path of lifelong discipleship.

Our experiences with the Holy Spirit have been pivotal. They mark the shift from belief to empowerment. There came a time in my life, Volker, when I became discontent with a powerless Christian walk. I longed for what I read in the book of Acts: miracles, boldness, encounters with the living God. Then one day, while driving and listening to worship music, the presence of the Holy Spirit overwhelmed me. It felt like electricity flowing through my body. I suddenly gained clarity about who the Holy Spirit is and how deeply involved He wants to be in my life.

My encounter, as Dorine, came in a season of intense prayer. I yearned for a deeper relationship with God, one that went beyond the rituals of faith. As I pressed into His presence, I experienced the infilling of the Holy Spirit. I began to speak in tongues and felt an undeniable surge of power and joy. That experience transformed my approach to prayer, worship, and ministry.

Together, we now see that salvation was only the beginning. There is so much more in Christ. We believe discipleship must include transformation by the Holy Spirit, not just intellectual assent or outward rituals. Too often, mainstream churches stop at conversion. However, the Bible calls us to a life of greater purpose, obedience, and spiritual authority. That can only happen when the Holy Spirit is allowed to baptise, fill, and lead us.

This is why we share our testimonies. Not to point to ourselves, but to glorify God and demonstrate the fullness of salvation. We aim to demonstrate the profound impact of Christ on lives and the urgent need for the world to recognise this truth.

As you read our stories, we encourage you to reflect on your faith. Have you encountered Jesus personally? Has the Holy Spirit transformed your heart? Are you walking in your purpose and calling? We believe the answers to these questions are not only important, but eternal.

Let us invite you to go deeper. To rediscover the meaning of salvation. To live it out fully. And to be stirred by a burden for evangelism, knowing that someone else is waiting for the good news that changed your life and ours.

Background–The Core of Christian Faith in Short and Sweet

God is, has always been, and will always be God. This unchanging truth is foundational to our faith. According to Scripture, there came a time when one of the archangels, Lucifer, desired to be like God and to exalt himself above the Most High. Though he once held a significant position, likely connected to worship in the third heaven, his pride led to rebellion. As a result, God cast him down along with a third of the angels who had joined his cause.

When Satan and his followers were expelled from heaven, they were thrown down to the earth. In time, God chose to bring divine order to the chaos that had filled the earth. Genesis 1:2 describes it as *"formless and empty"* in Hebrew, *tohu wa-bohu*. Amid this disorder, God created man in His image, a masterpiece that reflected His beauty and authority. This act of creation infuriated Satan, who responded by deceiving Adam and Eve in the Garden of Eden.

Through deception, Adam and Eve disobeyed God, and sin entered the world. Their fall resulted in a severed relationship between God and man. Because God is holy and cannot coexist with sin, humanity was banished from Eden and fell under a curse.

From that moment, mankind began striving in their strength, even attempting to build a tower that reached the heavens. God responded by confusing their language, halting their unified rebellion. This event underscores the power of the spoken word and God's sovereignty over human ambition.

Meanwhile, Satan devised another plan. He sought to corrupt human DNA by sending fallen angels to cohabit with women, resulting in a race of giants, such as Goliath. In response, God initiated a cleansing through Noah and the flood, preserving righteousness and restarting His plan.

Later, God chose to reveal His heart by pursuing a covenant relationship with mankind. He called Abraham, establishing him as the father of many nations. From Abraham, the nation of Israel was born a people whom God called His own and referred to as His bride. Because of this special relationship, Satan directed his hatred toward Israel (1 Chronicles 21).

Israel eventually found itself in slavery in Egypt for over 430 years. God then raised Moses to lead His people out of captivity and into the land He had promised. Through signs and wonders, God delivered Israel, led them through the wilderness, and gave them laws to guide their relationship with Him and with each other.

Upon reaching the Promised Land, it was divided among the twelve tribes. Although God desired to rule His people directly, they demanded a king, wanting to resemble the nations around them. During the period of the kings, disobedience to God's commands was frequent. To correct and guide them, God sent prophets. A few individuals, such as judges, kings, and prophets, were anointed with the Holy Spirit, which empowered them for their divine assignments.

Despite these interventions, the relationship between God and man continued to decline, leading to the exile and scattering of the Israelites. Nevertheless, even in this, God's plan of redemption was already unfolding. During the time of the kings, He foretold the coming of the Messiah who would fulfil the law and restore holiness.

After a period of divine silence lasting more than 400 years, the angelic hosts announced the birth of Jesus Christ. At the age of thirty, He was baptised and filled with the Holy Spirit, marking the beginning of His public ministry. During the next three and a half years, Jesus revealed the nature and principles of God's Kingdom.

Jesus, fully God and fully man, was born of Mary and conceived by the Holy Spirit. His death on the cross was the ultimate fulfilment of the law. As the perfect sacrifice, He became the Lamb of God, and through His atonement, the power of sin and the works of the devil were destroyed.

Scripture reveals that after His death, Jesus descended into Hades, took back the keys of death and authority from Satan, and returned in glory to sit at the right hand of the Father. As He promised, the Holy Spirit was poured out on the day of Pentecost, so that every believer could walk in the same authority and power that Jesus demonstrated.

The Holy Spirit is the One who renews our dead spirit and makes us alive in Christ. Jesus said:

"Very truly I tell you, no one can see the kingdom of God unless they are born again." (John 3:3, NIV)

When we receive Christ, we are born again, and the Spirit of God dwells within us.

We see two distinct workings of the Holy Spirit in the life of a believer. First, the Holy Spirit dwells within us to produce the character, or fruit, of the Spirit. Galatians 5:22-23 says:

"But the fruit of the Spirit is love, joy, peace, forbearance, kindness, goodness, faithfulness, gentleness and self-control." (Galatians 5:22-23, NIV)

Romans 8:9 adds:

"If anyone does not have the Spirit of Christ, they do not belong to Christ." (Romans 8:9, NIV)

The indwelling Spirit leads us to become more like Christ over time. This transformation is evidence of a sanctified life.

Secondly, the Holy Spirit comes upon us for power, the gifts of the Spirit. Acts 1:8 declares:

"But you will receive power when the Holy Spirit comes on you; and you will be my witnesses..." (Acts 1:8, NIV)

According to 1 Corinthians 12, the gifts of the Spirit include prophecy, healing, speaking in tongues, wisdom, and others. These gifts equip us for ministry and spiritual warfare. This empowerment, often referred to as the baptism in the Holy Spirit, enables us to operate in the supernatural and continue the work of Jesus as described in Mark 16.

The Holy Spirit also prompts us to gather as believers in congregational communities that represent the Kingdom of God on earth. Jesus Himself appoints and anoints individuals to serve in leadership roles such as apostles, prophets, evangelists, pastors, and teachers, so that the Body of Christ may be equipped and edified.

To be filled with the Holy Spirit is to be positioned for victory in the spiritual battle we face daily. Only by the gifts of the Spirit can we overcome the enemy and destroy his works.

This understanding is at the heart of *The Apostolic Mandate: Bringing the Kingdom of God to Your Sphere of Influence*. We write with two primary goals. First, to offer a deep and clear understanding of the Apostolic Mandate through Scripture, Church history, and sound theology. Second, to help believers practically activate this mandate.

Throughout this book, we share real-life stories, teaching insights, and reflection points to encourage you to live out this calling in your sphere. You do not need a platform or a title, just a willing heart and the Spirit of God within you. We charge you to reflect Christ, serve faithfully, and influence the world around you for His glory. This is not merely a message; it is a commissioning.

How Do You NOT Become a Born-Again Christian?

John 3:16 is perhaps the most well-known summary of the gospel message. Yet, when we read it within its proper context, particularly alongside verses 14 and 15, it reveals a much deeper theological truth. Jesus does not offer a vague or sentimental statement about God's love for the world. Rather, He anchors that love in a specific historical and typological event: the lifting up of the bronze serpent in the wilderness, as recorded in Numbers 21:4-9.

This connection is not incidental. It is essential to understand the nature of salvation and challenge any doctrine that suggests salvation is automatically applied to all. In particular, it challenges the teaching of universal reconciliation, which asserts that everyone will ultimately be saved, regardless of their beliefs. Jesus's own words make it clear that while salvation is indeed offered to the world, its benefits are reserved for those.

The Typological Framework: The Bronze Serpent (Numbers 21:4-9)

Jesus intentionally references the wilderness account from the book of Numbers to illustrate the nature of His redemptive work. In that story, the Israelites had sinned against God and were judged through the sending of venomous snakes. Many began to die. In response, God instructed Moses to fashion a bronze serpent and raise it on a pole. Anyone who looked upon it in faith was healed and lived.

This story powerfully combines both judgment and mercy. The judgment was severe and tangible. The mercy was miraculous but conditional. The bronze serpent was available for all to see, yet not everyone received its benefit. Only those who looked were healed. The provision was sufficient, but it was not universally applied. This event becomes the interpretive key that unlocks the meaning of John 3:14-16.

The Lifting Up of the Son of Man

In John 3:14, Jesus said, *"Just as Moses lifted up the snake in the wilderness, so the Son of Man must be lifted up"* (John 3:14, NIV).

The phrase "lifted up" refers not only to the crucifixion but also to the exaltation of Christ, as confirmed later in John 12:32-33. Jesus was drawing a clear typological parallel between Himself and the bronze serpent. Just as those who looked at the serpent were healed, so those who believe in Him would receive eternal life.

John 3:15 continues this line of thought: *"that everyone who believes may have eternal life in him."* Then comes the famous verse: *"For God so loved the world that he gave his one and only Son, that whoever believes in him shall not perish but have eternal life"* (John 3:16, NIV).

The original Greek, *"οὕτως γὰρ ἠγάπησεν ὁ θεὸς τὸν κόσμον,"* is best translated as "In this way God loved the world," referring directly back to the lifting up of the Son of Man. It is not love in the abstract, but love demonstrated through action.

The Offer and the Condition: "Whoever Believes"

The heart of this passage lies not only in the scope of the offer but in the condition of its reception. Twice, Jesus uses the phrase "whoever believes" as to how eternal life is received. He does not suggest that all will be saved. Rather,

He declares that those who believe will be saved. This is not merely a theological nuance; it is at the heart of the gospel.

As Augustine once said, "God made you without you, but He will not justify you without you." Faith is not a passive inevitability. It is an intentional response to the grace that God initiates.

In the wilderness, not everyone was healed automatically. Only those who obeyed God's instruction and looked upon the bronze serpent were healed. In the same way, only those who place their trust in Christ are saved. The love of God is indeed extended to all, but the effect is limited to those who respond in faith.

Rejection of Universal Reconciliation

The doctrine of universal reconciliation claims that all people will ultimately be saved and restored to God, regardless of whether they repent or believe in Jesus Christ. However, this idea stands in direct contradiction to the clear teaching of Jesus in John 3 and throughout the New Testament. Scripture consistently presents salvation as a gift that must be received by faith.

The repeated emphasis on believing in Christ, *as stated in John 3:16, "whoever believes in Him shall not perish"* (NIV), makes it unmistakably clear that salvation is not automatic. It is not granted by default, nor is it the inevitable outcome for all humanity. The love of God offers redemption to all, but only those who believe are saved. Any teaching that dismisses this truth undermines the urgency of repentance, the necessity of faith, and the reality of eternal separation from God.

Belief is Essential, Not Optional

The phrase "whoever believes" is not a poetic flourish. It is a theological demand. If salvation were guaranteed for all, the urgency of belief would be meaningless. The lifting up of Christ would have no requirement attached to it. However, Jesus speaks with purpose. His words reveal that the call to believe is not optional. It is essential.

John Calvin once wrote, "Christ was given for all, that whosoever believes in Him should not perish. Nevertheless, although He is offered to all, yet all do not receive Him." This affirms the biblical balance: Christ's death is sufficient for all but effective only for those who believe.

Perishing is a Real Possibility

John 3:16 presents a profound and sobering contrast: *"shall not perish but have eternal life."* This is not a poetic device or rhetorical flourish. It is a declaration of eternal consequence. Jesus is not offering a suggestion, but a divine warning.

Later in the same chapter, He intensifies the message: *"Whoever believes in the Son has eternal life, but whoever rejects the Son will not see life, for God's wrath remains on them"* (John 3:36, NIV). The language is clear. To reject the Son is not to remain neutral; it is to remain under judgment.

This truth is echoed throughout Scripture. In Matthew 7:13-14, Jesus speaks of two gates: *"wide is the gate and broad is the road that leads to destruction, and many enter through it. But small is the gate and narrow the road that leads to life, and only a few find it."* The reality of perishing is not figurative. It is the tragic destiny of those who persist in unbelief.

Eternal life is God's promise to those who believe, but the alternative, separation from God and eternal judgment, is just as real. To preach the gospel without acknowledging this truth is to offer half a message. The call to salvation carries urgency precisely because the danger is real. Jesus did not come only to enhance life; He came to rescue us from perishing. Furthermore, that rescue is received through faith in Him alone.

The Typological Precedent

The bronze serpent in the wilderness was a symbol of divine mercy made available during a time of judgment. Yet, its healing power was not universal. Many still perished because they did not obey God's command to look. Athanasius, writing against the Arians, stated: "Although He suffered for all, yet all do not receive the benefit, but only those who are partakers of the Spirit of Christ." The consistent witness of Scripture affirms that salvation comes only through faith in Jesus Christ.

Universal reconciliation assumes that individuals can be saved without personal repentance or belief. However, the New Testament does not allow for that possibility. Every call to salvation includes the demand for repentance, faith, and obedience.

The Heart of the Gospel

John 3:14–16 is one of the most powerful declarations in the entire Bible. It reveals a God whose love is not passive but sacrificial. He gave His Son to be lifted up, not for ceremony but for salvation. However, just as in the days of Moses, the provision does not guarantee the outcome. Only those who look to Christ in faith are saved.

Any teaching that severs salvation from belief does violence to the structure of Jesus's teaching. It turns divine love into a blanket that covers unbelief and undermines the necessity of repentance. Jesus speaks clearly and urgently. Perishing is a real outcome. Belief is the decisive condition. Moreover, the love of God, displayed in the lifting up of His Son, invites a response.

The gospel is offered to all, but it is only applied to those who trust in the One who was lifted up.

Discipleship and Purpose

Discipleship and purpose are inextricably linked aspects of a believer's walk with God. They are not optional elements of salvation, but essential expressions of a life truly transformed by the Gospel.

Having encountered the saving grace of Jesus Christ and the power of the Holy Spirit, we both testify that salvation was not the end. It was the beginning of a life that demands renewal in mind, body, and spirit. We have come to understand that salvation must lead to transformation, and transformation must lead to purpose. That purpose is discovered, refined, and fulfilled through discipleship.

Volker often speaks about the need for holistic renewal, the kind that not only touches the heart but also awakens the believer to their calling. The Holy Spirit plays a vital role in this, guiding us into truth, revealing God's will, and empowering us to walk in it. For Dorine, discipleship has always been the foundation for spiritual maturity. Without it, faith becomes passive. Discipleship trains our ears to hear God's voice, shapes our character, and grounds our identity in Christ.

True discipleship involves more than personal devotion. It is obedience to Jesus's Great Commission. When He said, *"Go and make disciples of all nations…"*

(Matthew 28:19, NIV), He was not speaking only to the apostles. He was commanding all who would follow Him. Discipleship means walking alongside others, teaching them, nurturing them, and demonstrating what it looks like to live a Christ-centred life. It is about reproducing the life of Christ in others.

When we commit to discipleship, we allow God to work not just in us but through us. We grow personally, but we also become instruments of growth in the lives of others. Through teaching, mentoring, and modelling, we help raise others into maturity. This is not a task for the spiritually elite; it is the call of every believer.

Living out our salvation also means discovering and walking in the purpose for which God created us. Each of us is uniquely crafted, gifted with talents and passions, and assigned by God for His glory. Purpose is not a mystery reserved for a few. It is found by aligning our lives with God's Word and surrendering to His leading. Whether we are called to ministry, the marketplace, missions, or any area of influence, living with purpose means using all that we are to serve God and build His Kingdom.

We have learned that calling is not confined to pulpits or platforms. It may be expressed in raising a godly family, bringing justice in the workplace, encouraging a discouraged heart, or leading with integrity in our communities. The Holy Spirit enables us to identify these assignments and walk in them with boldness.

Including discipleship and purpose in our teaching on salvation is not an addition; it is a necessary extension of the gospel. Salvation leads us to transformation. Transformation calls us to purpose. Moreover, purpose leads us to serve, disciple, and impact lives for eternity.

As we live a life guided by the Spirit and rooted in the Word, we find that our purpose is not only fulfilling but also fruitful. It brings meaning, clarity, and joy to our faith. It draws others to Christ. Moreover, it aligns our lives with God's redemptive plan for the world.

Transformed and Renewed

As believers, we understand that transformation and renewal are not abstract ideas but central truths that define the Christian life. They describe the ongoing work of God's grace in shaping us into the likeness of His Son. These are not mere theological concepts but living realities made possible through the redemptive work of Christ and the active presence of the Holy Spirit in us.

Transformation begins with a profound, inward change, a shift that affects our heart, mind, and character. It is the divine exchange where the old self, shaped by sin and separation from God, is replaced by a new nature rooted in righteousness and an intimate relationship with Him. The Apostle Paul wrote, *"Therefore, if anyone is in Christ, the new creation has come: The old has gone, the new is here!"* (2 Corinthians 5:17, NIV). This is not a metaphor. It is a supernatural reality. In Christ, we are not improved versions of our old selves; we are made entirely new.

Renewal, however, is not a one-time event. It is the continual process of spiritual growth that follows transformation. It involves aligning our thoughts, attitudes, and desires daily with the truth of God's Word. As Paul exhorts in Romans 12:2, *"Do not conform to the pattern of this world, but be transformed by the renewing of your mind. Then you will be able to test and approve what God's will is his good, pleasing and perfect will."* Renewal is a work of the Holy

Spirit, but it also requires our cooperation. It calls us to submit our minds to God, to meditate on His truth, and to cultivate spiritual disciplines that strengthen our walk.

The work of transformation and renewal touches every part of our lives. It revives our relationship with God, refines our character, and reorients our purpose. It reshapes how we treat others, how we speak, what we prioritise, and how we see the world around us. As our hearts are renewed, we begin to reflect more of Christ, His compassion, His holiness, His humility, and His courage.

This is not an automatic process. It requires intentional surrender. We must be willing to lay down our will, to allow the Holy Spirit to challenge, cleanse, and lead us. Spiritual maturity demands persistence. It is a lifelong process marked by both victories and trials. Nevertheless, through it all, we are strengthened by the assurance that God is committed to finishing the work He began in us.

As we are transformed and renewed, our lives begin to have a positive impact on those around us. We do not carry this change for ourselves alone. We become carriers of God's love, agents of healing, and vessels of His redemptive grace. In a world that is fractured and longing for hope, we are called to live as Christ's ambassadors, pointing others to the power of a changed life through Him.

This is the calling that compels us. We believe that transformation and renewal are not reserved for a select few. They are the inheritance of every believer. We have tasted this grace, and we continue to walk in it. Through God's mercy, we are being made new, and through His Spirit, we are being equipped to bring that same renewal to the world.

Transformation is the divine work that brings us from death to life. Renewal is the daily process that aligns us with God's will. Together, they empower us to live holy, fruitful lives that testify to the reality of Jesus Christ. As transformed and renewed sons and daughters, we are sent into the world not just to reflect Christ but to represent Him.

Living Out Salvation

Salvation is not merely a moment in time or a distant hope. It is a present and active reality that reshapes every part of our daily lives. As believers, we are called not only to receive salvation but to live it out, allowing the grace of God to transform our thoughts, attitudes, decisions, and actions from the inside out.

At the heart of living out salvation is a personal and ongoing relationship with Jesus Christ. We believe that Jesus, the Son of God, lived a sinless life, died on the cross as the sacrifice for humanity's sin, and rose again in victory over death. When we accept Him as Lord and Saviour, we are reconciled to God, cleansed of sin, and granted the gift of eternal life. This relationship with Jesus is the foundation of our Christian walk, and it informs everything else we do.

To live out our salvation is also to follow the teachings and example of Christ. Jesus instructed us to love the Lord our God with all our heart, soul, mind, and strength, and to love our neighbour as ourselves (Mark 12:30-31). This love is not simply emotional. It is revealed in how we live in compassion, forgiveness, kindness, humility, and service. As we grow in Christ, our lives should increasingly reflect His character, bringing glory to God in everything we do.

Another key element is obedience to the Word of God. Scripture is not only our source of doctrine; it is our daily guide. It reveals God's will and provides wisdom for righteous living. When we study and meditate on the Word, we learn His voice, we understand His heart, and we begin to conform our lives to His truth. As we align our thoughts, speech, and conduct with Scripture, we honour God and live in step with His Spirit.

Living out salvation is not a private pursuit. We are designed to walk this path in community. The Church, as the body of Christ, is the place where believers are nurtured, supported, and equipped for life and ministry. We are called to actively participate in the life of the Church through worship, fellowship, teaching, and service. In the community, we grow stronger, encourage one another, and carry out the mission of making disciples, just as Jesus commanded in Matthew 28:19-20.

This life of salvation also involves a deep commitment to holiness and spiritual growth. Sanctification is the process of becoming more like Jesus, and it is a lifelong journey of growth. It requires us to surrender to the work of the Holy Spirit, who convicts, purifies, and empowers us. We are called to put off the old self, to walk away from sin, and to pursue righteousness. As we yield to the Spirit, we are changed from glory to glory, becoming living witnesses of God's grace and truth.

We also recognise that our faith must reach beyond the walls of the Church. We are called to be salt and light in the world to influence our families, workplaces, and communities for the sake of the Gospel. Living out salvation means sharing our faith, demonstrating God's love through tangible acts of service, advocating for justice, and being present in places where hope is most needed. When we step into these spaces with the love and truth of Christ, we participate in God's redemptive work on the earth.

Living out salvation is not about religious performance. It is a holistic and Spirit-led way of life. It touches every area of our relationship with Christ, our obedience to His Word, our involvement in the Church, our pursuit of holiness, and our engagement with the world. It is a lifelong pursuit, sustained by grace and empowered by the Holy Spirit.

Every day we live as redeemed people is a testimony to the power of God's salvation. We are not only saved from something, but we are also saved for something. We are called to live fully for Christ, bearing fruit that lasts, and pointing others to the One who saves.

While the previous discussion covers many important aspects of living out salvation, there are a few additional points to be considered:

Perseverance

Perseverance is essential to living out our salvation. It is the grace-enabled strength that allows us to remain faithful to Christ through trials, temptations, and the testing of our faith. It is not something we achieve through human willpower. It is a steady reliance on God's power, His promises, and the encouragement found within the body of Christ.

Jesus Himself warned us, *"In this world you will have trouble. But take heart! I have overcome the world"* (John 16:33, NIV). He never promised a life free of hardship, but He did promise His presence and victory. As we walk out our salvation, we must adopt a posture of endurance, one that trusts in God even when the path is difficult or unclear.

We do not endure in isolation. Our perseverance is sustained by God's Spirit within us and supported by the fellowship of believers around us. When trials come, whether in the form of persecution, loss, personal struggle, or delay, we are called to remain steadfast. We hold tightly to the goodness of God and trust that He is at work, even when we cannot see it.

Temptation is another battleground that requires perseverance. The enemy seeks to draw us away from God through subtle enticements and distractions. To persevere in purity and truth, we must remain anchored in the Word, devoted in prayer, and connected to the community of faith. Resisting temptation is not about striving alone; it is about walking in the Spirit and choosing to honour God in every decision.

At the heart of perseverance is trust. We hold fast because we trust that God is faithful. He has said, *"Never will I leave you; never will I forsake you"* (Hebrews 13:5, NIV).

That assurance gives us strength. We know that *"in all things God works for the good of those who love him, who have been called according to his purpose"* (Romans 8:28, NIV). Even in seasons of darkness or silence, we continue to move forward, knowing that God has not abandoned us.

Perseverance also deepens our faith. James encourages us with these words: *"Consider it pure joy, my brothers and sisters, whenever you face trials of many kinds, because you know that the testing of your faith produces perseverance. Let perseverance finish its work so that you may be mature and complete, not lacking anything"* (James 1:24, NIV). Trials become tools in the hands of God, shaping us, refining us, and building endurance that strengthens our walk.

As we persevere, we are being conformed more fully into the image of Christ. Our lives become testimonies of His sustaining grace. We can comfort others with the same comfort we have received. We become witnesses not just in word, but in the way we endure with hope, walk with faith, and remain unshaken in our devotion to Christ.

Perseverance is not optional. It is the path of spiritual maturity. It is the mark of disciples who have set their eyes on Jesus and refuse to turn back. With God's help, we press on.

Prayer

Prayer is one of the most vital and sacred practices in the life of every believer. It is not just a spiritual discipline; it is our lifeline to God. Through prayer, we enter into personal communion with the Creator of the universe. It is where we draw near to Him, experience His presence, and open our hearts to be shaped by His will.

We understand prayer as a two-way conversation, not a ritual or religious formality. It is where we pour out our hearts before God, expressing our thoughts, emotions, fears, joys, and hopes. In that place of sincerity, we find that God is not distant. He is attentive. He listens, He responds, and He delights in our desire to be with Him.

Prayer is how we seek God's guidance and direction. In seasons of uncertainty or when faced with critical decisions, we can come before the Lord and ask for wisdom, trusting that He will direct our steps. As we pray, we learn to surrender our own will and desires, laying them at His feet in humility. In doing so, we allow our hearts to align with His purpose, and we trust that His ways are higher than ours.

It is also through prayer that we express our worship and thanksgiving. We come before Him not only to ask, but to honour Him, to acknowledge His faithfulness, His goodness, and His sovereign care in our lives. When we lift up our praise, we are reminded of who God is. We remember His mercies, His provision, and the immeasurable gift of salvation. Prayer cultivates gratitude. It strengthens our worship and keeps our hearts tender before the Lord.

Prayer is the place where we lay our burdens. Whatever weighs on us, our anxieties, concerns, struggles, or pain, we bring them to God. He invites us to do so, assuring us that He cares deeply for us. As Scripture says, *"Cast all your anxiety on him because he cares for you"* (1 Peter 5:7, NIV). In prayer, we find rest in His presence. We find comfort in His nearness, and we receive peace that surpasses understanding.

We have experienced how prayer opens the door to the presence of God. It is in those quiet moments, when we seek His face, that we encounter His love, His peace, and His strength. Prayer creates space for God to speak and for us to listen. It is where transformation begins. In prayer, we receive grace. We are renewed. And we are reminded that we are not alone.

As we continue to grow in prayer, we have seen how it becomes the conduit for personal transformation. Through prayer, we surrender more deeply to God. We invite Him to shape our hearts, refine our motives, and form Christlike character within us. Prayer allows the Holy Spirit to do a sanctifying work in us, producing growth, maturity, and spiritual fruit.

Living out salvation without prayer is impossible. Prayer sustains our walk, anchors our faith, and connects us to the One who empowers us. It is through prayer that we grow in intimacy with God and become vessels through which His love, power, and truth flow into the world.

Salvation For All and the Role of Evangelism

Salvation lies at the heart of the Christian faith. It represents the deliverance and redemption of humanity from sin and its consequences. Through salvation, we are reconciled with God and given the promise of eternal life.

However, this gift is not exclusive or selective. It is offered to all individuals, regardless of their background, ethnicity, or social status. This universal invitation reveals the depth of God's love and the boundless reach of His grace.

Yes, Jesus did speak about judgment and about what is traditionally understood as hell. One of the key terms He used is Gehenna (γέεννα), which referred historically to the Valley of Hinnom, just outside Jerusalem. This was a place where detestable practices such as child sacrifice once occurred, as mentioned in Jeremiah 7:31.

By the time of Jesus, Gehenna had become a symbol of divine judgment. He warned, *"Do not be afraid of those who kill the body but cannot kill the soul. Rather, be afraid of the One who can destroy both soul and body in hell"* (Matthew 10:28, NIV). He also said, *"Anyone who says, 'You fool!' will be in danger of the fire of hell"* (Matthew 5:22, NIV).

Jesus's references to judgment are not symbolic warnings without consequence. They affirm the reality of eternal judgment. Scripture speaks of a final evaluation for all people. For those who reject Christ, this judgment is one of condemnation and separation from God.

Revelation 20:12,15 describes this sober moment: *"The dead were judged according to what they had done... Anyone whose name was not found written in the book of life was thrown into the lake of fire."* Similarly, John 3:18 declares, *"Whoever believes in him is not condemned, but whoever does not believe stands condemned already..."*

For believers in Christ, judgment does not determine salvation that is already secure in Him. However, we will give an account of our work. Paul writes, *"For we must all appear before the judgment seat of Christ, so that each of us may receive what is due... whether good or bad"* (2 Corinthians 5:10, NIV).

This Bema Seat Judgment is not about punishment, but about reward. The works of each believer will be tested. As Paul writes in 1 Corinthians 3:15, *"If it is burned up, the builder will suffer loss, but yet will be saved even though only as one escaping through the flames."*

What does all of this mean for you? It means that the message of salvation is not just a theological concept; it is a life-and-death reality. If you have believed in Jesus Christ, your name is written in the Book of Life. If you have not, you are invited to receive Him by faith even now. The door is still open.

God's desire is clear: He wants all people to be saved. John 3:16 affirms this, saying, *"For God so loved the world that he gave his one and only Son, that whoever believes in him shall not perish but have eternal life"* (NIV). This is not theoretical love. It is love proven in action. Nevertheless, this gift must be received through belief.

That is why evangelism matters. Evangelism is not optional. It is the divine mandate to proclaim the Gospel of Jesus Christ to all nations. Jesus commissioned His followers, saying, *"Go and make disciples of all nations"* (Matthew 28:19, NIV). He called us to share what we have received to proclaim the life, death, and resurrection of Christ so that others might believe and be saved.

Evangelism takes many forms. It can happen in a one-on-one conversation, in a pulpit, on social media, or through acts of compassion and service. The method may vary, but the message remains the same. Jesus Christ is the way, the truth, and the life, and no one comes to the Father except through Him (John 14:6). As believers, our task is to present that truth with love, clarity, and boldness.

If you are a follower of Christ, we urge you to see yourself as His ambassador. Speak of Him when prompted. Share your testimony when the opportunity comes. Let your life reflect His love so powerfully that others are compelled to ask you for the reason behind your hope. As Peter wrote, *"Always be prepared to give an answer... for the hope that you have"* (1 Peter 3:15, NIV).

Evangelism is not about coercion. It is not about winning arguments. It is about presenting an invitation to experience the same salvation that changed your life. And it is the Holy Spirit who convicts hearts, draws people to the Father, and transforms lives. You carry the message. He does the work.

Salvation is available for everyone. Our role is to make it known.

Conclusion

In this chapter, we have explored the profound and practical reality of salvation. Through our testimonies and reflections, we have shared what it means to be found by grace and transformed by God's power.

Dorine shared how salvation is not something we could ever earn. It is a divine rescue mission, rooted in our need and fulfilled through Christ's sacrifice. Her story reminded us that we must first recognise how lost we truly are in order to appreciate the magnitude of the salvation we have received.

Volker emphasised the responsibility that comes with salvation. It is not a private treasure to be kept hidden, but a living truth that must be proclaimed. Through evangelism, we participate in God's redemptive plan. We extend the same invitation that once reached us to others who are still searching.

Together, we explored the ongoing work of salvation in our lives, including transformation, renewal, the calling to discipleship, and the discovery of purpose. We have looked at the need for perseverance through trials, the role of prayer as our spiritual lifeline, and the necessity of growing into maturity by the power of the Holy Spirit.

We also confronted the reality of judgment and the urgency of the Gospel. Salvation is a gift, but it is not automatic. It must be received by faith, and it must be shared in love. As believers, we are not only recipients of salvation, but also carriers of the message.

If you have received Christ, may you live boldly in that truth. Let salvation shape your character, choices, relationships, and mission. If you have not yet believed, we plead with you to consider the message of Jesus. Please respond to the invitation while it is still available. He came to seek and to save those who were lost. That includes you.

CHAPTER TWO

FOUNDATIONAL THEOLOGY IN CHURCH HISTORY

EVERY ENDURING STRUCTURE begins with a solid foundation. The same principle applies to theology. Before we can rightly understand the Apostolic Mandate and its charge to bring the Kingdom of God into every sphere of influence, we must first examine the foundational theology that shaped these truths throughout Church history.

In this chapter, we turn our attention to the early centuries of the Christian faith. We explore the theological groundwork laid by those who came before us, the Church Fathers and early Christian thinkers who wrestled with Scripture, preserved apostolic teaching, and contended for sound doctrine in a world that neither understood nor accepted the message of Jesus Christ.

Our goal is to take you back to the origins of what we now understand as the Apostolic Mandate. These were not ideas developed in isolation or through innovation. They were formed through prayer, persecution, the study of Scripture, and the power of the Holy Spirit working through men and women who loved Christ and His Church. Their lives and writings helped to clarify the role of the believer in a fallen world and the nature of God's Kingdom breaking into time through His people.

We will revisit the teachings and convictions of early Church leaders such as Ignatius of Antioch, Justin Martyr, Irenaeus of Lyons, and Augustine of Hippo. Their reflections on the character of God, the structure of the Church, and the mission of believers offer us profound insight into the theological roots of our faith. Although separated from us by centuries, their wisdom continues to resonate with the Church today.

Be encouraged to do more than read history. See these foundations for what they truly are: stepping stones that support the weight of your faith and calling. These men were not writing theory. They were interpreting revelation under the fire of persecution and the inspiration of the Spirit. They gave us the first language for expressing divine truths that still shape our understanding of discipleship, worship, holiness, and mission.

We believe that returning to these roots will bring clarity to our present responsibilities as followers of Christ. If we are to bring the Kingdom of God into our homes, churches, communities, and nations, then we must know where we stand and what we stand upon.

Understanding foundational theology gives us strength. It grounds us in the Gospel. It protects us from distortion. It reminds us that our faith is not a newly invented one, but rather deeply rooted in a rich and resilient heritage. To live out the Apostolic Mandate today, we must be tethered to the truths that have guided the faithful across generations.

As we open the pages of Church history, may your understanding be deepened, your convictions strengthened, and your passion for God's Kingdom reignited.

The Early Church Fathers and Theological Foundations

The early Church Fathers, along with Christian philosophers and theologians in the centuries following Christ's ascension, played a pivotal role in shaping the foundational theology of the faith. Much of what we understand about the Apostolic Mandate and the Kingdom of God draws from their interpretations of Scripture, their theological insights, and the integrity of their lived witness.

In the earliest days of the Church, these leaders devoted themselves to clarifying and preserving the teachings of Christ and His apostles. They approached the Apostolic Mandate not as an abstract idea but as a practical charge to spread the Gospel and bring the reality of God's Kingdom into every part of life.

The context in which they worked was often marked by persecution, cultural opposition, and internal pressures. These circumstances required them to address not only theological questions but also questions of identity, resilience, and continuity. What did it mean to be faithful to Christ in a society that rejected Him? How could the Church maintain its unity and purpose under external threat? These were not theoretical concerns. They were matters of life, faith, and spiritual responsibility.

Among those who helped form the theological backbone of early Christianity were Ignatius of Antioch, Justin Martyr, Irenaeus of Lyons, and Augustine of Hippo. Their voices continue to shape our understanding of Christian mission and identity.

Ignatius of Antioch wrote extensively on the importance of unity within the Church. He connected this unity directly to the divine relationship between the Father, Son, and Holy Spirit. This emphasis serves as a reminder that the Apostolic Mandate includes a call to foster reconciliation and harmony wherever we are sent. In living out the Kingdom of God, we also promote the unity that reflects God's nature.

Justin Martyr, who came to faith through philosophical inquiry, offered profound reflections on the Logos, God's divine reason and self-expression. He taught that every person, through the faculty of reason, holds the potential to engage with the divine Logos. His theology affirms that all people are made to bear witness to God's Kingdom, and that truth can be seen and proclaimed through every sphere of human life, regardless of one's social or professional context.

Irenaeus of Lyons is best known for his defence of Christian orthodoxy in his work *Against Heresies*. He presented Christ as the new Adam, the one who brings renewal where the first Adam brought rebellion. Irenaeus taught that through union with Christ, believers are empowered to live in obedience and to manifest God's will on earth. This vision of transformation is a direct expression of the Apostolic Mandate: as we are made new in Christ, we also become agents of renewal in the world around us.

Augustine of Hippo provided comprehensive theological reflections on the nature of God, the Church, and human society. His vision of the Church as the "City of God" showed how Christians are called to influence the world around them with Kingdom values while awaiting the full realisation of that Kingdom in eternity. He saw believers as citizens of heaven who live faithfully on earth, advancing God's reign through lives marked by love, justice, and truth.

Studying the early Church Fathers gives us more than historical insight. It provides us with a theological framework for understanding our roles today. These voices from the past continue to speak into the present, reminding us that the call to bring the Kingdom of God to our spheres of influence is deeply rooted in the Christian tradition.

The Ecumenical Councils and Doctrinal Formulation

No exploration of foundational theology would be complete without a careful study of the Ecumenical Councils. These crucial assemblies, convened during the first millennium of the Church's history, served as platforms for the Church's leadership to grapple with complex theological issues, formulate doctrines, and establish a consensus that would guide Christian belief and practice for centuries to come.

Seven Ecumenical Councils took place between the 4th and 8th centuries, beginning with the First Council of Nicaea in 325 AD and ending with the Second Council of Nicaea in 787 AD. These councils, attended by bishops from various Christian regions, were significant in shaping Christian orthodoxy and understanding the Apostolic Mandate.

The First Council of Nicaea addressed the Arian controversy regarding the nature of Christ's divinity. The resulting Nicene Creed asserted the consubstantiality of the Son with the Father, thereby confirming the understanding of the Trinity, which is crucial for grasping the Apostolic Mandate.

The Council of Constantinople (381 AD) expanded on the Nicene Creed, underscoring the role of the Holy Spirit and affirming His divinity. This Council's decision played a pivotal role in defining the Trinitarian nature of God, a cornerstone of Christian belief and a guiding principle in the execution of the Apostolic Mandate.

The Council of Ephesus (431 AD) and the Council of Chalcedon (451 AD) addressed the dual nature of Christ, which is both divine and human. Understanding Christ's dual nature is essential for interpreting the Apostolic Mandate, as it affirms that Christ, while divine, fully engaged with the earthly realm and encouraged His followers to do the same.

Later Councils, including the Second Council of Constantinople (553 AD), the Third Council of Constantinople (680-681 AD), and the Second Council of Nicaea (787 AD), dealt with various heresies and the role of icons in worship. Each of these contributed to the unfolding understanding of how believers should engage with the divine and the world.

The doctrinal formulations of these Ecumenical Councils had practical implications for how Christians perceived their role in the world. By affirming doctrines such as the Trinity and Christ's dual nature, they emphasised that the divine is not detached from the world but is intimately engaged with it. This understanding reinforces the Apostolic Mandate's call to bring the Kingdom of God to our spheres of influence.

The Enlightenment and Challenges to Foundational Theology

As we step ahead into the Age of Enlightenment, also referred to as the Age of Reason, we encounter a new set of challenges to foundational theology. This period, spanning the 17th and 18th centuries, was marked by significant shifts in intellectual and cultural paradigms, with an emphasis on reason, science, and individualism.

Enlightenment thinkers often placed a premium on empirical evidence and rational thought, leading to a surge in scientific discoveries and innovations. Simultaneously, it also fostered a degree of scepticism and, in some quarters, an outright rejection of religious doctrines and dogmas, which were seen as incompatible with the new rationalist ethos.

Renowned philosophers such as Immanuel Kant, David Hume, and Voltaire questioned the credibility of religious faith, miracles, and divine intervention. The increasing focus on human reason often came at the expense of divine revelation, leading to a reinterpretation, if not a complete dismissal, of many traditional Christian teachings.

The Enlightenment period also gave birth to Deism. This belief system accepted the existence of a creator based on reason but rejected revealed religion, miracles, and direct divine involvement in the world. For Deists, the world was a clockwork mechanism set in motion by God but left to operate independently according to natural laws.

Such developments posed significant challenges to the understanding and application of the Apostolic Mandate. The stress on individualism and human autonomy often seemed at odds with the call to align oneself with God's will and bring His Kingdom to one's sphere of influence.

Nevertheless, the Church was not an idle bystander during the Enlightenment. Christian theologians and philosophers, such as Bishop George Berkeley and Christian Wolff, defended faith, offering nuanced responses that sought to reconcile Christian beliefs with the ideas of the Enlightenment.

Moreover, during this period of challenge and change, the Church was compelled to clarify and articulate its doctrines, thereby enriching and diversifying Christian theology. It prompted believers to reexamine the meaning and relevance of their faith in a changing world, and how they could live out the Apostolic Mandate amid these shifts.

Modern Theological Movements and Their Impact

Over the past two centuries, a range of theological movements has emerged across the global Church. These movements have shaped, challenged, and expanded our understanding of the Apostolic Mandate and the call to bring the Kingdom of God into every sphere of influence.

In the 19th century, the Historical-Critical method of biblical interpretation arose, particularly in Germany. This approach treated the Bible as a historical document and sought to understand it in light of its original context, including authorship, culture, and language. While this method raised questions about traditional interpretations, it also prompted deeper reflection and careful study. Many used it as a tool to uncover richness in Scripture that had long been overlooked, inviting the Church to engage more thoughtfully with the biblical text.

The tragedies of the 20th century, including the devastation of two World Wars and the Holocaust, compelled theologians to confront suffering, evil, and human depravity in new ways. Thinkers like Karl Barth advanced what became known as Neo-Orthodoxy, or the Theology of Crisis, which drew attention to God's complete sovereignty and humanity's profound dependence on divine grace. This theological shift pointed us toward the Kingdom of God as a radical hope, one that anchors us even in times of uncertainty and moral collapse. At the same time, Jürgen Moltmann's Theology of Hope reminded believers that our faith is grounded in God's promises and oriented toward His redemptive future.

In Latin America, the emergence of Liberation Theology in the mid-20th century responded to the cries of the poor and oppressed. This movement read the Gospel through the lens of social injustice and economic disparity. For many believers shaped by this theology, the Apostolic Mandate included not only the preaching of Christ but also the pursuit of justice, equity, and dignity for all people. The Kingdom of God was seen as a present reality breaking in through acts of compassion, advocacy, and transformation within society.

During the same period, voices within the Church began to rise, highlighting the need for equal recognition of women in theology and ministry. Feminist Theology and Womanist Theology emerged as critical responses to centuries of exclusion and misinterpretation. These movements emphasised the equal value and image-bearing nature of women. They invited the Church to revisit Scripture with renewed sensitivity and to include women's voices and leadership in the fulfilment of the Apostolic

Mandate. The call to bring the Kingdom of God into the world now included affirming the full participation of women in that mission.

In more recent years, the rise of Postmodern Theology has influenced how believers approach truth, meaning, and community. These theological current resists rigid definitions and value personal and cultural context. Postmodern perspectives invite the Church to express its faith through authenticity, humility, and genuine relationships. In this setting, the Apostolic Mandate is lived out through creativity, dialogue, and contextual expressions of the Gospel that speak to a pluralistic and questioning generation.

Each of these theological movements has contributed to the richness and complexity of the global Church's witness. They reveal that the Apostolic Mandate is not limited to evangelism or spiritual disciplines. It includes justice, equality, healing, reconciliation, and cultural engagement. God's Kingdom reaches into the systems that govern society, the narratives that shape our identity, and the structures that influence daily life.

As we consider these movements, we are reminded that God has always used voices from various corners of the world to shape His people and refine their mission. We are invited to learn from them, not to adopt every position they take, but to discern what aligns with the heart of God and to carry forward the truths that bring life and freedom.

The task before us is to live wisely and boldly in our time. By listening, learning, and seeking the Spirit's guidance, we can take part in the unfolding work of God's Kingdom. Our role is to understand the times in which we live and to faithfully express the Gospel in ways that are both faithful to Scripture and relevant to the world around us.

The Apostolic Mandate continues. It transcends generations and cultural boundaries. It calls each of us to be instruments of God's redeeming love in our unique settings.

Contemporary Issues in Foundational Theology

As we move further into the 21st century, the Church is encountering a wide range of issues that challenge and shape foundational theology. Rapid advancements in technology, global connectivity, increasing awareness of justice concerns, and the presence of diverse religious traditions require us to reflect more deeply on what it means to live out the Apostolic Mandate in our time.

One pressing area of engagement is the relationship between science and faith. Breakthroughs in cosmology, evolutionary biology, and genetics have stirred new discussions around creation, human identity, and the meaning of being made in the image of God. These developments invite thoughtful dialogue rather than fear. As believers, we recognise that both Scripture and creation reveal the character of God. When approached with discernment, scientific discovery can lead to a more profound appreciation of God's wisdom and design, equipping us to proclaim His Kingdom with depth and relevance.

The growing emphasis on social justice also calls for serious theological reflection. Issues such as economic inequality, racial injustice, gender equity, and environmental responsibility are no longer peripheral topics. They sit at the heart of what it means to reflect God's righteousness in the world. The Apostolic Mandate compels us to engage these realities with compassion, courage, and conviction. Addressing systems that oppress or marginalise others is not separate from our mission; it is a demonstration of the Kingdom of God in action.

Religious pluralism presents another layer of complexity. In today's global landscape, we live and work among people from many faith traditions. Our response is not one of withdrawal or compromise, but rather an intentional presence. We are called to speak the truth of Christ with love and clarity while honouring the humanity of those who believe differently. This context demands maturity and humility as we fulfil the Apostolic Mandate in ways that are faithful to the Gospel and respectful of others.

The digital world has become a powerful sphere of influence. With the rise of online churches, virtual gatherings, and social media platforms, new spaces have emerged for worship, teaching, and evangelism. These technologies present unique challenges in maintaining spiritual authenticity and depth. At the same time, they offer unprecedented opportunities to reach hearts and communities beyond physical borders. We are learning to plant seeds of the Kingdom in digital soil, trusting that God can work through screens as well as sanctuaries.

Conversations within the Church around sexual orientation and gender identity also demand thoughtful engagement. These discussions ask us to revisit foundational beliefs about human dignity, relationships, and the nature of love. While the Church must remain grounded in Scripture, we are also called to demonstrate the character of Christ, full of grace and truth. These are not questions to avoid. They require prayer, wisdom, and pastoral care as we strive to embody the heart of God in a world seeking clarity and compassion.

In facing these contemporary issues, we are reminded that theology is not static. It must be rooted, yet responsive. Our doctrine stands on the eternal truth of God's Word, and our practice must reflect the ongoing work of the Holy Spirit in our context. We are not preserving a tradition for its own sake. We are stewarding a living faith that reveals the reign of Christ in every generation.

The Apostolic Mandate remains unchanged. We are called to bring the Kingdom of God into every sphere of life. What changes is how we live that out amid new realities. As the world shifts, we listen to the Spirit, remain anchored in truth, and step forward in obedience, committed to being light in every place God sends us.

The Importance of Studying Foundational Theology

Engaging with foundational theology is essential to our walk with God. It serves as a compass, providing us with orientation, clarity, and stability in our faith. As we seek to live out the Apostolic Mandate by bringing the Kingdom of God into our spheres of influence, studying foundational theology becomes more than an academic pursuit; it becomes an expression of faithful discipleship.

Foundational theology anchors us in the core truths of the Christian faith. It provides a framework for interpreting Scripture, understanding Church tradition, and making sense of the Christian experience. As we grow in our knowledge of the nature of God, the person and work of Jesus Christ, the ministry of the Holy Spirit, and the mission of the Church, we are better equipped to walk in truth and to live with purpose. These doctrines do not exist in abstraction. They form the substance of our identity as believers and guide us as we live out the Kingdom of God in our daily contexts.

Through the study of theology, we also gain insight into the rich history of Christian thought and practice. From the teachings of the early Church Fathers to the theological developments that emerged in councils, reformations, and revivals, we see the unfolding of God's work through His people. Each season in Church history reveals a response to real questions, crises, and opportunities. This historical awareness deepens our appreciation for the Church's diversity and prepares us to engage thoughtfully with the challenges of our time.

Foundational theology prepares us to participate in conversations that matter. In a world shaped by many viewpoints and belief systems, both inside and outside the Church, we are often called to engage across lines of difference. A grounded understanding of our faith enables us to speak with both conviction and grace. It enables us to listen attentively, respond thoughtfully, and represent Christ faithfully in every conversation.

Even more, foundational theology shapes our spiritual formation. It draws us deeper into the knowledge of God. It refines how we think, how we worship, and how we make decisions. Theology is not confined to the intellect. It renews the heart and transforms the soul. As we study the truths of Scripture and reflect on the wisdom of those who came before us, we learn to discern God's voice and align our lives with His will.

Studying theology leads us into greater intimacy with the One we serve. It strengthens our convictions, clarifies our calling, and equips us to bring His Kingdom wherever He has placed us.

Through this pursuit, we step into our part in God's redemptive mission. We participate in something eternal, something that brings life, order, and truth into a world that needs them. This is the heart of the Apostolic Mandate. Moreover, it is through the study of theology that we are prepared to live it out.

Conclusion

This exploration of foundational theology across Church history, from the early teachings of the Church Fathers through the Ecumenical Councils, into the challenges of the Enlightenment, the rise of modern theological movements, and the complexities of contemporary issues, reveals a rich and layered heritage of Christian thought. Each historical period, with its unique concerns and contributions, has shaped the understanding of the Apostolic Mandate and deepened the call to embody the Kingdom of God within our spheres of influence.

Foundational theology is not a passive archive of past ideas; it is an active engagement with the past. It reflects a living engagement with divine truth, continuously refined through the Church's response to Scripture, culture, and unfolding human experience. The theological convictions we hold today have been shaped not by isolation but by centuries of Spirit-led inquiry, worship, and witness across diverse contexts.

Studying foundational theology equips believers with more than knowledge; it cultivates discernment, resilience, and spiritual depth. It anchors Christian identity and offers clarity in interpreting doctrine, navigating contemporary questions, and living a faith that is both rooted and responsive to the world. This engagement is essential not just for pastors or theologians but for every believer seeking to embody God's reign in daily life.

This was a call to active pursuit, not passive admiration. The truths uncovered here serve as a foundation to build upon, not a conclusion to rest in. May this study stir within you a greater hunger for God's Word, a stronger grasp of your faith, and a renewed sense of responsibility to carry His presence into the places you are called to influence. As you live out the Apostolic Mandate, may the foundation you now stand on give you the strength, clarity, and confidence to bear witness to the Kingdom of God with boldness and grace.

CHAPTER THREE

HOMILETICS: BIBLE EXEGESIS AND APPLICATION

THE TASK OF BRINGING the Kingdom of God into our sphere of influence begins with how we communicate its truth. Every setting, whether a pulpit, a classroom, a living room, or a digital platform, presents an opportunity to proclaim the Word with clarity and conviction. Homiletics, the sacred discipline of preaching, gives structure and depth to this task by helping us interpret the Scriptures and present them in a way that transforms minds and hearts.

Homiletics is not simply about delivering sermons. It is about rightly dividing the Word of truth, through careful exegesis and bringing that truth into contact with real-life situations through faithful application. Through this process, biblical messages move beyond historical reflection and become living instructions for faith, obedience, and spiritual formation. When Scripture is preached with understanding and relevance, it becomes a powerful agent for revealing the presence of God's Kingdom in everyday life.

This chapter offers a practical and theological exploration of homiletics. We will examine key principles of biblical interpretation, consider how to apply them to modern contexts, and reflect on what makes preaching both faithful to the text and meaningful to the listener. By engaging with these tools and insights, you will be equipped to handle the Word with integrity and to present it with conviction wherever you are called to speak.

Whether you are leading a congregation, facilitating a Bible study, or seeking to grow in your personal grasp of Scripture, homiletics provides a valuable path. It deepens your understanding, strengthens your voice, and aligns your message with the heart of God.

As we engage this chapter, may we be shaped not only as communicators of truth, but also as vessels through which that truth brings light to others.

Principles of Bible Exegesis

Bible exegesis is the disciplined practice of interpreting Scripture with precision and reverence. It is the foundational step in homiletics, forming the bridge between the written Word and its faithful proclamation. Through careful exegesis, we seek to uncover the original meaning of a text by examining what the biblical authors intended to communicate within their historical and literary settings. This work safeguards us from distortion, ensuring that the Word is handled with integrity and taught in truth.

Several guiding principles underpin effective exegesis. Each one serves to deepen our understanding of Scripture and sharpen our ability to communicate its message clearly and effectively.

Context is Key

No verse stands alone. Each passage exists within an immediate context surrounding verses as well as a broader literary and theological setting. Understanding how a verse fits within the chapter, the book, and the overarching narrative of the Bible is essential to interpreting it faithfully. This principle calls us to read Scripture holistically rather than fragmenting its meaning.

Literary Genre Matters

Scripture is a collection of diverse writings, including narratives, poetry, law, prophecy, wisdom, Gospels, epistles, and apocalyptic visions. Each genre has unique conventions. Recognising whether a passage is a parable, a legal code, or a historical account shapes how we read and understand its content. A psalm expresses truth differently than a letter from Paul; each must be approached with respect to its literary form.

Historical and Cultural Background

Scripture emerged from particular times and places. The customs, languages, political realities, and religious environments of ancient Israel, the early Church, and the Roman world all influence the meaning of the text. Studying these contexts helps us hear the text in its original voice and avoid projecting modern assumptions onto ancient messages.

Grammatical and Linguistic Precision

Language is the vessel of meaning. Words carry weight, and grammar provides structure. Careful attention to the syntax, sentence flow, and vocabulary—especially in the original Hebrew, Aramaic, or Greek—can uncover layers of insight. Word studies often reveal theological richness that may be hidden in translation.

Canonical Harmony

The Bible presents a coherent revelation. Each book contributes to the whole, and sound exegesis considers how a passage aligns with the broader narrative of Scripture. This principle encourages consistency, ensuring that interpretations remain anchored in the truth revealed throughout the canon.

Intertextual Echoes

Scripture frequently refers to itself. Prophecies fulfilled, allusions clarified, and themes developed across both testaments create a rich tapestry of meaning. Observing how later texts refer to earlier ones can illuminate both and provide depth to our preaching.

Prayerful Dependence on the Holy Spirit

Although exegesis involves intellectual effort, it is not merely an academic task. Scripture is Spirit-breathed, and its understanding requires spiritual receptivity. Through prayer, we invite the Holy Spirit to guide our study, purify our motives, and reveal the living Word within the written text. Illumination from the Spirit brings clarity and conviction that no amount of study alone can produce.

Applying these principles leads to a faithful engagement with the Bible. They remind us that we are not merely analysing text, but discerning God's voice. Such engagement forms the foundation for powerful preaching that speaks to the heart, shapes character, and calls people to participate in the life and reign of God within their daily spheres of influence.

Principles of Applying Biblical Truths

Understanding the original intent of a biblical text lays the foundation for preaching, yet the task does not end there. The heart of homiletics lies in leading listeners from ancient words into present realities.

Preaching is not a history lesson or a literary critique it is a divine appointment in which God speaks to His people through His Word. The purpose is to connect the truth of Scripture to the daily rhythms of life, helping individuals encounter the living God and respond with faith and obedience.

Effective application demands thoughtful reflection and spiritual attentiveness. The following principles support this sacred responsibility:

Anchored in Sound Exegesis

Every application must emerge from a faithful reading of the text. Without accuracy in interpretation, attempts at relevance become speculative and unreliable. Application is not a creative exercise detached from meaning; it is a natural extension of the message already embedded in the Scripture.

Connected to Real Life

The application speaks to the needs, questions, joys, and struggles that people face today. It involves listening not only to the text but also to the community. The preacher must understand both the biblical world and the contemporary context to draw out implications that speak directly to everyday life.

Flowing from the Central Message

The driving force of every sermon is the main truth of the passage. Application that deviates from this central message risks misrepresenting the text. Not every word or image within a passage demands application, but the core message always carries relevance for modern discipleship.

Clear and Practical

Application gains strength from specificity. Vague statements about "loving more" or "trusting God" fall flat unless listeners understand what that looks like in action. Concrete suggestions, whether they address behaviour, mindset, speech, or decision-making, give weight to the sermon and offer tangible direction.

Aware of Varied Realities

People listen from different starting points. A single message reaches parents and students, business leaders and the unemployed, the joyful and the grieving. While the truth remains the same, its implications unfold differently across circumstances. Application must acknowledge these layers without diluting the message.

Grounded in Grace

Biblical application grows best in the soil of grace. Preaching is not a tool to enforce burdens, but a call to freedom through Christ. Instruction rooted in guilt may produce momentary change, but grace nurtures lasting transformation. The invitation is always to respond out of love for God, not compulsion.

Aimed at Transformation

The objective of applying biblical truth is not merely to inform, but to reform. Preaching shapes lives. It calls for repentance, renews hope, and strengthens resolve. Application that awakens the conscience and stirs the will enables listeners to step into God's purposes with clarity and conviction.

Application is more than a technique; it is a form of shepherding. It calls for discernment, compassion, and wisdom. When approached faithfully, it becomes the means through which the eternal Word meets the present moment. In this sacred work, preachers serve as stewards of God's message, opening the Scriptures so that the Kingdom of God may take root in homes, workplaces, and communities.

By allowing the Word to be heard, understood, and lived, we fulfil the Apostolic Mandate not only by preaching it but by embodying it. Through faithful application, the Gospel moves beyond the pulpit and into the world.

Overemphasising Certain Doctrines or Cherry-Picking Verses

One of the ongoing challenges in homiletics is the tendency to highlight certain doctrines at the expense of others or to isolate Bible verses from their intended context. Whether done consciously or unintentionally, this approach distorts Scripture and hinders a faithful presentation of biblical truth. It can lead to misinterpretation, division, and the elevation of personal views over the integrity of the Word of God.

Doctrinal overemphasis often arises from personal preferences, cultural leanings, or denominational traditions.

While every preacher or teacher may have a particular theological lens, leaning too heavily into one emphasis can limit the Church's exposure to the fullness of God's counsel. A narrowed perspective risks forming believers with an incomplete view of God's character and Kingdom.

The practice of selecting isolated verses to reinforce personal convictions, often referred to as cherry-picking, poses another threat. This method treats Scripture as a set of disconnected statements rather than a coherent revelation. When verses are removed from their context or interpreted apart from the larger narrative of Scripture, they can be made to support nearly any claim, including those that conflict with the core message of the Gospel.

Several principles safeguard against these tendencies:

Honour the Full Counsel of Scripture

The Bible must be approached as a unified revelation. Its various books, voices, and literary styles all contribute to a larger message about God and His redemptive work. Presenting Scripture holistically allows the Church to engage its entire depth and breadth, drawing from the wisdom and tension that exist within its pages.

Practice Contextual Reading

Every verse belongs to a paragraph, every paragraph to a book, and every book to the overarching canon. Responsible interpretation considers literary form, authorial intent, and historical background. This approach safeguards Scripture from misuse and keeps its meaning grounded in truth.

Offer a Balanced Theological Diet

Healthy preaching and teaching encompass the variety of themes found in Scripture. From justice to grace, law to promise, discipline to comfort, the Bible speaks to the entirety of human experience. A balanced spiritual diet strengthens faith, nurtures growth, and guards against theological narrowness.

Cultivate Prayerful Humility

The Word of God demands reverence. Recognising our limitations, we approach the text with prayer and dependence on the Holy Spirit. Humility in interpretation invites deeper insight and guards against imposing personal agendas on sacred Scripture.

When Scripture is handled with integrity, its truth speaks clearly and powerfully. Avoiding doctrinal imbalance and verse isolation equips the Church to receive the fullness of God's message and to live it faithfully in every sphere of life.

Balancing the Tension Between Context and Application

In the practice of homiletics, one of the most delicate responsibilities is to reconcile the historical context of Scripture with its relevance for modern listeners. The Bible was written in specific cultural and temporal settings, yet its message continues to speak into new generations. The preacher's task is to steward this tension faithfully.

Effective preaching begins with respect for the original context of the biblical text. Understanding the circumstances, audience, and purpose behind a passage ensures that interpretation remains anchored in truth. This foundation must remain firm before any consideration of contemporary relevance.

From this grounding, we begin to discern timeless truth principles that reflect God's nature, human need, and the rhythm of redemption. These truths transcend the particularities of ancient life and speak into every generation.

To navigate this tension wisely, the following guidelines offer direction:

Commit to Exegetical Integrity

Interpretation must begin with a faithful reading of the text as it was originally given. Every application rests upon this first step. Where the original meaning is misunderstood, all that follows becomes misaligned.

Identify Timeless Truths

Scripture reveals principles that hold across generations. These can include God's faithfulness, human responsibility, the need for justice, or the call to love. Recognising these truths helps the Church apply Scripture without forcing ancient norms into modern settings.

Position Each Text Within the Broader Biblical Narrative

The story of Scripture follows a clear arc: creation, fall, redemption, and restoration. Placing a passage within this framework helps reveal its enduring significance and informs faithful application.

Understand the Role of Contextualization

Every act of teaching involves interpreting the text for a specific audience. The cultural, social, and spiritual realities of that audience shape how the message is received. Being conscious of this dynamic invites wisdom and discernment in communication.

Use Meaningful Illustrations and Analogies

Culturally resonant examples and stories serve as bridges between the world of the text and the lives of listeners. These should clarify truth, not dilute it, helping people grasp how Scripture speaks to their situation.

Maintain an Ongoing Posture of Listening

Interpreting and applying Scripture is not a one-time task; it is a continuous process. It requires continual engagement with both the Word and the world. Openness to new insights allows preachers to remain responsive to the Spirit's leading and to the evolving realities of those they serve.

Balancing context and application is the lifeblood of transformative preaching. It calls for faithfulness to the text and compassion for the listener. When done well, it creates a space where Scripture is not only heard but also lived, becoming a light in the present world and a witness to the enduring reign of Christ.

The Role of the Holy Spirit in Bible Study and Understanding

The Holy Spirit holds a vital role in the study and understanding of Scripture. The Bible itself is a product of divine inspiration, as affirmed in 2 Timothy 3:16. Engaging with its truths requires more than academic discipline or intellectual skill. It calls for spiritual dependence on the very Spirit who inspired its writing.

Inspiration

Scripture was not merely authored by human initiative. According to 2 Peter 1:21, men spoke from God as they were carried along by the Holy Spirit. The Bible carries divine origin and authority, having been shaped by the Spirit to reveal God's nature, His works, and His will. Its integrity and power flow from this supernatural source.

Illumination

While study tools and critical methods support biblical understanding, true comprehension is made possible through the illumination of the Holy Spirit. As stated in 1 Corinthians 2:12–14, the truths of God are spiritually discerned. The Spirit opens the believer's mind to see beyond the surface of the text and to grasp its depth. He enables a spiritual clarity that human reasoning alone cannot produce.

Conviction

As the Word is studied, the Holy Spirit brings conviction. This is not limited to intellectual agreement with Scripture but extends to the heart.

According to John 16:8, the Spirit reveals sin, righteousness, and judgment. Through this work, Scripture becomes a mirror through which readers see their need for repentance, renewal, and alignment with God's purposes.

Guidance

The Holy Spirit leads believers into truth, ensuring that interpretation remains faithful to the Word's intended meaning. John 16:13 confirms the Spirit's role in guiding into all truth. This guidance protects against error, helps interpret difficult passages in harmony with the broader counsel of God, and ensures applications are sound and spiritually edifying.

Empowerment

Biblical understanding is incomplete without obedience. The Holy Spirit empowers believers to live in accordance with the truth revealed in Scripture. As described in Ephesians 3:16, strength for obedience comes from the inner working of the Spirit. This divine enablement transforms knowledge into practice, shaping lives that reflect the character of Christ.

Communion

Studying the Bible in partnership with the Holy Spirit becomes an act of communion with God. Scripture is not approached merely as a text to analyse but as a living Word through which God speaks. The Spirit draws the reader into deeper fellowship with God, making the study of Scripture a place of spiritual encounter and formation.

Bible study, therefore, is not a purely intellectual discipline. It is a spiritual practice grounded in humility, guided by the Spirit, and aimed at transformation.

As we rely on the Holy Spirit in our study and application of the Word, we are equipped to fulfil the Apostolic Mandate, bringing the Kingdom of God to bear in every aspect of life.

Continuing Growth in Biblical Understanding

Biblical understanding is not a destination; it is a lifelong pursuit that unfolds through consistent study, spiritual openness, and faithful application of God's Word.

Scripture contains a wealth of wisdom that invites continuous exploration. Remaining engaged in this process enriches both our knowledge and our spiritual maturity.

Commitment to Lifelong Learning

Approaching Scripture as a lifelong student fosters humility and openness. Each reading offers new insights, and each season of life brings fresh perspective. A posture of learning keeps the heart receptive and the mind alert to deeper layers of meaning.

Regular Bible Reading and Study

Growth in understanding requires regular and intentional engagement with Scripture. Devotional reading nurtures the soul, while structured study builds theological depth. Both practices are essential in forming a well-rounded relationship with the Word.

Engagement with a Variety of Resources

The study of Scripture is enriched by tools that clarify and deepen comprehension. Commentaries, Bible dictionaries, theological texts, and scholarly works provide context and insight. These resources support responsible interpretation and broaden theological perspective.

Participation in Community

Biblical understanding flourishes in community. Discussions, teachings, and shared reflections offer opportunities to test interpretations, ask questions, and gain wisdom from the diverse experiences of fellow believers. Learning together strengthens accountability and nurtures growth.

Application of Biblical Truths

Understanding is strengthened through practice. As we act on the truths found in Scripture, those truths become rooted in our daily lives. Application reinforces comprehension and opens the way for deeper revelation.

Continual Prayer and Dependence on the Holy Spirit

The Spirit who inspired Scripture is also the one who illuminates it. Through prayer, we invite divine insight. As expressed in Psalm 119:18, we ask that our eyes be opened so that we may see the wonders of God's Word. The Holy Spirit faithfully guides us into truth, shaping both understanding and obedience.

Integration with Life Experience

With time, life's experiences shape how we engage Scripture. As seasons change, new layers of meaning emerge, allowing us to revisit familiar passages with greater depth and insight. Integrating biblical truths with real-life circumstances fosters maturity and wisdom.

The study of Scripture is not aimed at the accumulation of information. It is a pathway to spiritual formation and effective service in the Kingdom of God. As understanding grows, so does the capacity to reflect Christ and to advance His work in every sphere of influence. Let each encounter with Scripture move us closer to the fullness of God's purpose.

Conclusion

Homiletics, as the art and discipline of interpreting and applying Scripture, holds a central place in the fulfilment of the Apostolic Mandate. Through careful Bible exegesis and faithful application, the Word of God transcends the page and enters the hearts and lives of those who hear it. This chapter has underscored that preaching is not merely a transfer of knowledge but a sacred task that involves deep spiritual responsibility, theological precision, and pastoral sensitivity.

Sound exegesis ensures that Scripture is handled with integrity and accuracy. Accurate application allows biblical truths to speak into present realities with clarity and power. Both are sustained by the presence and guidance of the Holy Spirit, who reveals truth, convicts the heart, and empowers transformation. Avoiding the pitfalls of selective interpretation and maintaining balance between historical context and contemporary relevance are essential for faithful proclamation.

This work does not end at the pulpit. It continues in study rooms, small gatherings, personal reflections, and communal worship. The preacher, the teacher, and every believer who opens the Scriptures becomes a vessel through which the Kingdom of God takes visible form in everyday life.

CHAPTER FOUR

HERMENEUTICS - BIBLE INTERPRETATION AND APPLICATION

THE HERMENEUTICAL TASK is complex, given the Bible's diversity of authors, genres, and historical and cultural backgrounds. Yet, it is deeply rewarding, opening our eyes to the depth and richness of God's revelation, stirring our hearts with its transformative power, and guiding our steps with its divine wisdom.

By the way, we claim that the Bible consists of 70 books, considering the Psalms as a single book, rather than 66, as widely argued. Let us approach the task with humility, recognising the infinite depth of God's Word and our limited understanding. Let us also approach it with expectation, trusting that the same Spirit who inspired the Word will guide us into all truth and equip us to apply it in our lives and ministries.

Let us also remember that hermeneutics is not just a scholarly exercise, but a spiritual journey, one that deepens our communion with God and our commitment to His Kingdom. So, let us journey together, exploring the unsearchable riches of God's Word and learning to interpret and apply it for the advancement of His Kingdom in our spheres of influence.

Contextual Interpretation

One of the most fundamental principles in the study of hermeneutics is contextual interpretation. Scripture does not consist of isolated verses or statements. Instead, each part of Scripture is embedded within multiple layers of context, immediate, wider, and canonical, that influence its meaning. Ignoring these contexts can lead to misunderstandings, misinterpretations, and misuse of Scripture. By respecting these contexts, we can more accurately discern the intended meanings and apply them more appropriately in our contemporary setting.

Immediate Context: The immediate context includes the verses and passages surrounding the text under consideration. It often provides crucial information about the text's original purpose, audience, and meaning. Before jumping to conclusions about a text's meaning, we should first examine its immediate context.

Wider Context: The wider context includes the historical, cultural, social, and religious circumstances in which the text was written. It includes knowledge about the author, the recipients, the location, the time, and other factors that shaped the text's original production and reception. By understanding the wider context, we can avoid anachronistic readings that impose our modern perspectives on the ancient text.

Canonical Context: The canonical context refers to the text's position within the broader context of Scripture. The Bible is a diverse but unified book, with each part contributing to the overall biblical story and message. We should interpret individual texts in consideration of the broader biblical narrative, themes, and theology.

Practising contextual interpretation requires both diligent study and interpretive humility. We need to study because understanding the contexts requires knowledge of the biblical world, biblical languages, biblical literature, and biblical theology. We need humility because even with diligent study, our understanding of the contexts will always be partial and provisional. We must remain open to new insights and be willing to revise our interpretations in light of more compelling evidence or better reasoning.

As we strive to interpret the Bible contextually, we depend on the Holy Spirit's guidance, remembering that He inspired the original contexts and understands them perfectly. We also remember our Apostolic Mandate, seeking to translate the ancient contexts into our modern context in a way that faithfully represents the biblical message and effectively communicates it to our spheres of influence.

Tools For Biblical Interpretation

Interpreting the Bible is a rich and rewarding task, yet it also presents a significant challenge. The Scriptures were written in different languages, in different cultures, and in different periods than our own. Consequently, we need a variety of tools to help bridge these gaps and unlock the meaning of the biblical text.

The following tools are crucial for accurate and effective biblical interpretation:

Biblical Languages: Knowledge of the original languages of the Bible, Hebrew, Aramaic, and Greek, is invaluable for accurate interpretation. It enables a deeper understanding of the text that often cannot be fully captured in translation. Tools such as interlinear Bibles, language lexicons, and language courses can help in this area.

Bible Commentaries: Commentaries provide detailed explanations of biblical texts, verse by verse, drawing on a wealth of scholarly research. They can provide insights into the historical context, the original languages, literary features, theological implications, and practical applications of the text.

Bible Dictionaries and Encyclopaedias: These resources provide information on a wide range of biblical topics, including people, places, concepts, customs, and events. They can help clarify unfamiliar terms, explain cultural practices, and provide background information that enhances the understanding of the text.

Bible Atlases: An atlas can help visualise the geography of the biblical world, giving insights into the locations, distances, topography, climate, and other geographical factors that play a role in the biblical narrative.

Bible Concordances: A concordance lists the locations where each word appears in the Bible, making it a valuable tool for word studies and tracing themes and concepts throughout Scripture.

Bible Software: Various software programs and online platforms offer a wide range of resources for Bible study, including digital Bibles, language tools, commentaries, dictionaries, atlases, and more. They also provide powerful search and analysis tools that can greatly enhance your study of Scripture.

Theological Literature: Books, articles, and lectures on biblical theology, systematic theology, historical theology, and practical theology can provide deeper insights into the biblical message and its relevance for various areas of life and ministry.

Community: Finally, one of the most valuable tools for biblical interpretation is the community of fellow believers, both contemporary and historical. By engaging in dialogue with others, we can gain new perspectives, avoid personal biases, and enrich our understanding of the biblical text.

Using these tools effectively requires both commitment and discernment: commitment to diligent study and lifelong learning, and discernment to evaluate different views and to integrate various insights into a coherent understanding of the biblical message. As we use these tools under the guidance of the Holy Spirit, we will be better equipped to fulfil our Apostolic Mandate, interpreting and applying God's Word in our spheres of influence.

Approaches to Biblical Interpretation

There is a broad range of methods and approaches that scholars and Bible readers employ to interpret the Scriptures. Each of these approaches offers a different lens through which to view and understand the text, and each has its unique strengths and potential pitfalls.

Here are some key approaches to biblical interpretation:

Literal Approach: The literal approach interprets the text at face value, basing its understanding on the text's plain and obvious meaning. This approach respects the author's intention and the text's historical and grammatical context. However, it can be prone to oversimplification, failing to account for symbolic, figurative, or metaphorical language.

Historical-Critical Approach: The historical-critical approach aims to interpret the text within its original historical and cultural context. It uses critical methods to reconstruct the historical circumstances, literary forms, and theological perspectives of biblical authors. While this approach can provide valuable insights, it can sometimes be overly sceptical or reductionistic, discounting the divine inspiration or canonical context of the text.

Theological Approach: The theological approach interprets the text in consideration of the broader biblical theology. It explores the text's contribution to the overall biblical message and its relevance for doctrinal or ethical issues. However, one must be careful not to impose systematic theological categories onto the biblical text.

Literary Approach: The literary approach focuses on the text as a work of literature, examining its elements and their interplay. It pays close attention to literary devices, genre conventions, narrative structures, and poetic features. This approach can illuminate the beauty, power, and subtlety of the biblical text, but must also respect the text's historical and theological dimensions.

Canonical Approach: The canonical approach interprets individual texts within the context of the entire biblical canon. It recognises the Bible's unity and diversity, as well as the interplay between its various parts. This approach can deepen our understanding of the biblical story and message, but should avoid forcing connections that are not warranted by the text.

Reader-Response Approach: The reader-response approach focuses on the reader's engagement with the text. It explores how the text resonates with individual readers or communities within their specific contexts and experiences. While this approach can highlight the personal and communal relevance of the Bible, it should not neglect the text's original meaning or universal truth.

Spiritual Approach: The spiritual approach views reading and interpreting the Bible as a spiritual practice, encompassing prayer, meditation, and spiritual transformation. It pays attention to the role of the Holy Spirit in inspiring, illuminating, and applying the text. This approach is central to our Apostolic Mandate, but should be balanced with rigorous study and critical thinking.

A well-rounded biblical interpretation draws on multiple approaches, using each as a tool to explore different aspects of the text. By doing so, we can gain a richer, deeper, and more nuanced understanding of the biblical text, enabling us to apply it more effectively in our lives and ministries.

Applying Hermeneutical Principles

Knowing the principles of hermeneutics is one thing, but putting them into practice is another. The application of hermeneutical principles involves both a methodical process and thoughtful discernment. Here are some practical steps for applying these principles in your Bible study and interpretation:

Begin your study with prayer. Ask God to open your heart and mind to His Word and to guide you in understanding and applying it. Depend on the Holy Spirit, who inspired the Scriptures and can illuminate their meaning to you.

Carefully read the text and observe what it says. Take note of the literary genre, the structure, the key terms, the main ideas, the characters, the setting, and any other features of the text. Utilise tools such as Bible translations, concordances, and lexicons to enhance your observation.

Study the various contexts of the text: the immediate context, the wider historical-cultural context, and the canonical context. Use tools like commentaries, Bible dictionaries, and Bible encyclopaedias to gain insights into these contexts.

Based on your observation and contextual analysis, interpret the meaning of the text. Seek to understand what the author intended to communicate to the original audience, and how that message fits into the broader biblical theology. Be aware of different interpretive approaches and use them judiciously to illuminate different aspects of the text.

Consider the implications of the text for your beliefs and practices. What does it teach about God, humanity, salvation, ethics, etc.? How does it challenge, encourage, comfort, or guide us? How does it connect with your personal experience or current situation?

Study how the text applies to your life and ministry. How does it speak to your specific context and circumstances? How can it inform your decisions, shape your character, guide your actions, or influence your relationships? Remember that the aim of Bible study is not only the transformation of ourselves, but also the transformation of the world around us.

Share your insights and applications with others. Engage in dialogue with fellow believers, whether in a Bible study group, a church service, an online forum, or a personal conversation. Learn from their perspectives, respond to their questions, and welcome their feedback.

Finally, integrate your biblical interpretation with your broader understanding of God, the world, and your mission. Let it inform your theology, your worldview, and your ministry. May it inspire your worship, devotion, and service. Let it fulfil your Apostolic Mandate, bringing the Kingdom of God to your sphere of influence.

Remember that applying hermeneutical principles is an ongoing process —a lifelong journey of learning, growth, and transformation. So be patient with yourself, be humble in your claims, and be passionate in your pursuit of God's truth. Be diligent in your study, be sensitive to the Spirit's guidance, and be bold in your application. Furthermore, through it all, may your love for God, His Word, and His world deepen and overflow.

Challenges in Biblical Interpretation

The task of biblical interpretation, while deeply rewarding, also presents certain challenges. These challenges arise from the complexities of the biblical text itself, the distance between the biblical world and our world, the diversity of readers and interpretations, and the practical demands of applying the biblical message.

The Bible was written in various times and cultures, in different languages, and for different audiences than our own. This historical distance can make it challenging to understand the original meaning of the texts and translate them into our contemporary context.

It shows a diverse range of cultural perspectives and practices, some of which may seem unusual or even offensive to us. Interpreting the Bible requires careful discernment of what is culturally specific and what is universally applicable.

The Bible encompasses a diverse range of literary genres, including narrative, poetry, prophecy, law, wisdom, apocalyptic, epistle, and others. Each genre has its conventions and requires its interpretive strategies. The Bible also employs a rich array of literary devices, including symbolism, metaphor, irony, and parable, which can add layers of meaning but also complicate interpretation.

The Bible speaks of profound and mysterious realities: God, creation, humanity, sin, redemption, covenant, kingdom, and more. Grasping these theological truths can challenge our intellectual capacities and spiritual sensitivities. It can also confront our existing beliefs and values, requiring us to change or expand our understanding.

Readers or students of the Bible often come to different interpretations of the same text, based on their different backgrounds, perspectives, assumptions, or interests. These interpretive differences can lead to confusion, disagreements, or even conflicts within the Christian community. They can also raise questions about the authority, clarity, or relevance of the Bible.

Applying the biblical message in our lives and societies is not always straightforward. It requires wisdom to discern the principles behind biblical commands or examples, courage to confront the societal norms or personal habits that contradict these principles, and creativity to embody these principles in our specific circumstances. It also requires patience and perseverance, as change often takes time and faces resistance.

Despite these challenges, we should not be discouraged or disheartened. Rather, we should see them as opportunities for growth, dialogue, and transformation. They drive us to study more diligently, to listen more attentively, to discuss more respectfully, and to pray more fervently. They remind us of our dependence on the Holy

Spirit, who inspired the Scriptures and can guide us in understanding and applying them. And they keep us humble, knowing that our interpretations are always partial and provisional and that our applications are always in need of correction and refinement. Ultimately, these challenges serve our Apostolic Mandate, deepening our engagement with the Bible, enriching our experience of God's truth, and equipping us to bring the Kingdom of God to our spheres of influence.

Hermeneutics and the Community of Believers

Hermeneutics, the art and science of biblical interpretation, is not a solitary endeavour. It is intrinsically tied to the community of believers. The Bible itself was written within a community context and was meant to be read, understood, and lived out within the context of community.

Here are several ways in which hermeneutics and the community of believers intersect:

Shared Tradition and Wisdom: Within the community of believers, a rich heritage of biblical interpretation, theological reflection, and practical wisdom is found. Engaging with this tradition provides valuable insights, perspectives, and interpretations that can deepen our understanding of the Bible. Learning from the wisdom of those who have gone before us helps us avoid individualistic or idiosyncratic interpretations.

Interpretive Dialogue: Engaging in dialogue and discussion with fellow believers fosters a more comprehensive and nuanced understanding of the Bible. As we interact with others, we gain different perspectives, challenge our assumptions, and refine our understanding of the world. This interpretive dialogue within the community helps us discern the collective wisdom of the Body of Christ.

Accountability and Correction: The community of believers provides accountability in biblical interpretation. It guards against individual biases, personal agendas, or skewed interpretations. When interpretations stray from the collective understanding of the community, there is an opportunity for correction and guidance, ensuring fidelity to the biblical message.

Cultural and Contextual Insight: Within the community, a diverse range of backgrounds, experiences, and cultural contexts exists. This diversity enriches our understanding of the Bible, as different perspectives shed light on the cultural nuances, contemporary applications, and relevant issues tied to the biblical text. The community helps us bridge the historical and cultural gap between the biblical world and our own.

Spiritual Discernment: The Holy Spirit is not limited to working in isolation but often moves within the collective discernment of the community. As believers come together in humility and prayer, seeking the Spirit's guidance, there is a heightened sensitivity to the Spirit's leading and illumination in the interpretation of Scripture. The community acts as a safeguard against individualistic or self-serving interpretations.

Collaborative Application: Hermeneutics extends beyond understanding the text to the application of biblical truths. Within the community, we can collaborate on how to apply the Bible's teachings in our individual lives, families, churches, and broader societal contexts. By working together, we gain wisdom, encouragement, and accountability in living out the transformative message of Scripture.

The community of believers plays a vital role in hermeneutics, ensuring that interpretation remains grounded in the larger body of Christ, accountable to the historic teachings of the Church, and sensitive to the leading of the Holy Spirit. By embracing the wisdom and insights of the community, we are better equipped to faithfully interpret and apply the Bible in our lives and fulfil our Apostolic Mandate together, bringing the Kingdom of God to our spheres of influence.

CHAPTER FIVE

ECCLESIOLOGY: THE 5-FOLD MINISTRY

ECCLESIOLOGY, THE STUDY of the Church, holds deep significance for every believer. It addresses the nature, purpose, structure, and ministry of the Church as instituted by God. Within this framework lies the 5-Fold Ministry, a biblical model designed to equip and empower the Church to carry out its Apostolic Mandate with clarity and effectiveness.

The 5-Fold Ministry unfolds the scriptural foundation and functional roles of the five ministry gifts: apostle, prophet, evangelist, pastor, and teacher. Each gift reflects a divine strategy for building, nurturing, and mobilising the Body of Christ. Their roles are not defined by status or control, but rather assigned to foster collaboration, spiritual growth, and readiness for service. The Church is strengthened when each function works in harmony, with every believer supported in discovering and activating their God-given calling.

We will confront prevailing misconceptions that have led to confusion, misuse, or resistance to this biblical framework. With practical insights, we will explore how to apply the 5-Fold Ministry across diverse congregational settings, ensuring that its power is realised in both structure and spirit.

Fold 1: Apostles

The office of the apostle holds a foundational role within the five-fold ministry. Derived from the Greek word *Apostolos*, meaning "one who is sent," the term reflects divine commissioning. Apostles are not self-appointed; God sends them with a mandate to establish, advance, and uphold the structures of the Kingdom. Their task is not confined to evangelistic expansion, but extends to laying doctrinal foundations, providing spiritual oversight, and fostering unity within the Church. Apostles lead with vision, build with conviction, and govern with spiritual authority under the Lordship of Christ.

Understanding the role of apostles begins with examining how Scripture defines and exemplifies this office. From Jesus's ministry to the formation of the early Church, the office of apostleship emerges as a distinct calling that integrates leadership, revelation, and mission.

Biblical Foundation of Apostleship

The apostolic office is firmly rooted in Scripture, dating back to Jesus Christ's appointment of the twelve. These men were more than followers; they were witnesses of His life, death, resurrection, and ascension (Matthew 10:14). Their mandate was foundational. They became the first builders of the Church, laying doctrinal stones that continue to guide the faith community today (Ephesians 2:20).

Beyond the twelve, the New Testament identifies other individuals who bore apostolic authority. Paul referred to himself as an apostle by divine appointment, underscoring that his commissioning came directly from Christ and not through human means (Romans 1:1; Galatians 1:1). His ministry among the Gentiles exemplified the apostolic calling to pioneer new frontiers and establish order where the Gospel had not yet taken root.

Additionally, names such as Barnabas, Epaphroditus, Andronicus, Junia, Timothy, and Titus appear in apostolic contexts, each playing vital roles in supporting, teaching, or strengthening the churches. Their contributions affirm that apostleship extended beyond the original twelve and continued as a vital function in the early Church.

The authority of apostles was not derived from popularity or personal charisma but from their divine commissioning and fruitfulness in ministry. Their teachings shaped doctrine, their writings were preserved as Scripture, and their counsel was received with reverence across early Christian communities. They functioned as stewards of revelation and overseers of order, acting as spiritual architects under Christ, the Chief Cornerstone.

While the original twelve apostles held a unique place in history, their role set a precedent for apostolic ministry that transcends time. Apostles today do not replace their foundation, but they carry forward the same DNA of divine sending, called to plant, govern, and equip with clarity, courage, and character.

Recognising the biblical pattern of apostleship equips the Church to discern, receive, and honour true apostolic leadership in the present age. It protects against counterfeit expressions and ensures that apostolic influence builds up rather than divides. As the Church honours this office, it aligns itself with God's architecture for growth, maturity, and mobilisation.

When apostolic ministry functions in its rightful place, the entire Body of Christ benefits. Leaders are trained. Churches are planted. Doctrines are protected. Unity is strengthened. The Apostolic Mandate to make Christ known and form mature disciples across every sphere is advanced with intentionality and order.

The Apostolic Anointing and Gifting

The apostolic office operates under a distinct anointing and gifting bestowed by the Holy Spirit. This empowerment is not ornamental; it is functional, equipping apostles with spiritual capacity to fulfil their divine assignment in the Church and across broader Kingdom territories. Understanding this anointing is key to appreciating the weight, reach, and responsibilities of apostolic ministry.

Apostolic ministry is not built on charisma or human appointment. Its legitimacy flows from a divine commissioning, rooted in spiritual authority, sustained by revelation, and marked by impact. Each dimension of the apostolic function reflects the Spirit's work through individuals who are aligned with God's purpose for the maturity and mobilisation of the Body of Christ.

Here are some key aspects to consider:

Commissioning and Authority

Apostles are commissioned by Christ and entrusted with authority that flows from alignment with Scripture and submission to the Lordship of Jesus. This authority is spiritual and has a directional function. It enables apostles to lay foundations, establish healthy governance, and provide covering for churches and leaders. Their authority is not domineering, but generative; it births, builds, and brings order where the Kingdom must take root.

Pioneering Leadership and Kingdom Vision

Apostles lead with vision. They see with spiritual clarity, often perceiving what has not yet been built. This visionary insight enables them to pioneer ministries, chart new territory, and mobilise resources for Kingdom advancement. Their leadership is marked by bold obedience, creative direction, and the ability to galvanise others toward a common Kingdom objective. Apostles are catalysts, often raised by God to initiate reform and stir movement in stagnant environments.

Spiritual Discernment and Insight

Apostolic anointing carries a heightened awareness of spiritual realities. Apostles discern atmospheres, identify root issues, and perceive the counsel of the Spirit. This discernment is not suspicion or opinion; it is revelation given for the health and purity of the Church. Through Spirit-led insight, apostles provide correction, wisdom, and prophetic guidance that guard the integrity of the Gospel and help the Church remain aligned with its mission.

Strategic Wisdom and Divine Architecture

Apostles are master builders. Their gift includes the ability to develop divine blueprints, implement systems, and bring strategic order to ministries and networks. Their thinking is structured yet spiritually dynamic. Whether in planting churches, establishing training centres, or forming apostolic teams, apostles move with clarity and foresight.

They discern timing, assign roles, and orchestrate movements that outlive their leadership.

Equipping and Multiplying Others

Apostolic ministry is not self-preserving; it is fundamentally reproductive in nature. Apostles carry a deep burden to equip others, raise leaders, and release individuals into their God-ordained assignments. They cultivate capacity in people and structures, ensuring that the work of ministry continues beyond them. This equipping is intentional, strategic, and Spirit-led, fuelling Kingdom advancement through trained and activated believers.

Cross-Cultural Perspective and Global Reach

Apostles often carry a burden that transcends cultural or geographical limitations. Their assignments involve reaching across languages, nations, and backgrounds to build bridges and unify the Church. They foster global partnerships, mobilise missionary initiatives, and plant cross-cultural works that reflect the fullness of God's heart for every tribe and tongue. Apostolic ministry thrives in diversity, fostering unity without erasing individual identities.

Demonstration of Power

Signs, wonders, and miracles frequently accompany the apostolic office. These manifestations are not displays of power for admiration, but affirmations of divine authority. The supernatural often marks the advancement of apostolic work, validating the Word preached and opening hearts to the reality of God's Kingdom. Miracles, healing, deliverance, and prophetic breakthroughs accompany the apostolic movement where faith is alive, and Christ is exalted.

A Broader Dispersion of Apostolic Grace

While the apostolic office is distinct, apostolic grace is not confined to a title. The Holy Spirit distributes apostolic functions to various individuals across the Body of Christ. Many believers operate with apostolic vision, strategy, or boldness, even without formal recognition. These individuals often exhibit leadership, innovation, and missional focus, contributing significantly to the advancement of God's purposes in their contexts.

Recognising the apostolic anointing and gifting enables the Church to honour what God is doing through His appointed vessels. It removes suspicion, breaks cycles of dishonour, and makes room for transformation. When apostles are released into their calling, the Church matures, ministries are aligned, and the Kingdom gains momentum.

We do not exalt individuals; we align with divine order. Apostolic ministry is a gift to the Church, not a platform for control. It is a movement of builders, sent ones, and vision-bearers, entrusted with the task of preparing the Body for effectiveness, unity, and maturity. This is part of the inheritance we receive through the Apostolic Mandate.

Relationship Between the Apostolic And Prophetic

The apostolic and prophetic ministries function as a foundational tandem in God's design for the Church. These two offices, while distinct in function, share a spiritual synergy that is essential for building, guiding, and preserving the integrity of the Church's mission. Their relationship is not merely cooperative; it is divinely orchestrated to establish God's purposes in the earth through revelation, direction, structure, and movement.

Shared Foundation in Christ

The ministries of apostles and prophets originate in Christ, the chief cornerstone. Scripture affirms this foundational relationship in Ephesians 2:20, where the Church is described as "built on the foundation of the apostles and prophets."

This foundation is not based on personal charisma or institutional rank, but on Christ's revealed will and the responsibility to uphold and communicate it with clarity and conviction. Together, apostles and prophets uphold the framework that keeps the Church aligned with its divine assignment.

Revelation and Directional Clarity

Prophets carry the grace to hear and declare the mind of God with accuracy and spiritual sensitivity. Their role involves delivering insight that often addresses the spiritual condition of the Church, societal matters, or upcoming seasons of change.

Apostles function with Kingdom vision, taking the revealed word and framing it into strategy, movement, and structural reform. Prophetic insight opens the heavens, and apostolic direction grounds that insight into practical transformation. This tandem ensures the Church both hears what God is saying and knows how to walk in it.

Guardianship and Alignment

In God's order, prophets and apostles provide a form of mutual spiritual accountability. Prophets carry the burden of truth and the courage to call out deviation from God's heart.

Their utterances bring alignment and purification, often calling the Church back to holiness and obedience. Apostles guard the overall movement and structure of the Church, ensuring that spiritual activity aligns with scriptural foundations and the direction of the Kingdom. In partnership, these ministries safeguard the Church against spiritual, doctrinal, and structural drift.

Establishing and Edifying the Church

Apostles build what prophets reveal. The apostolic office lays the groundwork for doctrine, discipleship, and governance. It frames the necessary systems and equips leaders who carry out Kingdom responsibilities.

Prophetic ministry builds on this foundation with edification, encouragement, and correction. It keeps the Church attuned to the heartbeat of heaven, ensuring that what is built remains alive, responsive, and holy. Together, they construct and sustain a living, Spirit-led Church.

Intercessory Depth and Strategic Prayer

Both apostles and prophets engage deeply in intercessory work. This is not optional; it is integral. Prophets carry the burden of the Lord in prayer, often sensing spiritual shifts before they occur. Apostles anchor these revelations in prayerful decrees and strategic actions. Together, their intercession tears down demonic resistance, opens new territories for the Gospel, and births Kingdom advancement in the spiritual and natural realms.

Collaborative Unity for Kingdom Advancement

Apostolic and prophetic functions thrive in environments of unity. When these ministries operate in spiritual harmony, the result is a Church that moves with divine accuracy and strength. An apostolic structure without prophetic sensitivity becomes rigid; prophetic activity without apostolic order risks disorder. Collaboration enhances both gifts. In shared submission to Christ and mutual honour, they strengthen one another and the Church they serve.

Posture of Humility and Mutual Submission

True apostolic and prophetic ministry flows from humility. Each recognises the grace at work in the other. There is no rivalry in divine function. Instead, there is a conscious effort to yield to the Spirit through one another's gifts. Mutual submission is not a sign of weakness; it is a mark of spiritual maturity. It keeps both ministries accountable and fosters an environment where truth, power, and love co-exist in balance.

Kingdom Impact Through Divine Synergy

When apostles and prophets walk in alignment, the Church experiences greater clarity, spiritual authority, and progress in fulfilling God's mandate. Cities are disciplined, territories shift, and hearts are turned toward the Lord. Their relationship forms a prophetic-apostolic synergy that prepares the Body of Christ for maturity, mission, and multiplication.

This divine partnership is not reserved for a few; it is a model for the Church. As we honour and cultivate the apostolic and prophetic ministries, we create an atmosphere where the Kingdom can be established with order, power, and purpose. Through their collaborative obedience, the Apostolic Mandate advances with strength and precision.

New Apostolic Movement Terminology

The New Apostolic Movement refers to a contemporary stream within Christianity that emphasises the active presence and function of the apostolic ministry in the Church today. This movement is rooted in a conviction that God continues to appoint apostolic leaders for the strengthening, expansion, and governance of the Church according to biblical patterns.

As the movement has grown, a distinct vocabulary has emerged to describe its core beliefs, structures, and practices. Below are key terms frequently associated with this movement:

Apostolic Network

These refer to relational associations of churches, ministries, and leaders united around shared apostolic vision and values. These networks are often non-denominational and function as collaborative communities rather than institutional hierarchies. They serve as platforms for connection, accountability, mutual support, and the strategic advancement of Kingdom initiatives.

Apostolic Alignment

This describes the intentional relational positioning of churches, leaders, or ministries under the spiritual authority and guidance of recognised apostolic leaders. Apostolic alignment is entered into willingly, reflecting a commitment to shared values, vision, and accountability for greater Kingdom effectiveness.

Apostolic Oversight

Apostolic oversight involves the spiritual care, direction, and counsel that apostolic leaders provide to those aligned with them. This oversight helps ensure that doctrine, practices, and leadership remain sound, biblically anchored, and ethically grounded. It fosters maturity, accountability, and clarity of vision within ministries.

Apostolic Teams

Apostolic teams are groups of leaders who serve alongside an apostolic leader to offer wisdom, counsel, and practical support. These teams function in unity to shape the vision, respond to challenges, and implement strategic actions that edify and expand the Church. The team dynamic reflects shared leadership and spiritual unity.

Apostolic Reformation

This term highlights the movement's call to return to New Testament patterns of Church governance and ministry. Apostolic Reformation involves a renewed recognition of apostles and the restructuring of Church life around biblical foundations. The focus is on spiritual restoration, mission advancement, and alignment with God's design for the Church.

Apostolic Sending

Apostolic sending refers to the commissioning of individuals or teams to plant churches, launch ministries, or carry out assignments in new regions. This sending affirms spiritual gifting, calling, and maturity. It represents a purposeful act of authorisation and blessing, with the expectation of fruitfulness and impact in the field of service.

Apostolic Succession

Apostolic succession speaks to the transference of responsibility, wisdom, and spiritual authority from one apostolic leader to the next. It ensures the continuity of leadership and vision across generations, preserving the integrity and strength of the apostolic ministry over time.

It is important to understand that while these terms are common within the New Apostolic Movement, their application may vary across regions, cultures, and Church expressions. The language used may differ, but the underlying emphasis remains on empowering the Church through biblically grounded, Spirit-led leadership.

Our understanding of these terms should always be guided by Scripture and confirmed by the fruit of transformed lives and advancing mission. Terminology serves to explain, not define, the move of God. At the heart of this movement lies the pursuit of God's original intent for the Church to be a maturing, sent, and empowered Body that lives out its Apostolic Mandate wherever it is placed.

Apostleship and Missions

Apostleship and missions are deeply connected expressions of the Church's calling to bring the Gospel to all nations. Apostles play a pivotal role in advancing this mission by carrying a vision that stretches beyond established territories and conventional boundaries. Their leadership, anointing, and insight are essential to the Church's global outreach and the fulfilment of the Great Commission.

Apostles often serve as initiators of mission efforts. Their spiritual DNA carries a mandate to establish Kingdom presence where it does not yet exist. With a readiness to reach unreached communities, they embrace the responsibility of sending, commissioning individuals and teams to plant churches, proclaim the Gospel, and demonstrate the power of the Kingdom in new regions. Their burden for the lost is marked by a sense of divine urgency that compels them to act.

Apostles are mobilisers by design. They identify and nurture the calling of those entrusted with the task of mission. Through teaching, impartation, and personal discipleship, they raise labourers who carry the Gospel across cultures. Apostolic leaders invest in preparation, release people into their assignments, and continue to provide guidance and oversight throughout the mission process.

Missions require more than zeal; they demand vision, structure, and strategy. Apostles bring these components together. With the ability to discern times and seasons, they offer leadership that is both prophetic and practical. They help prioritise territories, coordinate resources, and establish partnerships to ensure effectiveness and sustainability in outreach efforts.

One of the defining characteristics of apostolic missions is their awareness of and sensitivity to culture. Apostles understand that the Gospel must be communicated in a way that honours the cultural context without compromising biblical truth. This sensitivity allows the message of Christ to resonate deeply with communities, fostering genuine transformation rather than superficial conversion.

Missions inevitably involve confrontation with spiritual forces that resist the advancement of the Gospel. Apostles serve as spiritual gatekeepers, offering prayer support, guidance, and intercession to those in the field. Their presence often brings breakthroughs, enabling teams to overcome opposition and establish spiritual authority in difficult environments.

Apostolic missions are never meant to foster dependence. Apostles prioritise the development of local leaders who can shepherd their communities with strength and integrity. They raise leaders who understand their context, embrace their call, and build indigenous expressions of Church life that are sustainable and rooted in Scripture.

For apostles, missions are not complete without the establishment of local churches. They do not focus solely on evangelism but ensure that every new believer is discipled, grounded in the faith, and equipped to multiply. Apostolic missions yield churches that reflect the nature of the Kingdom, thriving, self-governing, and grounded in truth.

The relationship between apostleship and missions highlights the vital role that apostles play in mobilising, equipping, and empowering the Church for global outreach. Apostles provide visionary leadership, strategic guidance, and spiritual covering to ensure the effective spread of the Gospel to the ends of the earth. Through its apostolic ministry, the Church fulfils its Apostolic Mandate to bring the Kingdom of God to every nation, tribe, and tongue.

Apostles' Relationship with Pastors, Teachers, Prophets, and Evangelists

The relationship between apostles and the other ministry gifts, pastors, teachers, prophets, and evangelists, is essential for the complete functioning and edification of the Church. Each ministry gift carries a distinct role, yet all are designed to operate in harmony, complementing one another in service to God's people.

These ministry gifts function together to support the health and growth of the Church. Apostles provide vision, oversight, and strategic guidance. Pastors offer care and nurture. Teachers ground believers in biblical truth and discipleship. Prophets bring spiritual insight and direction. Evangelists focus on proclaiming the Gospel and drawing souls into the faith.

Apostles promote unity among these roles. They encourage collaboration that honours each gift's uniqueness while reinforcing their shared commitment to the Church's mission. When these gifts work together, the Church operates with greater clarity, purpose, and spiritual authority.

This relationship is governed by mutual submission. Each gift recognises the value of the others and submits to their function in humility. Apostles create space for growth and provide development opportunities, especially by equipping and empowering leaders in every area of ministry.

Apostles also help confirm and safeguard the work of pastors, teachers, prophets, and evangelists. Their discernment brings stability to ministry expressions, ensuring alignment with biblical truth and the overall vision of the Church. This guidance is vital in maintaining doctrinal soundness and protecting the flock from error.

Together, apostles and the other ministry offices multiply the Church's effectiveness. They raise new leaders, plant churches, and extend the reach of the Gospel. Their interdependence creates a Church that is whole, balanced, and spiritually vibrant. Each gift contributes a necessary strength, enriching the Church with wisdom, nurture, insight, and outreach.

Recognising and honouring this relationship helps the Church walk in unity and fullness. When these gifts are received and released in their proper place, the Body of Christ becomes a dynamic witness to the world and a faithful steward of the Apostolic Mandate.

Conclusion

The apostolic office remains foundational to the Church's design and divine mission. While apostles are often forerunners sent ones who carry vision, spiritual authority, and strategy, they are never meant to function in isolation. Their ministry flourishes in communion with prophets, pastors, teachers, and evangelists, each bringing a necessary dimension to the expression and effectiveness of the Body of Christ.

The strength of the apostolic calling lies not merely in pioneering or establishing but in nurturing a culture of alignment, accountability, and empowerment. Apostles call forth new territory, but they also call forth people leaders, communities, and generations into maturity, sound doctrine, and apostolic purpose. When their gift is received rightly and when apostles remain submitted to the Word and the Spirit, they serve as both foundation and catalyst, bringing alignment to the Church's mission and anchoring it to heaven's blueprint.

As we uphold the apostolic office, we are reminded that it is not defined by title or ambition but by the call to serve, to build, and to send. In honouring apostleship as God intended, we honour Christ, the true Apostle and High Priest of our faith (Hebrews 3:1), and we position the Church to rise in strength, clarity, and Kingdom impact.

Fold 2: Prophets

The office of the prophet holds a vital place within the Five-Fold Ministry. Prophets are called and anointed by God to speak His messages with clarity, conviction, and obedience. They bring revelation, insight, and spiritual direction that edify the Church and align it with God's purposes. Rooted in Scripture and active throughout the ages, prophetic ministry remains essential for discernment, correction, encouragement, and the unfolding of divine plans.

The prophetic office is not an accessory to church life; it is foundational to its growth and alignment.

Prophetic Ministry in the Life of the Church

Prophetic ministry holds a vital place in the life of the Church, releasing divine revelation, spiritual discernment, and direction. It enriches worship, discipleship, and mission, enabling believers to walk in greater clarity, conviction, and spiritual maturity.

At its core, prophetic ministry unveils God's heart and mind. Prophets are gifted to receive and articulate divine insight, revealing God's character, His intentions, and His call to His people. Through their voice, the Church discerns

God's guidance and gains timely instruction for both individual and corporate decisions.

One of the primary functions of prophetic ministry is to strengthen the Church through encouragement and edification. Prophets release words that affirm, uplift, and instil hope, reminding believers of God's love, faithfulness, and promises. This ministry often restores confidence and renews vision where discouragement or confusion may have taken root.

Prophets also serve as watchmen, endowed with sharp spiritual discernment. They expose deception, identify spiritual strongholds, and bring correction when necessary. Their role is not to condemn, but to align the Church with truth, foster accountability, and call God's people into holiness. In this way, prophetic ministry serves as a safeguard against compromise and spiritual drift.

Worship is profoundly enriched through prophetic expression. Prophetic songs, spontaneous prayer, and spirit-led declarations create a deep sense of intimacy with God. These moments often become sacred spaces where the presence of the Holy Spirit is tangibly felt, drawing the Church into deeper adoration and surrender.

In guiding the Church, prophets offer divine perspective that illuminates complex situations. They bring clarity to decision-making, counsel leaders with insight, and keep the Church attuned to God's strategic direction. Their voice acts as a spiritual compass, aligning the Body with heaven's rhythm.

Intercession is another hallmark of prophetic ministry. Prophets often carry a deep burden for the Church and the world, engaging in prayer that seeks breakthrough, deliverance, and the advancement of God's kingdom. Their intercession forms a spiritual covering, creating room for the power and authority of God to manifest in tangible ways.

Prophetic ministry is not limited to the prophets themselves. It equips and activates the broader Body to hear God, discern His voice, and operate in prophetic gifts. Prophets mentor, train, and release others to step into their prophetic calling, cultivating a culture where believers are sensitive to the Spirit and confident in their spiritual authority.

Knowing the importance of prophetic ministry allows the Church to grow in both depth and direction. When embraced with discernment and honour, it fosters intimacy with God, strengthens spiritual alignment, and releases power for Kingdom advancement. In fulfilling the Apostolic Mandate, prophetic ministry plays a vital role in shaping a Church that listens, obeys, and manifests the will of God in every sphere of influence.

Prophetic Books and Major Prophets

The prophetic books of the Old Testament offer essential insights into the ministry of prophets and continue to shape our understanding of prophetic function in the Church today. These writings contain messages, visions, and divine revelations given to chosen vessels who spoke to God's people in critical seasons.

Among these texts, certain prophets stand out for the volume and depth of their work, commonly referred to as the major prophets.

Prophetic Books: The prophetic books include Isaiah, Jeremiah, Lamentations, Ezekiel, and the Book of Daniel in the Hebrew Bible, also known as the Old Testament. These books contain the prophetic words and messages of the respective prophets, addressing various themes such as judgment, repentance, restoration, and the future Messianic hope.

Each book offers unique insights into the heart and mind of God, His plans for His people, and the call for obedience and faithfulness. Here is a brief overview of each of the prophetic books mentioned above:

Isaiah:

The Book of Isaiah is one of the longest prophetic books in the Old Testament and is often considered a masterpiece of Hebrew poetry. It encompasses a diverse range of prophecies and themes, addressing both the immediate historical context of the prophet's time and foreshadowing future events.

Isaiah's prophecies speak of God's judgment on rebellious nations, the need for repentance, the coming Messiah, and the ultimate restoration and glory of God's people. The book is renowned for its Messianic prophecies, such as the prophecy of the virgin birth (Isaiah 7:14) and the suffering servant (Isaiah 53), which find their fulfilment in Jesus Christ.

Jeremiah:

The Book of Jeremiah provides an intimate glimpse into the life and ministry of the prophet Jeremiah, who faithfully delivered God's messages to the people of Judah during a time of spiritual decline. Jeremiah's prophecies encompass both judgment and hope, as he warns the people of impending destruction due to their rebellion but also offers the promise of restoration and a new covenant.

The book reveals Jeremiah's struggles, personal anguish, and unwavering commitment to proclaim God's word despite opposition. It highlights the importance of repentance, obedience to God's commands, and trust in His faithfulness.

Lamentations:

Lamentations is a collection of poetic dirges traditionally attributed to the prophet Jeremiah. It mourns the destruction of Jerusalem and the Babylonian exile, expressing deep grief and sorrow over the consequences of the people's sins and the devastation they experienced.

The book serves as a reflection on the consequences of disobedience, the enduring faithfulness of God even in times of judgment, and the need for repentance and hope in God's mercy.

Ezekiel:

The Book of Ezekiel presents the visions, symbolic acts, and prophecies of the prophet Ezekiel during the Babylonian exile. Ezekiel's prophecies address the spiritual condition of the exiled Israelites, the judgment on the nations, the restoration of God's people, and the future glory of God's Kingdom.

The book contains vivid imagery and symbolic actions that convey powerful messages. It emphasises the sovereignty of God, the importance of personal responsibility, and the promise of spiritual renewal and restoration.

Daniel:

The Book of Daniel combines prophecy, apocalyptic visions, and historical accounts. It recounts the experiences of Daniel and his fellow exiles in Babylon, offering prophetic insights into future events.

The book includes well-known stories such as Daniel in the lion's den and the fiery furnace, as well as visions that reveal God's sovereignty over earthly kingdoms and the ultimate triumph of His Kingdom. Daniel's prophecies point to the coming Messiah and anticipate future events, including the rise and fall of empires and the final establishment of God's eternal reign.

These books remain invaluable to the Church. They testify to God's justice and mercy, calling believers to repentance and deepening our understanding of His redemptive plan. Their prophetic voice continues to echo, urging the Church to live faithfully and to hope unwaveringly in the fullness of God's promises. Through their teachings, believers gain a deeper understanding of God's faithfulness, His redemptive work, and His desire to bring His Kingdom to fruition.

Major Prophets: The major prophets, Isaiah, Jeremiah, and Ezekiel, are known for the extensive length and depth of their prophetic writings.

God called these prophets to deliver powerful messages to the nations and the people of Israel during times of spiritual crisis, impending judgment, and the promise of restoration. Their writings contain a blend of rebuke, warning, comfort, and Messianic prophecies that have profound significance for the Church and humanity.

Isaiah

Isaiah's prophetic scope is both wide and deep, encompassing God's dealings with Israel and the nations. His writings are central to the Church's understanding of the Messiah and the nature of God's covenant love. Isaiah outlines God's redemptive plan with precision and beauty, giving us hope in the promise of salvation and the coming glory of the Kingdom.

Jeremiah

Often referred to as the "weeping prophet," Jeremiah conveys the emotional weight of prophetic ministry. His persistent call to repentance, alongside God's promise of restoration, showcases both God's discipline and compassion. Jeremiah's example encourages perseverance in truth, even when it is resisted.

Ezekiel

Ezekiel's prophecies challenge complacency and offer vivid pictures of God's holiness and power. Through symbolic acts and profound visions, he emphasised the importance of spiritual renewal and divine order. His message of hope to a scattered people remains a beacon for all who long for restoration and revival.

These prophets are a timeless reminder of God's faithfulness, His desire for repentance and obedience, and his ultimate plan of redemption. They provide the Church with spiritual guidance, encouragement, and insights into the nature and character of God. Their messages continue to resonate with believers, urging them to seek God, live in righteousness, and participate in the fulfilment of the Apostolic Mandate.

Functions and Responsibilities of Prophets

The office of the prophet carries distinct responsibilities that uphold the spiritual vitality and direction of the Church. God entrusts prophets to release His word, uncover spiritual realities, and strengthen the Body through divine insight. Their functions are not rooted in personal ambition but in obedience to a sacred call that serves the purposes of God and builds up His people. The functions and responsibilities of prophets are explained below:

Receiving and Delivering God's Messages: Prophets are primarily responsible for receiving divine messages directly from God and faithfully delivering them to His people. They serve as intermediaries, conveying God's word, instructions, warnings, and promises to individuals, congregations, and nations. Prophets act as mouthpieces of God, speaking with authority and conviction.

Speaking Truth and Exhortation: Prophets are called to speak the truth fearlessly, even in the face of opposition. They confront sin, rebellion, and idolatry, calling people to repentance and obedience to God's commands. Prophets exhort, challenge, and encourage believers to align their lives with God's will, promoting spiritual growth and transformation.

Discerning Spiritual Atmospheres: Prophets possess a heightened spiritual discernment that enables them to perceive spiritual atmospheres, discern the motives and intents of the heart, and identify demonic influences. They bring clarity and insight into the spiritual dynamics at work, helping believers recognise and address spiritual strongholds and engage in effective spiritual warfare.

Providing Guidance and Direction: Prophets offer guidance and direction to individuals, congregations, and leaders, offering them a clear path forward. Through the prophetic ministry, they provide insight into decision-making processes, strategic planning, and the pursuit of God's purposes. Prophets help believers navigate through challenging situations, providing wisdom, clarity, and direction based on God's revealed will.

Interceding and Praying: Prophets have a deep intercessory burden, standing in the gap and praying on behalf of the Church and the nations. They engage in fervent prayer, interceding for spiritual breakthroughs, revival, and the fulfilment of God's purposes. Prophets partner with God in the work of reconciliation, healing, and transformation through intercessory prayer.

Confirming and Authenticating: Prophets play a role in confirming and authenticating the work of God. They affirm and validate the movements of the Holy Spirit, confirming the authenticity of spiritual experiences, prophetic words, and manifestations. Prophets help believers discern between true and false spiritual encounters and teachings, ensuring alignment with God's Word.

Edifying and Equipping: Prophets contribute to the edification and equipping of believers. They provide spiritual nourishment, encouragement, and comfort, building up the Body of Christ. Prophets help believers discover and activate their spiritual gifts, nurturing their prophetic sensitivity, and encouraging them to embrace their unique calling and destiny.

These functions and responsibilities of prophets serve to strengthen the Church, guide believers in their spiritual journey, and facilitate the fulfilment of the Apostolic Mandate. Prophets bring divine revelation, spiritual discernment, and direction from God, enabling the Church to walk in alignment with His will and experience His transformative power. By embracing and honouring the prophetic ministry, the Church is equipped to bring forth the Kingdom of God in greater measure.

Gifts of the Spirit in Prophetic Ministry

The prophetic ministry operates in conjunction with the gifts of the Holy Spirit, which empower prophets to fulfil their calling and responsibilities. These spiritual gifts enable prophets to convey God's messages effectively, discern spiritual truths, and edify the Church. The Spirit commonly manifested in prophetic ministry using these gifts:

Word of Wisdom: The gift of the word of wisdom allows prophets to receive and impart supernatural insights and divine wisdom concerning specific situations, decisions, or future events. This gift empowers prophets to offer practical guidance and strategic direction to individuals, leaders, and congregations, grounded in God's wisdom and revelation.

Word of Knowledge: Prophets with the gift of the word of knowledge receive supernatural understanding and insight into specific facts, information, or circumstances that are not known through natural means. This gift allows prophets to speak the truth, reveal hidden issues, and provide clarity and understanding to individuals or the Church as a whole.

Discerning of Spirits: The gift of discerning spirits equips prophets to perceive and distinguish between different spiritual influences and manifestations. Prophets with this gift can discern the presence of demonic activity, identify false teachings or deceptive spirits, and recognise the genuine move of the Holy Spirit. This gift helps ensure the authenticity and accuracy of prophetic messages.

Prophecy: The gift of prophecy is the primary gift associated with the prophetic ministry. Prophets with this gift receive and communicate messages from God that edify, exhort, and comfort individuals and the Church. Prophetic words may include predictions, encouragement, guidance, correction, and revelation of God's heart and intentions. The gift of prophecy strengthens faith, builds up believers, and brings alignment with God's purposes.

Interpretation of Tongues: Prophets with the gift of interpretation of tongues can interpret messages spoken in languages that are not understood, enabling the Church to understand and benefit from the spiritual utterances. This gift complements the prophetic ministry, bringing understanding and edification to the Body of Christ.

Faith: The gift of faith operates powerfully in the prophetic ministry, enabling prophets to trust in God's promises, believe in the impossible, and step out in boldness. Prophets with this gift inspire others to trust God and believe in His miraculous intervention. Their unwavering faith serves as an example and catalyst for the Church to embrace greater levels of faith and dependency on God.

Teaching: While teaching is not commonly associated with the prophetic ministry, prophets may also possess the gift of teaching. This gift enables prophets to explain, apply, and communicate the truths and principles of God's Word with clarity, authority, and spiritual insight. Prophets with the gift of teaching provide a solid biblical foundation for the prophetic messages, helping believers understand and apply them effectively.

These gifts of the Spirit empower prophets to effectively fulfil their calling, convey God's messages, and bring edification and alignment to the Church. As prophets operate in the gifts of the Spirit, they contribute to the spiritual growth, discernment, and transformation of individuals and the Body of Christ. The gifts of the Spirit amplify the impact of the prophetic ministry, ensuring that the Church walks in the power and anointing of the Holy Spirit as it fulfils the Apostolic Mandate.

Prophetic Ministry in the Modern Church

The prophetic ministry remains a vital part of the modern Church, providing a source of spiritual guidance, revelation, and encouragement. In the contemporary context, prophetic ministry manifests in various ways and plays a significant role in the life of believers and the Church as a whole.

Within the modern Church, the prophetic ministry operates in alignment with biblical principles and in response to the leading of the Holy Spirit. Prophets are recognised and affirmed for their spiritual giftings, character, and the fruit of their ministry. They are committed to the authority of God's Word and are guided by the principles of love, humility, and accountability.

Modern prophetic ministry involves the proclamation of God's truth, the discernment of spiritual atmospheres, and the activation of spiritual gifts. Prophets bring divine insight into the challenges and opportunities of the present age, encouraging believers to align their lives with God's purposes and the leading of the Holy Spirit.

Prophetic ministry in the modern Church serves to edify, exhort, and comfort believers. Through the prophetic word, believers are reminded of God's faithfulness, His promises, and His plan for their lives. The prophetic ministry also brings conviction and correction, helping believers grow in holiness and obedience to God's Word.

A spirit of collaboration and accountability characterises the modern prophetic ministry. Prophets often work in partnership with other ministries, such as pastors, teachers, evangelists, and apostles, to bring holistic ministry to the Church. They contribute to the equipping and activation of believers, fostering a prophetic culture where all members can discern and respond to God's voice.

The modern prophetic ministry also embraces the diversity of spiritual expressions. Prophetic worship, art, dance, and other creative forms are recognised as avenues through which the prophetic message can be conveyed and received. Prophetic ministry is not limited to verbal prophecy but encompasses various creative expressions that bring forth God's heart and truth.

In the modern Church, the prophetic ministry seeks to operate in balance and harmony with other ministry gifts. Prophets work alongside pastors, teachers, evangelists, and apostles, recognising the interdependence and synergy of these gifts. Together, they contribute to the health, growth, and mission of the Church, fulfilling the Apostolic Mandate to bring the Kingdom of God to every sphere of influence.

As the modern Church embraces the prophetic ministry, believers are equipped to hear God's voice, discern His leading, and walk in greater intimacy with Him. The prophetic ministry provides spiritual alignment, direction, and encouragement to individuals, congregations, and the broader Church. It empowers believers to live out their faith boldly and fulfil their God-given purpose in the world.

Challenges and Controversies in Prophetic Ministry

The prophetic ministry, like any other aspect of the Church, is not immune to challenges and controversies. While the prophetic gift is a powerful tool for edification and guidance, its operation can be subject to various pitfalls and misunderstandings. Here are some of the challenges and controversies commonly associated with prophetic ministry:

False Prophets and Deception: One of the most significant challenges in prophetic ministry is the presence of false prophets who claim to speak on behalf of God but propagate deception and false teachings. Such individuals can lead believers astray, sow confusion, and undermine the credibility of genuine prophetic ministry. Discernment and testing of prophetic words against God's Word are crucial for identifying false prophets and safeguarding against deception.

Misinterpretation and Misapplication of Prophecy: Prophetic words can sometimes be misinterpreted or misapplied, leading to confusion or disappointment. Believers may misjudge the timing or the context of a prophetic word, causing frustration and doubt. It is important to exercise discernment, seek confirmation and guidance from trusted spiritual leaders, and allow room for God's sovereign timing in the fulfilment of prophetic promises.

Lack of Accountability and Spiritual Covering: Prophetic ministry should ideally operate within the framework of accountability and spiritual covering. Without proper oversight, prophets may become isolated, vulnerable to pride, or prone to personal agendas. Prophets must submit to the guidance and correction of mature spiritual leaders, fostering a healthy environment for prophetic ministry.

Excessive Focus on the Supernatural: Prophetic ministry can sometimes become overly focused on supernatural manifestations or spectacular experiences, neglecting the foundational aspects of biblical teaching and character development. This imbalance can lead to spiritual sensationalism, with a focus on seeking signs and wonders rather than transforming lives and pursuing holiness.

Unbalanced Prophetic Pronouncements: Prophetic ministry must be exercised with humility and balance. Pronouncements of judgment or negative prophecies without a redemptive or edifying element can create fear, discouragement, and a negative perception of prophetic ministry. Prophets should strive to convey God's heart of love, mercy, and restoration while addressing sin and calling for repentance.

Unresolved Personal Issues and Impure Motives: Prophets, like any other individuals, may struggle with personal issues, woundedness, or impure motives that can hinder the accuracy and integrity of their prophetic ministry. It is essential for prophets to continually pursue personal growth, accountability, and a genuine desire to serve God and His people with humility and a pure heart.

Scepticism and Rejection: Prophetic ministry can be met with scepticism and rejection, both within and outside the Church. Some individuals may dismiss the prophetic gift altogether or have had negative experiences that lead to scepticism. It is crucial for prophets and the Church to demonstrate the authenticity and transformative impact of genuine prophetic ministry through humility, love, and a commitment to biblical truth.

Addressing these challenges and controversies requires a discerning and balanced approach to prophetic ministry. It is essential to prioritise biblical teaching, accountability, humility, and a genuine love for God and His people. By upholding integrity, seeking discernment, and operating in the power of the Holy Spirit, prophetic ministry can effectively contribute to the edification, guidance, and spiritual growth of the Church.

Conclusion

The prophetic office stands as a vital expression of God's voice within the Body of Christ. It is not a ministry of spectacle or self-exaltation, but one of deep responsibility, spiritual burden, and holy surrender. Prophets draw the Church into the counsel of God, reminding us of His heartbeat, His standards, and His desire for intimacy with His people. Through revelation, discernment, intercession, and instruction, they align the Church with the will of the Father and awaken her to both her identity and assignment.

As the Church continues to grow in maturity and stature, the need for authentic prophetic voices becomes even more critical. In a time where many are tossed by every wind of doctrine and distracted by worldly noise, the prophet's call is to lift our gaze to correct, to edify, and to anchor us once again in God's eternal purposes. Their presence in the Church is not optional; it is essential for clarity, conviction, and divine direction.

To embrace the prophetic is to embrace the voice of the Shepherd who still speaks through His vessels. When prophets are received with honour and discernment, and when their ministry is exercised in humility and truth, the Church is fortified, the mission is sharpened, and the Kingdom advances with divine precision.

Let us then honour the prophetic office not through flattery or fear, but through alignment with God's Word and a willingness to hear what the Spirit is saying to the Church today, for it is in hearing and obeying His voice that we remain a people led by the Spirit and grounded in truth.

Fold 3: Evangelists

The office of the evangelist carries the heartbeat of God for the lost. It is a calling saturated with urgency, compassion, and divine empowerment to proclaim the Good News of salvation to those who have not yet believed. Within the 5-Fold Ministry of the Church, evangelists play an irreplaceable role in mobilising the Body of Christ to reach beyond the walls of the sanctuary and into the fields that are ripe for harvest.

Evangelists are not only heralds of the Gospel; they are equippers, activators, and mobilisers. They inspire the Church to embrace its Great Commission mandate not just as a biblical concept but as a daily, practical lifestyle. Their ministry brings vitality to outreach, stirs boldness among believers, and reorients the Church toward her missional posture. In this fold, we explore the nature, calling, and contribution of evangelists to the Church, along with the biblical foundations and practical qualities that define their effectiveness.

Characteristics and Qualities of an Evangelist

The office of an evangelist is marked by specific characteristics and qualities that enable them to effectively fulfil their calling of proclaiming the Gospel and leading others to Christ. Evangelists need to bare the characteristics and qualities such as these:

Passion for the Lost:

An evangelist is fuelled by a deep passion and burden for those who have not yet experienced the transformative power of the Gospel. They possess a genuine love for people and a relentless desire to see them reconciled to God. This passion drives them to actively engage in evangelism, sharing the message of salvation with boldness and compassion.

Effective Communicator:

Evangelists can clearly and effectively communicate the Gospel to diverse audiences. They possess strong verbal communication skills, using relatable language and illustrations to convey the message of salvation. They adapt their approach to connecting with different cultures, age groups, and backgrounds, ensuring that the Good News resonates with their listeners.

Biblical Knowledge:

The power of evangelists is grounded in a solid understanding of God's Word, particularly the foundational teachings of salvation, grace, repentance, and faith. They possess a comprehensive knowledge of biblical principles and doctrines, enabling them to answer questions, address doubts, and present a well-rounded understanding of the Gospel message.

Boldness and Courage:

Boldness and courage in sharing the Gospel, regardless of opposition or rejection, are part of being an evangelist. They are not easily deterred by resistance or discouragement but remain steadfast in their commitment to proclaim the truth. An evangelist relies on the power of the Holy Spirit to overcome fear and boldly declare the Gospel message.

Empathy and Compassion:

An evangelist exhibits genuine empathy and compassion for the struggles, pains, and needs of those they encounter. They approach evangelism with sensitivity, demonstrating care and understanding of people's life circumstances. Their compassion helps to create a safe and welcoming environment, allowing individuals to open their hearts to the message of hope and redemption.

Cultural Relevance:

An effective evangelist understands the cultural context in which they are ministering. They adapt their approach to meet people where they are, using culturally relevant methods and examples to communicate the Gospel effectively. They are aware of the diverse backgrounds, values, and worldviews of their audience, ensuring that the message remains relatable and applicable to them.

Discipleship Oriented:

The calling of an evangelist extends beyond conversion. It seeks to lead people to Christ through discipling and nurturing new believers. It recognises the importance of follow-up, mentoring, and guiding individuals in their journey of faith. An evangelist equips new converts with foundational teachings, connects them with a local church community, and encourages their spiritual growth and development.

Collaboration with the Church:

An evangelist works in collaboration with the local church, recognising the importance of the Body of Christ in fulfilling the Great Commission. They partner with pastors, leaders, and fellow believers, utilising their evangelistic gifts and passion to support the overall mission and outreach of the church. An evangelist understands the value of unity and the collective effort in advancing God's Kingdom.

These characteristics and qualities equip evangelists to effectively fulfil their calling and carry out the work of evangelism. By embodying these traits, evangelists become powerful instruments of transformation, leading countless individuals to encounter the saving grace of Jesus Christ and contributing to the fulfilment of the Apostolic Mandate.

The Supernatural Nature of the Gospel

The Gospel, at its core, is a message infused with supernatural power. It embodies the transformative and life-giving work of the Holy Spirit. The supernatural nature of the Gospel is evident in various aspects of its proclamation and impact.

Firstly, the Gospel itself is a supernatural message. It declares the good news of God's redemptive plan for humanity, offering forgiveness, reconciliation, and eternal life through faith in Jesus Christ. This message surpasses the natural limitations of human wisdom and understanding, transcending cultural, societal, and religious boundaries. It speaks to the deepest needs and longings of the human heart, addressing sin, brokenness, and the search for meaning and purpose.

Furthermore, the Gospel operates in the realm of the supernatural through the work of the Holy Spirit. It is the Holy Spirit who convicts hearts of sin, draws individuals to Christ, and brings about spiritual transformation. The supernatural power of the Holy Spirit accompanies the proclamation of the Gospel, opening blind eyes, softening hardened hearts, and causing spiritual rebirth. It is the Spirit who imparts faith, produces repentance, and seals believers with the assurance of salvation.

The supernatural nature of the Gospel is also seen in the signs, wonders, and miracles that accompany its proclamation. Throughout the New Testament, we see Jesus and the early disciples performing miracles and demonstrating God's power as a testimony to the truth of the Gospel. Miracles such as healing the sick, raising the dead, and casting out demons served as tangible manifestations of God's Kingdom breaking into the present world. These supernatural acts validated the message of the Gospel, drawing people to faith and demonstrating the authority and power of Jesus Christ.

Moreover, the Gospel brings about supernatural transformation in the lives of believers. It is not merely a set of moral teachings or religious rituals, but a message that has the power to change hearts, minds, and lifestyles radically. Through the work of the Holy Spirit, the Gospel produces spiritual regeneration, renewing the inner being and empowering believers to live a life that is pleasing to God. It brings about freedom from the bondage of sin, empowers believers to walk in righteousness, and releases them into their God-given purpose and destiny.

The supernatural nature of the Gospel challenges our naturalistic worldview and calls us to embrace the reality of the spiritual realm. It reminds us that the Gospel is not just a human invention or a religious philosophy but a divine revelation that operates in the supernatural power of God. It invites us to step into a realm where the miraculous and the extraordinary become a part of our everyday lives as we trust in God's promises and rely on the Holy Spirit's guidance and empowerment.

As believers, we are called to embrace and proclaim the supernatural nature of the Gospel. We are called to demonstrate our power through acts of love, compassion, and the manifestation of spiritual gifts. The supernatural dimension of the Gospel is not limited to a select few but is accessible to all believers who walk in faith and obedience. It is through the supernatural work of the Gospel that we participate in the fulfilment of the Apostolic Mandate, bringing the Kingdom of God to every sphere of influence and witnessing the transformational power of Jesus Christ in the lives of those around us.

Outreach and Evangelism Practicum

Engaging in practical outreach and evangelism is vital for believers to actively participate in fulfilling the Great Commission and the Apostolic Mandate. A practicum in outreach and evangelism involves applying the principles and strategies of sharing the Gospel effectively.

Before engaging in outreach and evangelism, it is essential to spend time in prayer, seeking God's guidance, wisdom, and empowerment. Prayer aligns our hearts with

God's heart and invites the Holy Spirit to work through us. It prepares us to be sensitive to divine appointments, open to opportunities, and discerning of the Holy Spirit's leading.

Effective outreach and evangelism are rooted in building genuine relationships with people. This involves getting to know individuals, listening to their stories, and demonstrating care and love. By building relationships, trust is established, a safe space for sharing faith is created, and doors are opened for meaningful conversations about the Gospel.

The core of outreach and evangelism is the proclamation of the Gospel. This involves articulating the message of salvation through Jesus Christ, sharing personal testimonies, and explaining the significance of faith in Him. The Gospel should be communicated in a clear, relevant, and sensitive manner, addressing the needs and questions of those being reached.

Operative outreach necessitates creative and contextually relevant approaches. It involves considering the cultural, social, and personal contexts of the individuals we are engaging with. This may include using creative methods such as storytelling, visual media, community projects, or practical acts of service to demonstrate the love and power of the Gospel in a way that resonates with the target audience.

During the outreach and evangelism process, individuals may have questions, doubts, or objections about the Gospel. It is essential to listen attentively and respectfully, addressing their concerns with grace and truth. Equipping oneself with biblical knowledge, apologetics, and an understanding of common objections enables effective navigation of these conversations.

Outreach and evangelism should not end with a single encounter or proclamation. It is crucial to emphasise the importance of discipleship and follow-up. This involves connecting individuals with a local church community, providing resources for spiritual growth, and walking alongside new believers as they navigate their faith journey.

The Outreach and Evangelism Practicum requires a posture of continuous learning and adaptation. It is essential to evaluate and learn from each experience, seeking feedback and guidance from mentors and experienced evangelists. Adapting to different contexts, refining strategies, and staying current with relevant resources and training are essential to maintaining ongoing effectiveness in outreach.

By engaging in an outreach and evangelism practicum, believers become active participants in the Church's mission to reach the lost with the Gospel. This experience transcends theory and empowers individuals to put their faith into action, positively impacting lives and transforming communities. Through practical outreach, believers witness firsthand the power of the Gospel to bring hope, healing, and salvation to those in need.

The Impact of Evangelism

Evangelism has a profound impact on individuals, communities, and the world at large. It brings about transformation, renewal, and the expansion of God's Kingdom. The impact of evangelism is highlighted by:

Salvation and New Life: The primary impact of evangelism is the salvation and transformation of individuals. As the Gospel is proclaimed, people can respond to the message of God's love, forgiveness, and redemption through faith in Jesus Christ. This decision leads to a radical transformation, as they are born again and experience the newness of life in Christ. Through evangelism, countless lives are eternally changed as individuals are reconciled with God.

Spiritual Growth and Discipleship: Evangelism is not limited to the initial conversion experience. It also plays a vital role in the ongoing spiritual growth and discipleship of believers. As individuals embrace the Gospel, they are integrated into a local church community where they receive teaching, mentoring, and opportunities for service. Evangelism contributes to the maturing of believers, equipping them to grow in their faith, discover their spiritual gifts, and become effective disciples of Jesus Christ.

Community Transformation: The impact of evangelism extends beyond individual lives and reaches into the broader community. As the Gospel transforms individuals, they carry the values of the Kingdom of God into their families, workplaces, and social networks. This transformational influence has the potential to bring about positive change in areas such as morality, social justice, compassion, and community development. Evangelism can contribute to the healing and restoration of broken communities, fostering unity and reconciliation.

Revival and Spiritual Awakening: The consistent and widespread practice of evangelism has historically been linked to periods of revival and spiritual awakening. When believers are actively engaged in sharing the Gospel, seeking the lost, and praying for spiritual breakthroughs, it creates an atmosphere for God's presence and power to move in extraordinary ways. Revivals and spiritual awakenings often result in increased conversions, deep repentance, and a renewed hunger for God among believers.

Global Impact and Missions: Evangelism has a global impact, transcending cultural, geographic, and linguistic barriers. The Gospel has the power to reach every nation, tribe, and tongue, bringing people from all backgrounds into a relationship with God.

Evangelism fuels the mission efforts of the Church, resulting in the establishment of churches, the training of leaders, and the mobilisation of believers for cross-cultural missions. The impact of evangelism extends to remote corners of the earth, as believers respond to the call to bring the Gospel to unreached people groups.

Transformation of Worldviews and Societal Values: Evangelism challenges and transforms worldviews and societal values. As the Gospel is embraced, it brings a fresh perspective on life's purpose, meaning, and moral foundations. It challenges cultural norms and practices that contradict God's truth, promoting righteousness, justice, and compassion. Evangelism influences societies by instilling values such as love, forgiveness, humility, and social responsibility, leading to positive social change and the pursuit of the common good.

The impact of evangelism is vast and far-reaching. It has the potential to transform individuals, communities, and even nations. Through the faithful and intentional proclamation of the Gospel, lives are forever changed, spiritual growth is fostered, communities are transformed, and God's Kingdom expands. Evangelism remains a vital aspect of fulfilling the Apostolic Mandate, as believers continue to bring the Good News to every sphere of influence, ushering in the transformative power of Jesus Christ.

Training and Equipping Evangelists

Raising evangelists within the Church requires intentional discipleship, spiritual impartation, and practical preparation. The evangelist's calling is not self-sustained; it must be sharpened, stewarded, and supported by the Body of Christ. Scripture offers compelling examples of how evangelists were prepared, empowered, and released not only with passion but with sound doctrine and Spirit-filled power.

One of the clearest biblical models is Philip the Evangelist (Acts 8). Initially chosen as one of the seven to serve tables (Acts 6:5), Philip was faithful in small things before being launched into greater exploits. His public ministry in Samaria, marked by preaching, healing, and mass conversions, was not the product of impulsive action but of proven faithfulness and preparation.

His encounter with the Ethiopian eunuch (Acts 8:26-40) reveals not only spiritual sensitivity but also theological readiness. Philip understood Scripture well enough to explain Isaiah's prophecy and lead a royal official to Christ. From Philip's life, we see that effective evangelism grows from biblical literacy, spiritual sensitivity, and a readiness to act when led by the Spirit.

In training evangelists today, the Church must adopt this holistic approach. *First,* evangelists must be discipled in sound doctrine. They should be thoroughly acquainted with the central tenets of the Gospel redemption, the atonement, the resurrection, and the Kingdom of God. This training combines theological education with the ability to present truth in clear, life-changing language. Like Apollos, who was "mighty in the Scriptures" (Acts 18:24-26), but still needed Aquila and Priscilla to explain the way of God more accurately, evangelists today must be both fervent and teachable.

Second, they must be spiritually formed through prayer, fasting, and a deep relationship with the Holy Spirit. Jesus Himself prepared His disciples through extended time in His presence, teaching, modelling, and commissioning. Before He sent them out two by two (Mark 6:7-13), He ensured they were equipped with authority, instruction, and spiritual insight. Likewise, evangelists must be sent, not merely released. The Church must ensure they are formed in godly character and tested in obedience before they are commissioned for public ministry.

Third, the Church must invest in experiential training. Evangelists learn not only in classrooms but also in real-life settings, such as fields, where the Gospel is preached, conversations are had, and hearts are won. Jesus trained His disciples on the move. He preached, healed, and cast out demons before their eyes and then said, "Go and do likewise." Paul took Timothy and others on ministry journeys, allowing them to see, do, and eventually lead. Such practical immersion is irreplaceable. Today's Church must replicate this pattern by hosting evangelistic missions, street outreaches, digital campaigns, and one-on-one mentorship opportunities.

Fourth, the process of equipping must include spiritual impartation and commissioning. Paul exhorted Timothy not to neglect the gift that was in him through the laying on of hands (1 Timothy 4:14). Evangelists often carry gifts of healing, words of knowledge, and bold proclamation. These need activation in the community, not isolation. Apostolic and prophetic leaders must identify, lay hands on, and prophetically release evangelists into their assignment with covering and accountability.

Finally, evangelists must be trained in how to integrate their work into the local church. Philip did not create a separate movement; after his ministry in Samaria, the apostles Peter and John were sent to consolidate the work (Acts 8:14-17). Evangelism and pastoral care must flow together. Training must therefore include lessons in humility, collaboration, and the importance of submitting evangelistic fruit to local shepherds for discipleship and growth.

Training and equipping evangelists is not about producing performers; it is about shaping servants who carry fire, truth, and wisdom into the world. As the Church invests in this task, we raise messengers who not only proclaim salvation but demonstrate the Kingdom with power and integrity, fulfilling the Apostolic Mandate in every place where darkness still reigns.

Support and Collaboration Within the 5-Fold Ministry

The ministry of the evangelist finds its greatest effectiveness when exercised in mutual support and collaboration with the other offices within the 5-Fold Ministry. While evangelists are uniquely gifted to proclaim the Gospel and draw souls into the Kingdom, their impact is maximised when they function in unity with apostles, prophets, pastors, and teachers. Together, these ministry gifts form a complete and cohesive leadership structure that equips the Church for maturity and mission.

Evangelists often carry the initial spark of salvation, leading many to Christ and stirring hearts with the urgency of repentance and reconciliation. However, this work requires apostolic vision to direct it, prophetic insight to affirm and discern it, pastoral care to nurture the fruit, and sound teaching to root the new believers in doctrine and discipleship. Without such collaboration, the gains of evangelism may be compromised by shallow growth or spiritual confusion.

In the early Church, we see such collaboration at work. Philip, identified in Acts 21:8 as an evangelist, led a powerful outreach in Samaria (Acts 8:5-8), resulting in many conversions and signs. Yet when the apostles in Jerusalem heard of this revival, they sent Peter and John to support the new believers, laying hands on them so they could receive the Holy Spirit (Acts 8:14-17). This illustrates the beauty of collaboration: the evangelist initiates the move, and the apostolic and prophetic dimensions come alongside to complete the work and establish spiritual order.

Prophets can strengthen evangelists by providing timely insights and discerning spiritual atmospheres in regions or populations that are yet to be reached. They may receive specific directions from the Holy Spirit that sharpen the strategy or timing of evangelistic campaigns. Likewise, pastors ensure that the people won by the evangelist are not left vulnerable or isolated. They offer the relational support, shepherding, and communal structure needed for new believers to be integrated into the life of the Church. Teachers play a critical role in grounding converts in biblical truth, ensuring that the initial enthusiasm of salvation matures into lasting faith and obedience.

When each office honours and uplifts the other, the result is Kingdom advancement with depth and endurance. Evangelists benefit from this shared labour by being more effective in their assignments and more secure in their calling. They are not isolated firebrands but vital members of a divine framework that reflects the wisdom and order of God.

In today's church, fostering intentional collaboration within the five-fold ministry requires humility, mutual recognition, and consistent communication. Churches that operate with this model tend to be more holistic in their mission and more resilient in their growth. By understanding the interdependence of these ministry offices, we foster a healthy, united, and powerful Church culture that advances the Gospel.

Fold 4: Pastors

The office of pastors occupies a vital place within the 5-Fold Ministry, entrusted with the care, guidance, and spiritual oversight of God's people. Pastors are called to shepherd the flock, nurturing believers in their faith and walking with them through every stage of their spiritual growth.

In this section, we examine the nature of the pastoral office, its responsibilities, and its enduring relevance in the life of the Church. We also highlight the biblical foundation of this calling, the essential qualities of a faithful pastor, and the central role pastoral ministry plays in advancing the Apostolic Mandate.

Shepherd's Heart and Love for the Flock

At the heart of pastoral ministry lies the shepherd's heart, a unique blend of love, compassion, responsibility, and spiritual authority that reflects the character of Christ. This heart is not born out of ambition or title, but from a divine burden to care for God's people with tenderness and conviction.

The shepherd's love is patient, sacrificial, and enduring, shaped by the nature of Christ Himself, who described His ministry in the most tender terms: *"I am the good shepherd. The good shepherd lays down his life for the sheep"* (John 10:11, NIV).

Jesus, as the ultimate Shepherd, demonstrated what it means to lead with both strength and gentleness. He pursued the one lost sheep, restored the wounded, and stayed close to the weary. His ministry was not marked by control, but by care, not by dominance, but by a deep understanding of each individual under His watch.

The shepherd's love is not general or abstract; it is personal. Jesus knew His sheep by name and called them individually. This intimacy is central to a pastor's role, which includes knowing the people, praying for them, feeding them the Word of God, protecting them from deception, and walking with them through life's valleys and mountaintops.

The shepherd's heart is especially attentive to the weak and the broken-hearted. Pastors are not only teachers or administrators; they are carriers of comfort. They feel deeply the weight of their congregation's trials and walk closely in seasons of grief, correction, celebration, and transition.

This kind of love is not soft; it is durable. It bears with people, believes the best, and continues to show up, even when it is unacknowledged. The apostle Paul expressed this dimension of pastoral love in his letter to the Thessalonians:

"We were gentle among you, just as a nursing mother cares for her children. So, we cared for you, because we loved you so much, we were delighted to share with you not only the gospel of God but our lives as well" (1 Thessalonians 2:7-8, NIV).

Such affection is not born of mere emotional connection; it is born from divine assignment. A true pastor does not simply work in ministry; they are called to a people. Like Moses interceding for Israel or David watching over his father's sheep, they carry a sense of spiritual responsibility that cannot be delegated. Their love compels them to feed the sheep even when it costs them everything to weep with those who weep, to rejoice with those who rejoice, and to remain faithful even when the flock strays.

In a world increasingly marked by performance-driven leadership, the pastor's heart remains a countercultural symbol of steady, enduring love. Pastors are not managers of religious spaces; they are shepherds of souls. Their authority is anchored in their ability to care deeply and truthfully, offering not just teaching but presence, not just guidance but genuine affection. Theirs is the work of nurturing the Body of Christ into maturity with wisdom, patience, and unwavering love.

The shepherd's heart also reflects a protective instinct. Jesus said, *"The hired hand is not the shepherd and does not own the sheep. So, when he sees the wolf coming, he abandons the sheep and runs away"* (John 10:12, NIV).

A pastor does not abandon the people when challenges arise. They stand watch, confronting false doctrines, warning of spiritual danger, and ensuring that the flock remains grounded in truth. This role requires both tenderness and courage, a balance that only flows from abiding in Christ, the True Shepherd.

Finally, a pastor's love seeks multiplication. It is not content with keeping sheep safe; it seeks to raise more shepherds. Just as Jesus trained and released His disciples to tend to His people after His ascension, today's pastors are called to pour into others, equipping and mentoring them to care for the next generation. Their love is not possessive; it is generative. It creates room for others to grow and lead, because the focus is never on building personal influence but on expanding the reach of Christ's care to more lives.

In every way, the shepherd's heart reflects the ministry of Jesus. As pastors serve today, their highest model remains the One who left the ninety-nine for the one, who washed feet, who bore the cross, and who continues to intercede for His flock. In embracing the shepherd's heart, pastors do not just lead; they embody the love of Christ and reveal the Kingdom of God through every act of spiritual care.

The Ministry of a Pastor

The ministry of a pastor is one of the most tender yet weighty assignments in the Body of Christ. It is a calling to shepherd, nurture, equip, and lead God's people into maturity, unity, and obedience.

This ministry is not merely about public preaching or church administration; it is about the faithful stewardship of souls, the day-to-day guidance of believers, and the cultivation of a healthy, thriving spiritual community. Pastoral ministry, when carried out under the leadership of the Holy Spirit, becomes a living expression of Christ's ongoing care for His Church.

At its core, the ministry of a pastor is pastoral, not positional. It is rooted in the biblical imagery of shepherding, where the pastor watches over the flock not as a hired hand, but as one entrusted by the Chief Shepherd, Jesus Christ. In 1 Peter 5:2–3 (NIV), the apostle exhorts, *"Be shepherds of God's flock that is under your care, watching over them not because you must, but because you are willing, as God wants you to be… not lording it over those entrusted to you, but being examples to the flock."*

This scripture beautifully captures the heart posture required of every pastor: willingness, humility, responsibility, and exemplary living.

One of the foundational ministries of a pastor is teaching and preaching the Word of God. Pastors are responsible for feeding the flock with sound doctrine, rightly dividing the Word, and helping believers apply biblical truths to everyday life. Their teaching nourishes the soul, shapes character, and equips the Church for effective ministry.

However, this teaching is not confined to the pulpit. It is often most powerful in one-on-one discipleship, small groups, counselling sessions, and spontaneous conversations. Every teaching moment becomes an opportunity to anchor hearts in Christ.

Another vital function of pastoral ministry is spiritual oversight and guidance. Pastors are called to lead the congregation with spiritual discernment, prayerful decision-making, and biblical wisdom. They must sense the spiritual climate of the people, perceive threats to the flock's well-being, and provide direction that aligns with God's purpose for the community. They serve as spiritual fathers and mothers, helping individuals discern their path, make godly choices, and remain faithful in every season.

The ministry of a pastor also includes counselling, comforting, and caring. Many believers come to church not just to worship, but to find healing, hope, and help. A pastor's listening ear, compassionate heart, and prayerful support become a source of great strength. Whether it is walking with a family through grief, guiding a couple through marital strain, or praying with someone facing discouragement, the pastor becomes a vessel through which God's presence and peace are made known. These quiet, often unseen acts of love are the heartbeat of true ministry.

Pastors are also mobilisers and equippers. According to Ephesians 4:11-12 (NIV), *"Christ himself gave the apostles, the prophets, the evangelists, the pastors and teachers, to equip his people for works of service, so that the body of Christ may be built up."*

This means the pastor's role is not to do all the ministry alone, but to train and release others to function in their God-given gifts. A healthy pastoral ministry involves leadership development, discipleship, and equipping others to teach, lead, serve, and reach out to others. The Church flourishes when every member is empowered, and it is the pastor who helps foster that growth.

Moreover, pastoral ministry entails the responsibility of intercession and spiritual oversight. True pastors labour in prayer for their people, often in secret. They cover their church in intercession, praying for protection, healing, direction, and revival. Like Moses lifting his hands on behalf of Israel or Paul weeping over the churches he planted, pastors carry the spiritual well-being of the flock in their hearts. Their prayers break strongholds, birth vision, and bring God's will into manifestation.

Additionally, the ministry of a pastor includes guarding the flock from deception. In Acts 20:28-30, Paul warns the

Ephesian elders to be on guard, for *"savage wolves will come in among you and will not spare the flock."*

Pastors must have a discerning spirit to recognise error, false doctrine, and unhealthy influences. They must have the courage to speak the truth, uphold biblical standards, and protect the integrity of the Gospel. This watchman aspect of pastoral ministry is not always celebrated, but it is essential for the long-term spiritual safety of the Church.

In all these functions, pastors serve with humility and dependence on Christ. They are not perfect, nor are they meant to be the centre of the Church. Their task is to reflect Jesus, point people to Him, and walk in obedience to His calling. The ministry of a pastor is sustained not by talent or charisma, but by communion with God, a servant's heart, and the daily filling of the Holy Spirit.

The ministry of a pastor is characterised by servant-heartedness, self-sacrifice, and a genuine love for God's people. It is a calling that requires dedication, humility, and a deep dependence on the Holy Spirit. Pastors are entrusted with the responsibility of nurturing the spiritual growth of the flock, fostering unity, and leading the congregation in fulfilling the Apostolic Mandate. Through their ministry, pastors have a significant impact on the lives of individuals, families, and communities, bringing hope, healing, and transformation through the love of Christ.

Challenges and Opportunities for Pastoral Ministry

Pastoral ministry is a sacred calling that presents both challenges and opportunities for those who are called to shepherd God's people. The role of a pastor is multifaceted, involving spiritual leadership, care for the congregation, teaching and preaching, and guiding the community towards spiritual growth.

However, along with the immense joy and fulfilment that pastoral ministry brings, there are also unique challenges that pastors face. These challenges include navigating the complexities of human relationships, addressing theological and doctrinal questions, providing pastoral care in times of crisis, and managing the practical demands of leading a church.

Yet, amidst these challenges, the pastoral ministry also offers profound opportunities for spiritual impact, personal growth, and the privilege of being a vessel through which God's love and grace can be poured out.

Challenges in Pastoral Ministry:

The pastoral ministry, while noble and deeply fulfilling, is not without its trials. Shepherding God's people requires more than love and willingness; it demands resilience, spiritual maturity, and unwavering dependence on the Lord. Pastors often find themselves navigating complex challenges that test their endurance, character, and obedience to their calling.

Recognising these challenges is not to discourage those called to this office, but to prepare them to lean more heavily on Christ, who remains the Chief Shepherd and sustainer of His under-shepherds.

One of the greatest challenges in pastoral ministry is carrying the emotional and spiritual weight of others. Like Moses, who interceded on behalf of the Israelites, pastors often feel a deep responsibility to stand in the gap for their congregation. Whether it is comforting the grieving, counselling the broken, or confronting sin in love, pastors are constantly pouring out.

Over time, this can lead to emotional exhaustion and spiritual depletion, especially if they neglect to rest and abide in the presence of God. The apostle Paul often expressed the burden he carried for the churches (2 Corinthians 11:28), reminding us that spiritual leadership comes with an invisible load that only God fully understands.

Another frequent challenge pastors face is criticism and misunderstanding. Despite their sacrifices and sincerity, pastors may be misjudged, unfairly criticised, or held to unrealistic expectations. Congregants sometimes expect their pastors to be flawless, available at all times, and agreeable in all matters. When decisions are made that are unpopular, even if biblically sound, pastors can become targets of discontent.

The prophet Jeremiah experienced this deeply, lamenting that his obedience to God often made him a reproach among his people (Jeremiah 20:8). For pastors today, walking in integrity while navigating the opinions of others requires humility and a heart anchored in God's approval, not man's applause.

Pastoral ministry can also be lonely. Many pastors find it challenging to form close friendships within their congregations, fearing they may be misunderstood or compromised. The position of leadership can sometimes create emotional distance, making it difficult for pastors to find safe spaces to share their struggles and vulnerabilities. Without intentional relationships, accountability, and mentorship, pastors can easily feel isolated and disconnected from their community.

Even Jesus, in His most sorrowful moment in Gethsemane, found His closest disciples asleep when He asked them to watch and pray with Him (Matthew 26:40). This underscores the reality that spiritual leadership is often marked by seasons of solitude.

Maintaining a healthy balance between ministry and family life is a common struggle. The demands of pastoral work, preaching, counselling, administration, visitation, and crisis management can easily encroach on time with one's spouse and children. If left unchecked, this imbalance can strain the pastor's home and contradict the biblical requirement that a pastor must manage his household well (1 Timothy 3:4-5). Pastors must be intentional in setting boundaries, honouring their roles as spouses and parents, and modelling what a Christ-centred family looks like.

Pastors are on the frontlines of spiritual battle. Because they shepherd God's people and guard the spiritual gates of their communities, they are frequent targets of the enemy. Temptation, discouragement, fear, division, and attacks on their integrity or health are all tactics used to weaken their resolve.

Ephesians 6:12 reminds us that *"our struggle is not against flesh and blood, but against rulers, against the authorities, against the powers of this dark world and against the spiritual forces of evil in the heavenly realms."* Pastors must be equipped with spiritual armour, strengthened through prayer and fasting, and covered by the intercession of the saints.

The risk of burnout is high in pastoral ministry. The constant demands, coupled with emotional strain, can lead to physical, mental, and spiritual fatigue. Without sabbath rest, personal retreat, and ongoing spiritual renewal, pastors may lose their passion and effectiveness. Elijah, after calling down fire from heaven and confronting Baal's prophets, fell into despair and asked to die (1 Kings 19:4).

It was only after rest, nourishment, and a renewed word from God that he regained strength to continue. Likewise, modern pastors need rhythms of renewal to prevent burnout and collapse.

Many pastors also face financial limitations, especially in smaller congregations or under-resourced communities. When compensation is inadequate, pastors may feel pressured to work additional jobs or carry financial burdens that limit their capacity for ministry. This can create stress and feelings of neglect, especially when their sacrifices go unacknowledged. Churches are called to honour and provide for those who labour among them (1 Timothy 5:17-18), but when that support is lacking, the challenge becomes deeply personal.

Pastors are often entrusted with the vision and direction for the church. However, implementing change can be met with resistance, especially when it disrupts tradition or comfort zones. Leading people into new seasons requires not only spiritual insight but also relational wisdom and patience. Moses faced ongoing resistance from the Israelites despite leading them out of bondage. Likewise, pastors must lead with grace, aware that change in people's hearts and habits takes time.

Despite all these challenges, the ministry of a pastor remains one of divine privilege. Each trial is an invitation to deeper intimacy with God, greater dependence on the Holy Spirit, and a more refined character. Challenges do not disqualify pastors; they shape them.

Furthermore, in all things, the faithful pastor can rest in the promise of Christ: *"My grace is sufficient for you, for my power is made perfect in weakness"* (2 Corinthians 12:9).

Opportunities in Pastoral Ministry

Though pastoral ministry is marked by sacrifice and tested by many challenges, it is also filled with sacred and transformative opportunities. Every trial faced by a pastor paves the way for deeper trust in God and greater fruitfulness in the lives of His people.

The pastoral office is a platform through which God's love, wisdom, and power are continually revealed. In the hands of a faithful shepherd, this ministry becomes a vessel of revival, healing, and lasting impact both in the local church and far beyond.

One of the most profound opportunities available to pastors is nurturing spiritual maturity in others. Through preaching, teaching, mentoring, and counselling, pastors are entrusted with shaping souls for the Kingdom of God. The apostle Paul likened this to labouring until Christ is formed in believers (Galatians 4:19).

Pastors guide people from milk to meat, from immaturity to rootedness, seeing lives transformed by the Word and the Spirit. This is not a theoretical task; it is hands-on discipleship that echoes the ministry of Jesus, who patiently taught His disciples and drew them closer to the heart of the Father.

Pastors have the opportunity to influence not only individuals but entire families and communities. Through weddings, child dedications, home visits, and family counselling, they minister across generations. By upholding biblical values and speaking life into homes, pastors serve as stabilising voices in a society often shaken by confusion and brokenness. In communities where division or despair prevail, the pastor becomes a symbol of unity, healing, and hope. This shepherding presence strengthens the moral and spiritual fabric of a people.

The pulpit offers one of the greatest opportunities for declaring eternal truths. Pastors are uniquely positioned to proclaim the unchanging gospel in a constantly shifting world. They do not merely deliver speeches; they declare the living Word of God. Through faithful preaching and teaching, pastors illuminate Scripture, correct error, exalt Christ, and release faith into the hearts of hearers. This sacred task brings joy to the pastor's heart as they witness conviction, salvation, and transformation unfold week after week.

Pastoral ministry creates a divine opportunity to raise the next generation of leaders. Just as Paul mentored Timothy and Titus, pastors today are spiritual fathers and mothers to emerging ministers, worship leaders, evangelists, and intercessors. They provide wisdom, accountability, and impartation to those called to serve. Through structured training and intentional relationships, pastors become conduits for multiplication, not just maintaining the church, but preparing it for generational impact.

When people walk through the darkest seasons of life, grief, illness, betrayal, or loss, pastors are often the first ones called. These moments, though difficult, are powerful ministry opportunities. A prayer at a hospital bed, a word of comfort at a funeral, or simply sitting in silence beside a grieving soul all carry eternal weight.

Pastors bring the presence of Christ into moments where human strength has failed. As the hands and heart of the Good Shepherd, they embody Psalm 34:18: *"The Lord is close to the broken-hearted and saves those who are crushed in spirit"* (NIV).

A pastor does more than oversee programs; they shape the atmosphere of worship, prayer, generosity, and faith within the congregation. They cast vision and model what it means to love God fully and serve people selflessly. Whether introducing spiritual disciplines, fostering intercession, or teaching stewardship, pastors set the tone for corporate growth and development. This spiritual culture becomes the environment in which revival can take root and flourish.

In this era of increased connectivity and collaboration, pastors have greater opportunity than ever to partner with other ministers, churches, and movements. Conferences, networks, and interdenominational initiatives allow pastors to unite in fulfilling the Great Commission. Through these partnerships, the local church becomes part of a global work that spreads the gospel, serves the poor, and advances the Kingdom in places its congregation may never physically reach.

Ultimately, the pastoral ministry serves as a space for the pastor's spiritual formation. While they pour into others, God is constantly shaping them, refining their character, expanding their wisdom, and increasing their sensitivity to the Holy Spirit. The demands of the role stretch the pastor's capacity, but they also deepen dependence on God. The pulpit, the counselling room, and the altar each become a classroom where the pastor is both teacher and student in God's gracious curriculum.

The pastoral calling is not a burden to endure but a holy trust to steward. Every sermon preached, every hand held, every seed sown in tears holds within it the promise of the Kingdom harvest. Jesus, the Good Shepherd, walks closely with His under-shepherds, sustaining them, rejoicing with them, and leading them beside still waters. The opportunities are as vast as the fields are ripe, and to those who faithfully shepherd His flock, there awaits an unfading crown of glory (1 Peter 5:4).

Synergy Between Pastors and Other Ministry Gifts

The strength of the Church is not found in isolated functions but in the unified, Spirit-led collaboration of its diverse ministry gifts. Within the Five-Fold Ministry, apostles, prophets, evangelists, pastors, and teachers, each office contributes uniquely to the edification of the Body of Christ.

Pastors, as shepherds of the flock, play a pivotal role in nurturing, guiding, and protecting the people of God. Their effectiveness is significantly enhanced when their ministry works in harmony with the other gifts God has placed within the Church.

Pastors are entrusted with the continual care of believers. They walk closely with individuals and families, discipling them through life's seasons and ensuring that the local church remains grounded in love, sound doctrine, and accountability. While their ministry is deeply relational and community-focused, the full maturing of the saints requires complementary expressions of leadership and spiritual equipping. This is where synergy comes into full effect.

Apostles carry a pioneering grace to plant churches, establish doctrine, and build spiritual infrastructure. While pastors nurture the daily life of the congregation, apostles provide the wider vision and structural guidance needed to keep the church aligned with Kingdom priorities. Together, the apostle and pastor ensure that both the structure and the soul of the church are sound. The apostle may identify territories to advance into, while the pastor prepares the people to live out that mission. This partnership balances expansion with stability.

Prophets bring revelation, discernment, and direction from the heart of God. They often challenge the church to remain spiritually alert and obedient to divine instruction. Pastors, on the other hand, help process and apply prophetic insight within the local body. They discern how to shepherd the people through seasons of correction, transition, or encouragement that may be brought forth through the prophetic word. A healthy synergy between pastors and prophets ensures that prophetic messages are not only received but also stewarded with wisdom and love.

For instance, when the prophet Agabus warned of a coming famine (Acts 11:28), it was the local church leadership, including pastors, who mobilised the response to care for believers. In this way, the prophetic voice awakened vision, and pastoral hands provided for them.

Evangelists are God's frontline messengers, anointed to proclaim the gospel and bring souls into the Kingdom. Their fire and boldness ignite outreach and expansion. However, without the nurturing care of pastors, the fruit of evangelism risks being scattered rather than established. Pastors provide a home for the new believer, a place where they can be discipled, healed, and grounded in faith. The evangelist gathers, and the pastor grows. Together, they fulfil the Great Commission by ensuring that salvation leads to transformation and maturity.

This synergy is visible in the ministry of Philip the evangelist (Acts 8), whose preaching brought many to faith in Samaria. It was then necessary for apostles and leaders to follow up, grounding the believers in the broader teaching and fellowship of the Church.

Teachers are gifted to expound the Word of God with clarity and depth, equipping believers with sound doctrine and spiritual understanding. While pastors care for the heart, teachers illuminate the mind. A church that is both loved and well-taught becomes strong and resilient in the face of deception and adversity. Pastors and teachers work side by side, one tending to the wounds and joys of life, the other anchoring believers in biblical truth. Their combined efforts create a spiritually balanced, well-fed church.

Paul himself noted this unity of function in Ephesians 4:11-13, where the five offices are described as being given for the equipping of the saints, the work of ministry, and the building up of the Body of Christ. None of these roles can fully function in isolation. Each is a stream that flows into the wider river of God's redemptive purpose for the world.

Synergy in ministry is not about hierarchy but harmony. Pastors do not control or compete with other offices; instead, they cultivate an atmosphere where every gift is recognised, honoured, and allowed to flourish. Just as the natural body requires the cooperation of all its parts to function effectively, so does the Body of Christ depend on the collaborative work of its spiritual leaders. When pastors create room for apostles to build, prophets to speak, evangelists to reach, and teachers to teach, the church becomes whole and effective.

This interdependence leads to a healthy spiritual ecosystem, where no single gift is exalted above others, and every office operates in mutual submission under Christ, the Chief Shepherd and Head of the Church.

The Significance of Pastors in Church and Community

Pastors play a significant role not only within the church but also in the broader community. Their impact extends beyond the walls of the church building as they serve as spiritual leaders, counsellors, and agents of positive change.

Pastors provide spiritual leadership within the church, guiding believers in their faith journey and helping them grow closer to God. They shepherd the congregation, offering wisdom, biblical teaching, and pastoral care. Through their leadership, pastors create an environment conducive to spiritual growth, inspiring individuals to develop a vibrant relationship with God and live out their faith in practical ways.

Pastors offer pastoral care and support to individuals and families within the church community. They provide guidance, comfort, and encouragement during times of crisis, grief, and personal struggles. Pastors lend a listening ear, offer prayerful support, and provide a safe space for individuals to share their burdens and concerns. Their presence and care bring comfort and healing to those in need.

They serve as moral and ethical guides, helping individuals navigate life's challenges and make decisions in alignment with biblical principles. They provide biblical counsel and offer guidance on issues such as relationships, family, work, and personal integrity. By upholding and modelling biblical values, pastors contribute to the moral fabric of the community, promoting virtues such as love, honesty, and compassion.

Pastors are actively involved in the community, seeking opportunities to serve and make a positive impact. They engage in acts of service, social justice initiatives, and outreach programs, addressing the needs of the marginalised, disadvantaged, and vulnerable populations. Pastors mobilise the church community to participate in community development projects, foster unity, and serve as agents of positive change in society.

Bridge Builders and Peacemakers through fostering unity within the church and the community. They promote reconciliation, forgiveness, and understanding, seeking to mend broken relationships and promote harmony. Pastors actively work towards racial reconciliation, socioeconomic unity, and cultural appreciation, helping to build a more inclusive and diverse community.

Pastors advocate for justice, equality, and compassion in the face of social injustices and cultural challenges. They address issues such as poverty, discrimination, human rights, and systemic inequalities. Pastors raise awareness, educate their congregations, and empower individuals to actively participate in efforts to bring about positive social change.

They also invest in leadership development within the church, identifying and equipping emerging leaders to take on new responsibilities. They provide mentorship, discipleship, and opportunities for individuals to develop their leadership skills and increase their influence. Pastors empower others to serve in various capacities, cultivating a new generation of leaders who can impact the church and the community.

Crisis Response, Spiritual Guidance, and support during times of crisis, including natural disasters, pandemics, or community-wide emergencies. They offer solace, hope, and a spiritual perspective during challenging circumstances. Pastors serve as a stabilising presence, helping individuals navigate uncertainty and find strength in their faith.

The significance of pastors in the church and community lies in their unique ability to inspire, guide, and empower individuals to live out their faith in transformative ways. Through their spiritual leadership, pastoral care, community engagement, and advocacy, pastors make a lasting impact on individuals' lives and contribute to the betterment of the community at large. Their commitment to the Apostolic Mandate brings the Kingdom of God to every sphere of influence, bringing hope, healing, and transformation to the church.

Mentoring and Apprenticeship for Aspiring Pastors

Pastoral ministry is not a calling to be stepped into lightly or without preparation. It demands not only spiritual maturity but also emotional intelligence, biblical literacy, and a shepherd's heart refined through experience.

One of the most effective ways to cultivate such readiness in aspiring pastors is through intentional mentoring and apprenticeship. These two elements, relational guidance and practical engagement, serve as bridges between calling and competence, ensuring that those entering pastoral ministry are not only passionate but prepared.

Mentoring provides the relational foundation upon which pastoral identity is built. A seasoned pastor, acting as a mentor, offers the aspiring pastor insight drawn from real ministry experience. This includes sharing both victories and failures, walking through personal challenges, and providing spiritual accountability. Like Moses mentoring Joshua, Elijah preparing Elisha, or Paul nurturing Timothy, mentorship in ministry transfers more than information; it imparts character, discipline, and spiritual perspective.

Paul's letters to Timothy are perhaps the clearest biblical model of pastoral mentoring. He not only instructed Timothy in doctrinal matters but also guided him in conduct, leadership under pressure, and guarding the faith.

In 2 Timothy 2:2 (NKJV), Paul wrote, *"And the things that you have heard from me among many witnesses, commit these to faithful men who will be able to teach others also."* This principle of generational transfer is essential for raising strong pastoral leaders.

Apprenticeship, on the other hand, complements mentoring by placing aspiring pastors in environments where they can observe, participate, and eventually lead under the supervision of experienced mentors. This hands-on model allows them to develop essential pastoral skills, preaching, teaching, counselling, leading prayer meetings, officiating services, and managing church dynamics. Apprenticeship fosters spiritual agility, enabling them to respond to real-life situations such as conflict resolution, crisis care, or congregational growth with wisdom and grace.

Jesus Himself used this model with His disciples. He invited them to follow Him, not only to hear His teachings but to watch Him heal, pray, serve, and love. Over time, He sent them out in pairs, allowing them to practice ministry with accountability (Luke 10:1-19). This approach of exposure, empowerment, and feedback shaped them into the early pastors and leaders of the Church.

The benefits of mentoring and apprenticeship also extend to spiritual formation. These relationships encourage aspiring pastors to confront their inner lives, examine their motives, develop healthy spiritual disciplines, and cultivate humility. It is in these safe, structured settings that they learn how to carry spiritual authority without pride, how to serve without exhaustion, and how to teach without striving. This growth is not always found in academic settings but is often forged in the quiet consistency of walking with a mentor who leads by example.

Churches and leadership networks have a responsibility to create intentional pathways for mentorship and apprenticeship. This includes identifying potential pastors early, pairing them with suitable mentors, providing structured learning experiences, and offering consistent evaluations. Doing so ensures the continuity of strong, biblically grounded leadership in the Church and prevents spiritual burnout by preparing ministers before the weight of ministry is placed on their shoulders.

In a time where spiritual shepherds are needed more than ever, mentoring and apprenticeship are not optional luxuries; they are essential. They secure the future of the pastoral office by cultivating leaders who not only know the Word but also know how to walk with people, listen to God, and live with integrity. These future pastors become not just church leaders, but spiritual fathers and mothers who reflect the compassion, authority, and wisdom of the Chief Shepherd, Jesus Christ.

Fold 5: Teachers

The office of teachers within the 5-Fold Ministry plays a vital role in equipping believers with sound doctrine, biblical understanding, and practical wisdom for living out their faith. Teachers serve as educators and communicators of God's Word, guiding individuals in their spiritual growth and helping them develop a solid foundation of biblical knowledge.

In this office, the focus is on imparting truth, facilitating discipleship, and nurturing a deep understanding of God's Word. Through their teaching ministry, teachers play a significant role in fulfilling the Apostolic Mandate.

Teaching as a Spiritual Gift

Teaching is not only a role or function within the 5-Fold Ministry, but it is also recognised as a spiritual gift bestowed upon us by the Holy Spirit. The gift of teaching is a special endowment that enables individuals to communicate and impart knowledge, wisdom, and understanding of God's Word effectively. Those who possess this gift have a profound passion for studying and interpreting Scripture, as well as a desire to share its truths with others.

The gift of teaching is characterised by the ability to explain complex concepts clearly and understandably, to provide insightful and relevant applications of biblical truths, and to inspire others to grow in their faith. Teachers with this spiritual gift possess a profound reverence for

God's Word and a dedication to upholding its authority and accuracy.

Furthermore, the gift of teaching goes beyond the dissemination of information. It involves creating an atmosphere conducive to learning, fostering a love for God's Word, and encouraging individuals to apply its principles to their lives. Teachers with this gift possess the capacity to engage and captivate their audience, making the Scriptures come alive and facilitating transformative encounters with God.

The gift of teaching is not limited to formal educational settings. However, it extends to various contexts within the church, such as Sunday school classes, small group studies, discipleship programs, and preaching ministries. Teachers with this gift can profoundly impact lives, equip believers, and help them deepen their understanding of God's Word, ultimately leading to spiritual maturity and a more profound relationship with God.

It is important to recognise and nurture the gift of teaching within the Body of Christ. By embracing and utilising this gift, teachers contribute to the overall growth and edification of the church. They play a significant role in empowering believers to live out their faith, defending biblical truths, and equipping others for ministry.

Teachers with the spiritual gift of teaching are essential in fulfilling the Apostolic Mandate, as they bring clarity, understanding, and application of God's Word to every sphere of influence. Their commitment to excellence in teaching and their dedication to sound doctrine serve to build up the Body of Christ, preparing believers to impact their communities and bring about the Kingdom of God.

Preparing and Delivering Teachings

Preparing and delivering teachings is a crucial aspect of the teaching ministry within the five-fold ministry. It involves a deliberate process of study, prayer, and effective communication to ensure that the message being delivered is clear, accurate, and impactful. The steps in preparing and delivering teachings go as follows:

Study and Research: Teachers dedicate time to studying and researching the Scriptures, seeking to understand the context, meaning, and application of the biblical passages they teach. They engage in in-depth study, consult commentaries and resources, and rely on the guidance of the Holy Spirit to gain a comprehensive understanding of the text.

Prayerful Preparation: Teachers approach their preparation with prayer, seeking God's wisdom and guidance to discern the main message and insights they will share with their audience. They rely on the Holy Spirit to illuminate their understanding of the Scriptures and to guide them in delivering a teaching that aligns with God's heart and purposes.

Structuring the Content: Teachers carefully structure their teachings, organising the content logically and coherently. They outline key points, develop supporting arguments, and arrange the material in a way that facilitates comprehension and retention for the listeners. This structure helps to present the message in a clear and accessible way.

Application of Biblical Truths: Effective teachings go beyond the dissemination of information and strive to provide practical application of biblical truths. Teachers help individuals understand how the teachings relate to their everyday lives, addressing real-life challenges and offering guidance for personal transformation. They illustrate principles with relevant examples and encourage reflection and action steps for further application.

Engaging Delivery: Teachers employ effective communication techniques to engage their audience during the delivery of their teaching. They employ various methods, including storytelling, illustrations, visual aids, and interactive elements, to captivate the listeners' attention and enhance their understanding. They speak with clarity, enthusiasm, and genuine passion for the topic, inspiring a hunger for deeper spiritual growth.

Sensitivity to the Audience: Teachers consider the needs, backgrounds, and maturity levels of their audience. They tailor their teachings to meet the specific needs of the individuals they are addressing, ensuring that the message resonates with their context and challenges. They communicate with sensitivity, empathy, and an awareness of the diverse perspectives and experiences within the congregation.

Continual Growth and Feedback: Teachers embrace a mindset of continual growth and improvement in their teaching ministry. They seek feedback from trusted mentors, peers, and members of the congregation, valuing constructive criticism and suggestions for enhancing their teaching effectiveness. They engage in self-reflection, evaluating their delivery, content, and impact to refine their approach.

Prayer and Spirit-led Delivery: Throughout the entire process of preparing and delivering teachings, teachers rely on the power of prayer and the leading of the Holy Spirit.

They invite the Holy Spirit to guide their preparation, anoint their delivery, and impact the hearts of the listeners. They understand that true transformation comes from the work of the Spirit and not merely through human effort.

By investing time and effort into preparing and delivering teachings, teachers contribute to the growth, edification, and equipping of the Body of Christ. Through their faithful stewardship of the message entrusted to them, they empower believers to live out their faith, deepen their understanding of God's Word, and actively participate in the fulfilment of the Apostolic Mandate.

Teaching Methods and Approaches

Within the framework of the 5-fold ministry, teaching methods and approaches hold a significant role in equipping and edifying the body of Christ. Just as apostles, prophets, evangelists, pastors, and teachers are called to equip believers for the work of ministry, teachers within the 5-fold ministry have a unique responsibility to facilitate transformative learning experiences that nurture spiritual growth, deepen understanding of biblical truths, and empower individuals to live out their faith. This chapter explores the intersection of teaching methods and the 5-fold ministry, examining how different teaching approaches can align with and enhance the specific giftings and purposes of each ministry gift.

From prophetic teaching that inspires revelation and encounters with God's truth to pastoral teaching that nurtures and guides individuals on their spiritual journey, this chapter explores the various ways in which teaching can complement and synergise with the diverse roles within the fivefold ministry. Join us as we explore the power of teaching methods to empower believers, strengthen the Church, and advance the Kingdom of God, guided by the 5-fold ministry.

Expository Teaching: This method involves systematically explaining and unpacking a specific passage or book of the Bible. Teachers carefully analyse the text, highlighting its context, historical background, and literary features. They strive to present a clear and accurate interpretation of the Scripture, guiding listeners through its meaning and application.

Topical Teaching: Topical teaching focuses on specific themes, subjects, or theological concepts found throughout Scripture. Teachers gather relevant passages and explore their connections, presenting a comprehensive understanding of the topic. This approach enables a more in-depth examination of specific aspects of faith and offers practical guidance for applying biblical truths.

Narrative Teaching: Narrative teaching involves using storytelling techniques to communicate biblical truths. Teachers utilise stories and narratives from the Bible to engage listeners, drawing them into the rich narratives of God's work in history. This approach helps individuals connect emotionally with the characters and events, making the teachings more relatable and memorable.

Interactive Teaching: Interactive teaching methods encourage active participation and engagement from the audience. Teachers incorporate discussions, small-group activities, and Q&A sessions to foster dialogue and reflection. This approach enables the sharing of insights, questions, and personal experiences, thereby fostering a dynamic learning environment that promotes mutual growth and learning.

Visual Aids and Media: Visual aids and multimedia resources enhance the teaching experience by utilising visual and audio elements. Teachers utilise PowerPoint presentations, videos, images, and props to illustrate concepts, provide visual cues, and enhance comprehension. These visual aids capture attention, reinforce key points, and create a more engaging and memorable learning experience.

Lecture-style Teaching: Lecture-style teaching involves a structured and informative delivery of content. Teachers present the material in a lecture format, sharing knowledge, insights, and practical applications. This method is effective for conveying complex concepts, providing in-depth explanations, and offering a comprehensive overview of a subject.

Socratic Method: The Socratic method involves asking thought-provoking questions to stimulate critical thinking and encourage deeper exploration of the topic. Teachers guide the audience through a series of well-crafted questions, leading them to draw their conclusions and discover insights. This approach promotes active engagement, encourages analytical thinking, and fosters personal reflection.

Multi-sensory Approaches: Multi-sensory approaches incorporate various senses to enhance the learning experience. Teachers engage students by using a combination of visual aids, music, object lessons, drama, and hands-on activities that cater to visual, auditory, and kinaesthetic learning styles. This approach appeals to different learning preferences, making the teachings more accessible and memorable.

Teachers need to tailor their teaching methods and approaches to the needs, preferences, and learning styles of their students. By utilising a variety of methods and approaches, teachers create a dynamic and engaging learning environment, fostering a deeper understanding and application of God's Word. Ultimately, the goal is to facilitate spiritual growth, equip believers, and inspire them to live out their faith in impactful ways as they fulfil the Apostolic Mandate.

Teachers As Life-long Learners

The teaching office within the 5-Fold Ministry is not merely a function of delivering information or clarifying doctrine; it is a sacred stewardship of truth, requiring a continual posture of learning, humility, and refinement. A true teacher in the Body of Christ is first and foremost a lifelong learner, submitted to the authority of Scripture, open to the leading of the Holy Spirit, and committed to growing in both knowledge and grace.

In the New Testament, we find that the role of a teacher is one of great responsibility. James 3:1 (NKJV) cautions, *"My brethren, let not many of you become teachers, knowing that we shall receive a stricter judgment."* This weighty call demands diligence, not only in teaching others but in cultivating one's growth. Teachers must remain teachable, knowing that their authority to instruct flows from their own willingness to be instructed.

Jesus Christ Himself modelled the life of a master teacher who remained in communion with the Father, seeking divine wisdom in all things. Though He was fully God, He continually communed with the Father, demonstrating that those who teach must always be in the posture of receiving. In Luke 2:46-47, even as a child, Jesus is found in the temple, *"sitting in the midst of the teachers, both listening to them and asking them questions."* This posture of engagement, both speaking and listening, illustrates that even the wisest remain learners.

Lifelong learning for a teacher goes beyond the accumulation of theological facts or the memorisation of Scripture. It involves a deepening sensitivity to the times, a discerning heart for the Body of Christ, and a commitment to rightly dividing the Word of truth. A teacher must be willing to study beyond convenience, to wrestle with difficult passages, to engage different perspectives, and to seek the heart of God behind every lesson they prepare. Their preparation is not for performance, but for transformation, both theirs and that of the hearers.

The Apostle Paul embodies this ideal vividly. Despite being an erudite scholar of the Law and a chosen vessel of divine revelation, Paul continually expressed his dependence on the Spirit and his pursuit of deeper knowledge of Christ. In Philippians 3:10 (NKJV), he declares, *"that I may know Him and the power of His resurrection..."* not as a beginner, but as a mature apostle hungry for more. His example reminds us that spiritual maturity is not the end of learning; it is the beginning of deeper longing.

Teachers who are committed to lifelong learning remain relevant and refreshed. They avoid stagnation by remaining curious, prayerful, and open to the Holy Spirit's illumination. The questions of others do not threaten them; instead, they welcome inquiry because they are learners themselves. Their learning flows into their teaching, making their ministry alive, anchored, and anointed.

A lifelong learner understands the need to grow not just in theology but in wisdom, character, and practical ministry. They read widely, listen deeply, and reflect often. They embrace feedback, seek mentorship, and adapt their methods without compromising truth. In doing so, they become not only instructors of knowledge but facilitators of transformation in the lives of others.

In today's ever-shifting cultural and spiritual landscape, the Church does not need teachers who recite yesterday's truths. It needs teachers who are daily renewed by God's Word, deeply rooted in doctrine yet adaptable in method, and passionately pursuing God's mind and heart. These teachers disciple others not from a place of superiority, but from shared pursuit. Their authority is not in how much they know, but in how deeply they have allowed truth to shape them.

To be a teacher in the 5-Fold Ministry is to accept a lifelong call to both instruct and be instructed to feed others while remaining hungry for righteousness. The maturity of the Church is tied to the faithfulness of its teachers to keep learning, growing, and sharpening their spiritual understanding. In this way, they become wise stewards of revelation, nurturing believers into wholeness and equipping them for the work of ministry in alignment with the Apostolic Mandate.

The Hub Model: A Proposal

The model we have designed and introduced in this section provides an overview of the core elements of the biblical NAR doctrine and also contains a suggested model extension: the aspect of the apostolic–prophetic role. This proprietary Apostolic–Prophetic Hub illustration proposes an organisational model of the apostolic–prophetic role as a concept for deploying effective leadership (see Figure 01 below). This understanding establishes an alternative leadership model within contemporary Christianity, which is noticeably distinct from the traditional leadership models of Protestantism, Catholicism, and evangelical Christianity.

The term hub model has been chosen because a hub is defined as the effective centre of a network. Just as a hub airport is a large airport from which people can travel to many other local airports (for instance, Heathrow's function as Europe's main international hub), a hub in theological terms is an apostolic–prophetic centre responsible for the spiritual development and order within a certain region or to use Wagner's term, sphere.

In this sense, a hub model is presented below, which encompasses all five functions of the five–fold ministry, including the covenant relationship between the apostle and prophet, as discussed in this chapter. Leading scholars from the NAR movement argue that churches and Christian ministries need effective leadership models which are theologically grounded in the doctrine of the offices of apostle and prophet, as described in the New Testament.

The fundamental concept of such a leadership model is the understanding, as was discussed above, that the defunct governmental office of New Testament polity, namely the apostleship and the other four functions, are being reassigned.

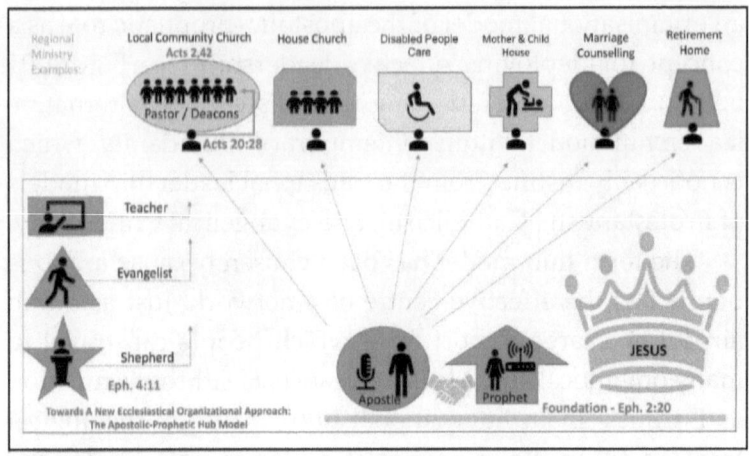

Figure 01: The Apostolic–Prophetic Hub Model

The central doctrine is that, as indicated in the Figure, Jesus Christ Himself has bestowed upon some Christians, men and women of His choosing, the spiritual governmental gifting of apostle, prophet, evangelist, pastor, and teacher. These five offices are serving and equipping in character and constitute a team authorised by God, whose function is to work together to spiritually activate churches, ministries and Christians for effective service in every sphere of life (these are indicated in the Figure by example spheres, such as a retirement home, marriage counselling, disabled people care, house churches and the local community church), in order to establish the principles of the heavenly kingdom on earth increasingly.

The serving characteristic is indicated in the Figure by arrows, which point from the five–fold ministries to the Christian ministries and churches at the top of the illustration. The apostle is the primus inter pares in such a team.

The apostle and prophet have, as mentioned above, a special foundational function for church building processes, as they are independent of any denomination. The traditional reading of the term "church" is defined within the context of the NAR doctrine, as ecclesia, meaning where Christians meet by the principles outlined in Acts 2:42 (NIV): "They devoted themselves to the apostles' teaching and fellowship, to the breaking of bread and prayer."

Where this activity takes place, there is ecclesia, as suggested in the Figure. It could be a congregation with 500 people, a house church with 10 people, or any other Christian ministry; they can all become part of the regional network of an apostleship. They all would be part of apostolic oversight. The figure illustrates the widespread use of the term 'church' and refers to Acts 2:42.

In this way, the Apostolic–Prophetic Hub model depicts the covenant between the apostle and prophet by referring to the biblical statement in Ephesians 2:20 (NIV), "Built on the foundation of the apostles and prophets, with Christ Jesus himself as the chief cornerstone."

Apostles and prophets, as dual leadership teams, play a fundamental role in the foundation of any form of church, from the times of the New Testament through to the present. The Figure underlines this aspect by using the symbol of one person's hand being extended to another, indicating the need for synergistic cooperation between the apostle and the prophet. A vertical apostle and his surrounding team have a God–given mandate for a particular sphere or region.

Pastors of local churches, as part of a local elders' team and shown in the Figure with the reference to Act 20:28, will recognise the authority of an apostle and his external team when looking for spiritual covering, and will feel comfortable under that particular apostleship's authority, agreeing with the consent of the local elders' team to a regional apostle, as displayed top left in the Figure.

The focus of a local pastor will be on shepherding the members of the local congregation. In contrast, the pastor of the five-fold ministry will focus on training local pastors, caring for them, and providing guidance on how to handle special counselling challenges. Any local leader who directly cares for a group of Christians should have a shepherd's strong love for his sheep.

The apostle and the other five-fold members will therefore be part of a local congregation themselves, submitting to the authority of the local elders' team. The entire system of apostolic oversight must be a voluntary network, based on trust, respect, transparency, and mutual submission. It can then be called a regional Apostolic-Prophetic Hub as it is not part of a local congregation, but placed organisationally outside of any local church (the Figure shows a frame around the five functions, separating them from the different spheres at the top of the illustration), to serve the corporate body of Christian believers within a region and to instantiate and reify godly order so that the ecclesia will bloom and flourish.

The Five-Fold Coordinated Efforts to Edify the Church

God, in His infinite wisdom, appointed five distinct ministry offices to govern, grow, and guide the Church: apostles, prophets, evangelists, pastors, and teachers. These are not titles for spiritual superiority, but functional graces entrusted to men and women to mature the Body of Christ.

Each office has its unique mandate, yet none was meant to operate in isolation. The true strength of the Five-Fold Ministry lies in its unity and coordination, a divine interplay designed to edify, equip, and perfect the saints.

The Apostle Paul, writing under the inspiration of the Holy Spirit, explains in Ephesians 4:11–12 (NKJV): *"And He Himself gave some to be apostles, some prophets, some evangelists, and some pastors and teachers, for the equipping of the saints for the work of ministry, for the edifying of the body of Christ."*

The edification of the Church does not come from one office functioning alone, but from the convergence of these five streams of grace flowing together in one direction toward the maturity and fullness of Christ in His people.

The Apostle functions as a divine architect. Apostles carry vision, divine blueprints, and governmental authority. They lay the foundational truth, establish spiritual order, and set direction. In coordinating efforts, the apostle ensures that the other ministry gifts are operating within a shared sense of purpose, safeguarding the unity of the faith and anchoring all ministry activity in Christ's redemptive mission.

The Prophet discerns and declares the heartbeat of God. Prophets bring spiritual sensitivity, timely warnings, and divine encouragement. They ensure the Church remains aligned with heaven's voice, exposing error and revealing God's perspective on current events, people, and purposes. When coordinated with apostolic strategy, prophetic insight strengthens the Church's faith and sharpens its discernment, empowering believers to walk in truth with spiritual precision.

The Evangelist ignites the outward flame of the Church. Evangelists are gifted to proclaim the Gospel with fervour, drawing the lost into the Kingdom. Their role in coordinated ministry ensures that the Church does not become inward-focused or stagnant. Evangelists bring urgency and clarity to the message of salvation, while pastors and teachers ensure those who come in are nurtured and grounded in the Word. When evangelistic fervour is supported by pastoral care and sound teaching, the fruit of salvation is sustained and multiplied.

The Pastor provides care, counsel, and community. Pastors carry the shepherd's heart, ensuring that believers are protected, fed, and healed. Their coordination role involves making space for each ministry gift to function without friction, while also safeguarding the flock from confusion, error, and neglect. Pastors disciple the heart while teachers train the mind. When both work in tandem, believers grow in wholeness, stability, and relational maturity.

The Teacher builds the framework of understanding. Teachers labour to unpack the truths of Scripture in practical, doctrinally sound, and spiritually transformative ways. Their coordination ensures that what is taught aligns with what is being preached and prophesied. Teachers bring doctrinal cohesion to the efforts of apostles and prophets, and they support the spiritual formation that pastors and evangelists initiate.

When these five gifts work together in humility and honour, the Church becomes unstoppable. The apostolic office lays the foundation. The prophetic keeps the direction pure. The evangelistic extends the reach. The pastor nurtures the soul. The teaching builds the mind. Together, they coordinate a divine system of checks, balances, and collaboration that keeps the Church both stable and advancing.

This coordination requires intentionality. It requires that ministry leaders communicate frequently, pray together, and remain submissive to the headship of Christ. It means resisting the temptation to elevate one gift above another and instead celebrating the full spectrum of grace that Christ has distributed among His people.

As Paul writes in Ephesians 4:16 (NIV), *"From him the whole body, joined and held together by every supporting ligament, grows and builds itself up in love, as each part does its work."*

In today's Church, the call is not merely to function, but to function together. Apostles must make room for teachers. Evangelists must value the intercession of prophets. Pastors must honour the vision of apostles, and teachers must appreciate the spontaneous move of the Spirit through prophets and evangelists. When coordination replaces competition, and collaboration overcomes isolation, the Church is edified in power, unity, and maturity.

The five-fold offices were never meant to be silos; they are a divine symphony. When they are coordinated well, the melody of heaven becomes unmistakably clear, drawing souls, healing wounds, training disciples, and expanding the Kingdom. This is the fullness of Christ made manifest through His Body on Earth.

Purpose and Function of the Five-Fold Ministry

The Five-Fold Ministry is not a denominational concept, or a hierarchical structure devised by human systems. It is a divine framework instituted by Christ Himself to establish, strengthen, and sustain the spiritual maturity of His Church.

According to Ephesians 4:11-13 (NKJV), *"And He Himself gave some to be apostles, some prophets, some evangelists, and some pastors and teachers, for the equipping of the saints for the work of ministry, for the edifying of the body of Christ..."* These ministry offices are not merely titles or positions of prestige; they are active expressions of God's grace at work to form Christ in His people.

At the heart of the Five-Fold Ministry is equipping. Each gift functions as a divine tool for preparing believers, not to remain passive recipients of religious instruction, but to rise as active participants in the work of the Kingdom. The Church is not a platform for spectatorship; it is a living Body made up of many members, each with a unique calling and contribution. The Five-Fold Ministry exists to awaken, train, and activate those callings so that the whole Body may operate in spiritual effectiveness and authority.

Another central function of the Five-Fold Ministry is edification the spiritual building up of the Body of Christ. This is not limited to emotional encouragement or doctrinal teaching. Edification involves the development of spiritual maturity, sound doctrine, character strength, and alignment with the heart and will of God. It includes both correction and comfort, challenge and counsel, so that the Church may grow into *"a perfect man, to the measure of the stature of the fullness of Christ"* (Ephesians 4:13, NKJV).

The Five-Fold Ministry also serves to bring unity of the faith. In a world where divisions abound and doctrines are often distorted, these offices collaborate to bring clarity, cohesion, and consistency to the Church's beliefs and practices. Apostles lay doctrinal foundations, prophets align the Church to God's voice, evangelists proclaim the unchanging Gospel, pastors shepherd the hearts of believers, and teachers instil sound doctrine. In unison, they foster unity rooted in truth, not compromise.

Furthermore, the Five-Fold Ministry functions to protect the Church from spiritual deception. Ephesians 4:14 warns us of being *"tossed to and fro and carried about with every wind of doctrine."* The coordination of these five ministries acts as a safeguard against false teachings, spiritual immaturity, and doctrinal error. They function together to keep the Body stable, grounded, and discerning.

Another significant purpose is to ensure the Church reflects the full expression of Christ on earth. Jesus operated in all five offices He was the Apostle of our faith (Hebrews 3:1), the Prophet without honour in His own country (Luke 4:24), the Evangelist who came to seek and save the lost (Luke 19:10), the Good Shepherd (John 10:11), and the Teacher of truth and wisdom (John 3:2). In distributing these offices to the Church, Christ gave of Himself so that His fullness might be expressed collectively through His people.

In the end, the Five-Fold Ministry is Christ's strategy for Kingdom advancement. Its function is not limited to pulpit ministry. Rather, it is intended to release grace across every sphere of society: church, family, business, education, government, and the arts. When the saints are properly equipped, they carry the influence of the Kingdom wherever they go. This is the Apostolic Mandate: to disciple nations, not merely to fill church buildings.

In summary, the purpose and function of the Five-Fold Ministry is to:

- ⌘ Equip the saints for active ministry
- ⌘ Build and strengthen the Body of Christ
- ⌘ Promote unity in the faith and knowledge of Christ
- ⌘ Safeguard the Church from deception and instability
- ⌘ Reveal the fullness of Christ through coordinated grace
- ⌘ Extend Kingdom influence beyond the Church into the world

When the Five-Fold Ministry operates in humility, maturity, and collaboration, the Church becomes a radiant Bride, prepared and positioned for her final assignment. This divine framework, established by Christ, is essential for preparing the Church not only to survive the present age but to thrive in power, purity, and purpose until He returns.

The Maturity and Character Required to Operate in the Five-Fold Offices

The operation of the Five-Fold Ministry is not merely a function of spiritual gifting; it is a sacred responsibility that demands spiritual maturity and unwavering Christlike character. While gifts may be distributed freely by the grace of God, the fruit of the Spirit is cultivated over time through surrender, obedience, and a life rooted in the Word and presence of God.

Scripture reminds us in Romans 11:29 (NKJV) that "the gifts and the calling of God are irrevocable," but gifting without maturity can damage the flock instead of building it up.

Each office, including apostle, prophet, evangelist, pastor, and teacher, wields spiritual influence that can shape lives, doctrines, and destinies. For this reason, those who fill these roles must be grounded in humility, accountability, and a lifestyle that reflects the heart of Jesus.

Apostles must carry authority with meekness, not dominance. Prophets must speak truth with love, not arrogance or bitterness. Evangelists must preach with compassion, not self-promotion. Pastors must shepherd with patience, not control. Teachers must instruct with grace, not intellectual pride. These callings are not platforms for power but postures of servanthood.

Spiritual maturity is evidenced not by eloquence or miracles but by the capacity to carry weight with integrity. It shows in how leaders handle correction, how they steward influence, and how they endure seasons of silence and testing.

Paul's counsel to Timothy is still relevant: "Take heed to yourself and the doctrine. Continue in them, for in doing this you will save both yourself and those who hear you" (1 Timothy 4:16, NKJV). In other words, the leader must be anchored before attempting to anchor others.

All Five-Fold ministers are called to live above reproach. Their personal lives, families, finances, and relationships must reflect holiness and accountability. The credibility of their office is often judged not by their sermons but by their consistency when no one is watching. Their authority flows not just from what they say, but from how they live.

In an age where charisma can easily eclipse character, the Church must return to valuing maturity over popularity and spiritual depth over public recognition. A true Five-Fold minister is not formed on a stage; they are shaped in secret, refined by submission, and matured through fellowship with Christ. Only then can they rightly divide the Word, rightly lead God's people, and rightly reflect the image of the One who called them.

Maturing Believers Through Shared Ministry

The true power of the Five-Fold Ministry lies not in the platform of a few but in the equipping of many. According to Ephesians 4:12, these ministry gifts were given "for the equipping of the saints for the work of ministry, for the edifying of the body of Christ." Their primary assignment is to mature believers, not keep them dependent, but release them into purpose.

When the Church adopts a shared ministry approach, believers transition from being spectators to active participants. Apostles activate boldness and vision in others. Prophets stir sensitivity to God's voice. Evangelists ignite a passion for souls. Pastors cultivate care and community. Teachers impart wisdom and understanding. Together, they lay a foundation that helps every believer identify their spiritual gifts, grow in grace, and serve effectively.

Mature believers are not only spiritually sound but emotionally stable, biblically informed, and missionally engaged. False teachings or trends no longer sway them. Instead, they grow into the full stature of Christ, able to discern truth, extend love, and contribute to the advancement of God's Kingdom. The Five-Fold Ministry ensures that no gift remains dormant, and no calling goes unfulfilled. When each part does its share, the whole body flourishes.

The Role of the Holy Spirit in the Five-Fold Ministry

At the very heart of the Five-Fold Ministry lies the dynamic, active presence of the Holy Spirit. No office, whether apostle, prophet, evangelist, pastor, or teacher, can function effectively apart from the Spirit's empowering, guiding, and sustaining work. It is the Holy Spirit who calls, equips, and anoints individuals for these sacred assignments, and it is by His wisdom and strength that the Church is led into all truth, unity, and maturity.

From the birth of the Church in Acts 2, we witness the Holy Spirit as the initiator of spiritual gifts and the establisher of leadership. The apostles did not move in human strength or institutional authority; they were filled with the Holy Spirit and spoke as He gave them utterance. Their boldness, discernment, and ability to organise the early Church were all products of divine enablement.

The Holy Spirit is not just a source of power; He is the teacher, comforter, and revealer of truth (John 14:26, NKJV). In prophetic ministry, it is He who gives utterance and unveils the mind of God. In evangelism, it is He who convicts hearts and draws souls to salvation. In pastoring, it is He who produces the fruit of love, patience, and gentleness. In teaching, it is He who gives understanding and depth of insight. The Spirit does not merely assist the Five-Fold gifts; He breathes life into them.

Moreover, the unity of the Five-Fold Ministry is sustained by the Spirit. Without Him, ministry becomes mechanical and divisive. With Him, ministry becomes a symphony of grace, truth, and effectiveness. He brings alignment, softens hearts, exposes pride, and points all leaders back to Christ. Where the Spirit is truly honoured, the Five-Fold functions not in competition, but in complement.

Ministers who operate in these roles must remain yielded to the Spirit on a daily basis. This requires prayerfulness, sensitivity, and spiritual alertness. It also requires humility, a recognition that the office is not theirs to control, but a gift to be stewarded under the leadership of the Holy Spirit. It is He who sets the pace, determines the season, and assigns the measure of grace.

In the life of the Church, the Holy Spirit ensures that the Five-Fold gifts are not merely roles to be filled but expressions of Christ's ongoing ministry on earth. Through the Spirit, Jesus continues to build His Church, sending apostles, revealing Himself through prophets, calling people through evangelists, shepherding them through pastors, and instructing them through teachers.

To disconnect the Five-Fold Ministry from the Holy Spirit is to reduce it to a man-made structure. To stay in communion with the Spirit is to keep it alive, fruitful, and anchored in heaven's will.

The Centrality of Christ in All Five-Fold Functions

Christ is the cornerstone of the Church, and the Five-Fold Ministry exists solely to reveal, exalt, and serve Him. Each office apostle, prophet, evangelist, pastor, and teacher is not a platform for self-promotion or spiritual hierarchy, but a channel through which the person and work of Jesus Christ are revealed more fully to the Body of believers.

Ephesians 4:11-13 reminds us that Christ Himself gave these gifts to the Church. He is both the sender and the model. The apostle reflects Christ's authority and mission. The prophet reflects the voice and divine insight of God. The evangelist reveals His redemptive heart for the lost. The pastor mirrors His shepherding care. The teacher embodies His wisdom and command of truth. Each gift is an extension of Christ's ongoing ministry through the Holy Spirit.

When any part of the Five-Fold Ministry operates apart from Christ's nature, it loses both its power and its purity. It is not enough to function in gifting; each office must reflect Christ's humility, character, and submission to the will of the Father. Jesus, though equal with God, made Himself of no reputation and served even unto death (Philippians 2:5-8). This mindset must remain at the centre of every leader's posture in ministry.

The goal of the Five-Fold Ministry is not to exalt the minister but to mature the Church until it reflects the fullness of Christ (Ephesians 4:13). That means each gift must continually point people back to Jesus, His teachings, His example, His power, and His finished work on the Cross. True apostolic authority does not create allegiance to personalities or systems, but to the person of Christ.

True prophetic utterance confirms the Word made flesh. True evangelism calls people not just to religion but to repentance and faith in Jesus. True pastoring leads believers into a deeper love for Christ. True teaching unveils the mysteries of Christ with clarity and reverence.

Christ remains the unifying figure across all functions. He is not merely at the beginning of His ministry call. He is the reason and the end goal. As ministers serve in their respective offices, their hearts must remain anchored in His love, their minds renewed by His truth, and their ministries rooted in His lordship. Apart from Him, we can do nothing (John 15:5).

Where Christ is exalted, the Five-Fold Ministry flourishes. Where He is sidelined, ministry loses its meaning. Everything must flow from Him, through Him, and unto Him, for He is the head of the Church, and in Him all things hold together.

Restoring the Full Expression of Christ in the Church

The end goal of the Five-Fold Ministry is nothing less than the restoration of Christ's full expression in His Body. Ephesians 4:13 speaks of attaining "the unity of the faith and the knowledge of the Son of God, to a perfect man, to the measure of the stature of the fullness of Christ." This is not an abstract goal but a divine blueprint for the Church.

Each office represents a facet of Christ's ministry. Apostles carry His authority and mission. Prophets embody His voice and vision. Evangelists proclaim His redemptive power. Pastors reflect His compassion and guidance. Teachers reveal His truth and wisdom. When these five offices function together in harmony, the Church reflects Christ more fully to the world.

This restoration is both spiritual and practical. It realigns the Church with Heaven's priorities and activates the Body to function beyond the four walls. It moves the Church from being clergy-centred to Christ-centred. Every believer becomes a vessel of truth, love, and power. Every gathering becomes a space of activation and transformation. Every community touched by the Church becomes a potential ground for revival and Kingdom impact.

The Church was never meant to operate on a fragmented model. Restoring the full expression of Christ requires honouring all five gifts, submitting them to the Holy Spirit, and weaving them together for the sake of edification. As the Church moves in this rhythm, the world will see a more accurate representation of Christ, not divided or diluted, but glorious and whole.

Guarding Against Misuse and Misrepresentation

One of the greatest challenges facing the Five-Fold Ministry today is the misuse or misrepresentation of these sacred offices. Titles are often taken for granted without the weight of responsibility, and gifting is sometimes elevated above character. This distortion not only stifles spiritual growth but also creates confusion, division, and mistrust within the Body of Christ.

Guarding against misuse begins with sound doctrine. The Church must uphold the biblical standards for each office, ensuring that those who function within these roles have not only been called by God but are also biblically grounded and spiritually accountable. Ministry must be marked by service, not self-exaltation. Christ rebuked those who loved to be called "Rabbi" but did not carry the heart of a servant (Matthew 23:6-12). In the same way, apostles, prophets, evangelists, pastors, and teachers must never forget that they are stewards, not owners, of the grace they carry.

Discipleship, mentorship, and local church accountability are essential safeguards against spiritual drift. No one should operate independently of the Body. Those in Five-Fold Ministry must be rooted in local fellowship, submitted to spiritual oversight, and open to correction. By creating a culture of humility and accountability, the Church preserves the purity and power of the Five-Fold structure.

Summary Table: A Practical Reference for the Five-Fold Ministry

To grasp the full spectrum of the Five-Fold Ministry, the following summary table provides a concise comparison of each office: Apostle, Prophet, Evangelist, Pastor, and Teacher. This visual reference complements the details in this chapter, allowing for a side-by-side understanding of the unique function, biblical foundation, core qualities, and potential pitfalls of each role. Scripture quotations are taken from the New International Version (NIV) to ensure accessibility and clarity.

Whether you are a church leader, Bible student, ministry trainer, or a believer seeking clarity on your calling, this table offers a snapshot that reinforces learning and encourages prayerful reflection. Biblical examples are included to inspire study and personal application.

Office	Function	Scriptural Reference	Core Qualities	Common Pitfalls to Avoid	Biblical Examples
Apostle	Lays foundations, pioneers new works, governs and oversees spiritual growth.	*Ephesians 2:20* – "built on the foundation of the apostles and prophets, with Christ Jesus himself as the chief cornerstone."	Visionary, courageous, fatherly, grounded in doctrine	Controlling leadership, elitism, and spiritual pride	Paul, Peter, Barnabas
Prophet	Declares God's word, brings correction and spiritual insight, edifies and aligns the Church.	*1 Corinthians 14:3* – "But the one who prophesies speaks to people for their strengthening, encouraging and comfort."	Spiritually discerning, truthful, bold, and intimate with God	Harshness, emotionalism, isolation from accountability	Samuel, Elijah, and Agabus
Evangelist	Proclaims the Gospel to the lost, equips believers for outreach	*2 Timothy 4:5* – "Do the work of an evangelist, discharge all the duties of your ministry."	Passionate, persuasive, compassionate, bold in faith	Shallow discipleship, individualism, and over-fixation on numbers.	Philip the Evangelist, Peter (Acts 2), Jesus (Luke 19:10)
Pastor	Shepherds the flock, offers care, disciples believers in community	*John 10:11* – "I am the good shepherd. The good shepherd lays down his life for the sheep."	Nurturing, wise, approachable, servant-hearted	Burnout, people-pleasing, resistance to change	Jesus (The Good Shepherd), Timothy, Moses
Teacher	Grounds the Church in truth, explains Scripture with clarity and depth	*James 3:1* – "Not many of you should become teachers because you know that we who teach will be judged more strictly."	Knowledgeable, patient, disciplined, humble	Intellectual pride, doctrinal imbalance, and lack of practical application	Apollos, Paul, Ezra

Table No.1: Five-Fold Ministry Summary

How to Use This Table

This summary table can serve as a versatile tool in various settings:

Personal Study: Reflect on your gifts and spiritual leanings. Use the table to identify the traits that resonate with you and seek God's guidance for growth and maturity.

Leadership Development: Equip emerging leaders by discussing each role, its responsibilities, and scriptural anchors. The table is a springboard for mentorship and discipleship conversations.

Group Training or Seminars: Use it as a worksheet in teaching settings. Each column can prompt discussion, case study analysis, or even intercessory prayer over different offices within your ministry.

Strategic Planning: Church leaders can use the table to evaluate whether all five ministry functions are active and supported within their teams, and to foster stronger synergy across callings.

The table is to be complemented by the rest of the content of this chapter. Use it prayerfully and consistently to sharpen discernment, promote unity, and empower the Church to function in alignment with Ephesians 4:12: *"to equip his people for works of service, so that the body of Christ may be built up"* (NIV).

Let it guide you in understanding roles, honouring and releasing them for the edification of the Body and the advancement of God's Kingdom.

CHAPTER SIX

WOMEN CALLED AND COMMISSIONED

"In the last days, God says, I will pour out my Spirit on all people. Your sons and daughters will prophesy..."
—Acts 2:17 (NIV)

THROUGHOUT EVERY AGE, the hand of God has rested upon those He has chosen, often in ways that challenge human tradition and expectation. There is something profoundly powerful about witnessing a life that has been marked by divine calling, a life that, regardless of background or position, becomes a vessel for God's purposes.

When heaven speaks and commissions a soul for service, no boundary, social, cultural, or institutional, can override that assignment. The call of God is sovereign, and when He commissions, He also equips. These calling births courage, stirs conviction, and sets individuals apart for a work that is bigger than themselves. It invites surrender, demands faith, and unfolds in ways that reveal the heart of God through the obedience of those who say yes.

The call of God has never been limited by gender. Throughout Scripture and Church history, we find God appointing women to play significant roles in His redemptive plan. From Deborah the judge and prophetess in the Old Testament, to Mary the mother of Jesus, to the women who were first at the tomb on Resurrection morning, the Bible testifies to a God who entrusts His mission to both men and women.

In the New Testament Church, women prayed, prophesied, taught, hosted congregations in their homes, and stood boldly alongside the apostles as co-labourers in Christ.

The Biblical Perspective

From the opening pages of Scripture, we encounter a God who creates both male and female in His image and entrusts them with shared dominion and purpose (Genesis 1:27-28, NIV). This foundational truth affirms that women were never an afterthought in God's design, but rather co-bearers of His image and co-labourers in His mandate. The biblical narrative is rich with accounts of women who responded to God's call, not as secondary participants, but as vital instruments in His redemptive work.

Throughout the Old Testament, we find women raised by God for leadership, counsel, and prophetic ministry. Deborah, a judge and prophetess (Judges 4:4-5, NIV), led Israel during a time of national turmoil. Both men and women recognised her authority, and her discernment was so trusted that military leaders refused to go into battle without her.

Then there was Huldah the prophetess, who was consulted regarding the Book of the Law during King Josiah's reforms (2 Kings 22:14-20, NIV). Her words carried divine authority, and the king and his court responded with repentance and national revival. These are not mere footnotes; they are bold declarations that God speaks through whomever He chooses.

In the New Testament, the ministry of Jesus reaffirmed the dignity, calling, and capacity of women. He shattered cultural norms by allowing women to sit under His teaching, as Mary did at His feet (Luke 10:39, NIV), and by entrusting them with revelation, as seen when He first revealed His identity as the Messiah to the Samaritan woman (John 4:25-26, NIV). Women supported His ministry, stood by Him at the cross, and were the first to proclaim His resurrection, commissioned directly by the risen Christ Himself (Matthew 28:7-10, NIV).

The early Church continued in this spirit. In Acts 21:10-11 (NIV), the prophet Agabus is mentioned, and shortly after, we are reminded of Philip's four unmarried daughters who prophesied (Acts 21:9, NIV). Paul commended women like Phoebe, a deacon of the church in Cenchreae (Romans 16:1, NIV), and Junia, who was "outstanding among the apostles" (Romans 16:7, NIV), offering evidence that women held influential roles in ministry, even in apostolic circles.

The biblical perspective is neither silent nor ambiguous about God's call upon women. Though cultural restrictions may have fluctuated through history, Scripture itself consistently reveals a pattern: when God calls, He commissions, and when He commissions, He backs that assignment with grace, authority, and fruit. Women, like men, are called not based on gender, but based on divine purpose. The Church must return to this scriptural clarity and honour the call of God wherever it is found.

Historical Perspectives on Women in Ministry

Throughout history, the role of women in ministry has been marked by both vibrant expressions and imposed limitations, shaped not only by Scripture but also by cultural, traditional, and institutional factors. While there have been seasons of flourishing female leadership within the Church, there have also been long stretches where women's spiritual contributions were undervalued or even silenced. Understanding this history is essential for appreciating both the breakthroughs of today and the biblical consistency of women ministering with authority.

In the early Christian Church, women were actively involved in ministry. The New Testament bears witness to women who hosted house churches, taught doctrine, prophesied, and served as co-labourers with apostles. Phoebe, a deacon in the church at Cenchreae, was entrusted with delivering Paul's epistle to the Romans (Romans 16:1–2, NIV). Priscilla, along with her husband Aquila, instructed Apollos more accurately in the way of the Lord (Acts 18:26, NIV). Junia, mentioned in Romans 16:7 (NIV), is referred to as "outstanding among the apostles," indicating that apostolic recognition was not limited to men. These were not exceptions or anomalies; they were visible signs of the Spirit's inclusion and empowerment of women in leadership roles.

As the Church became more institutionalised, particularly after the Constantinian shift in the fourth century, formal positions of authority became increasingly male-dominated. Hierarchical structures developed, and access to ecclesiastical roles was often restricted to men. This shift was less about divine instruction and more about aligning Church governance with prevailing cultural and political norms. Nevertheless, women continued to lead in various capacities through monastic movements, missionary endeavours, prophetic ministries, and local pastoral care, though often without official recognition.

The medieval period, although restrictive in many areas, still featured notable female figures who exerted remarkable influence. Women like Hildegard of Bingen, Catherine of Siena, and Julian of Norwich were respected mystics, theologians, and advisors to Church leaders. Although their ministry often took place outside formal clerical structures, their writings and revelations had a lasting impact on generations. Their authority was spiritual, not positional, yet it was undeniable.

During the Reformation, new theological movements did not initially open ministry offices to women, but women still played crucial roles as evangelists, writers, and reformers. In later centuries, revival movements such as the Methodist revivals, the Holiness movement, and the Pentecostal awakenings gave fresh platforms for female ministry. Women like Phoebe Palmer, Maria Woodworth-Etter, Aimee Semple McPherson, and Kathryn Kuhlman were powerful examples of Spirit-filled leadership, often operating with apostolic and prophetic grace before such titles were widely used for women.

The twentieth century witnessed a significant rise in the global visibility of women in ministry, especially through the Pentecostal and Charismatic movements. These streams of the Church, with their emphasis on the gifts of the Spirit and the priesthood of all believers, often provided fertile ground for women to exercise leadership. Today, we see women pastoring churches, leading denominations, heading mission organisations, and discipling nations not as an act of rebellion, but as a continuation of God's call that has echoed through history.

Understanding these historical perspectives reveals that women in ministry are not a novelty, nor a concession to modernity. It is a recovery of something ancient, something biblical, and something Spirit-led. The Church, when aligned with the fullness of God's design, has always included both men and women as ministers of grace and truth. History, when read through a redemptive lens, affirms what Scripture has already made clear: God calls, commissions, and anoints whomever He wills, and He has not been silent over the women He has sent.

Women in Theological Education

Theological education has long been the training ground for those called to serve the Church in various capacities, offering the tools needed for sound doctrine, biblical interpretation, and pastoral care. For generations, however, access to formal theological study was restricted, particularly for women. These barriers were shaped not by Scripture itself, but by longstanding cultural, institutional, and patriarchal norms that dictated who could be educated for ministry.

Despite these challenges, women have consistently demonstrated a deep hunger to know God, study His Word faithfully, and engage with theology intellectually and spiritually. From early Christian communities to modern seminaries, the desire to understand and teach truth has burned within women who viewed education not as a means to seek status, but as a call to faithful stewardship of their gifts. The rise of women in theological education, especially in the last two centuries, represents a powerful re-emergence of a biblical norm: that all who are in Christ are invited to grow in wisdom and spiritual maturity.

In Scripture, we see women who model theological depth. Mary of Bethany sat at Jesus's feet in a posture of a disciple, absorbing His teaching while others were preoccupied with domestic tasks (Luke 10:39, NIV). Her desire to learn was not corrected, but commended by Jesus.

In Acts 21:9, we find Philip the evangelist's four daughters, who prophesied, an indication of their theological grounding and spiritual maturity. Priscilla, as previously noted, was actively involved in explaining doctrine and instructing one of the Church's most eloquent preachers in a deeper understanding of truth.

In the modern era, women began to access theological training in greater numbers through Bible colleges, missionary training schools, and eventually seminaries. Trailblazers such as Henrietta Mears, Elisabeth Elliot, and F.F. Bosworth's female co-labourers helped shift the perception that theological study was a male-only endeavour. Pentecostal and evangelical movements played a significant role in opening educational spaces for women, often propelled by the view that if God could pour out His Spirit on all flesh, He could certainly equip all who were willing to be trained.

Today, women are not only attending seminaries and theological colleges in record numbers, but they are also teaching, leading, and contributing scholarly work that shapes how the Church thinks and lives. They are writing commentaries, publishing academic research, training ministers, and mentoring both men and women for Kingdom work. In many institutions, the presence of women has enriched the learning environment by bringing perspectives rooted in lived experience, spiritual discernment, and pastoral sensitivity.

The inclusion of women in theological education is not merely about equal opportunity; it is about preparing the whole Body of Christ for effective ministry. When women are trained to divide the Word of truth rightly, the Church benefits from sound teaching, thoughtful leadership, and holistic care. Theological education empowers women to respond to their calling with clarity and confidence, anchored in biblical truth and spiritual authority.

This is not just an academic pursuit; it is a divine invitation. As women step into seminaries, classrooms, and teaching pulpits, they do so not to claim positions for the sake of equality, but to fulfil the commission given to every believer: to love the Lord with all their heart, soul, mind, and strength and to teach others to do the same.

Women's Contemporary Expressions of Apostolic Ministry

Across the globe today, women are arising with spiritual authority, clarity of vision, and apostolic boldness. While the term "apostolic" often evokes images of the early Church or male-dominated leadership, there is an undeniable resurgence of women operating in apostolic dimensions, planting ministries, discipling nations, stewarding prophetic insight, and advancing the Kingdom with precision and power. This is not a modern invention; it is a present manifestation of a timeless call.

An apostolic woman is not simply one with a title. She has been sent by God with a specific mandate, just like the apostles of old. She carries a divine burden to build, govern, align, and multiply the work of God. Whether she leads a church, mentors leaders, launches community initiatives, or mobilises missions across regions, her authority comes from obedience to the Holy Spirit and the fruit that follows her labour. Her impact is not measured by size but by spiritual weight and eternal influence.

The expression of this ministry takes many forms. Some women are apostles in the marketplace, establishing Kingdom values in business, education, media, or politics. Others are church planters and reformers, raising spiritual sons and daughters and ensuring healthy church governance. Still others lead apostolic hubs, places of teaching, healing, prayer, and commissioning, where believers are trained and released into their assignments.

These women often operate prophetically and pastorally as well, but it is the apostolic grace that causes them to think beyond the local congregation and invest in long-term transformation.

What distinguishes these contemporary apostolic women is not only their courage but also their clarity of purpose. They do not compete with men, nor do they minister in reaction to inequality. They serve from a place of divine conviction, aware that they are stewards of a call, not mere participants in a trend.

Their leadership is characterised by humility, strategic thinking, and a profound reliance on the Word and the Spirit. Many work quietly, discipling leaders behind the scenes. Others are more visible, leading global networks or apostolic teams. In both expressions, the mark of the apostolic is unmistakable: fruitfulness, alignment with biblical truth, and the multiplication of disciples.

This is not about elevating women above men, but about recognising that the same Holy Spirit who raised Christ from the dead empowers both sons and daughters to prophesy, lead, and build (Acts 2:17, NIV). The 21st-century Church is seeing this unfold in powerful ways. Denominations, mission agencies, and apostolic networks are now acknowledging and affirming the God-ordained work being carried out through women across the nations.

We are witnessing a time when women are no longer waiting for permission from tradition; they are moving forward by the power of the Holy Spirit. They are faithful to Scripture, submitted to godly counsel, and empowered to lead. Their presence is not a disruption of order but a restoration of biblical balance. This contemporary wave of apostolic women is not only reshaping ministry paradigms but also accelerating the fulfilment of the Great Commission.

Addressing Barriers Faced by Women Apostles

Women called to apostolic ministry often walk a path lined with both divine affirmation and human resistance. Though their mandate comes from God, their assignment is frequently challenged by societal norms, church traditions, and internal doubts. The role of an apostle demands spiritual authority, leadership, and often pioneering work responsibilities, which for many are seen as unconventional or even unacceptable when held by a woman. These barriers, while real and complex, are not insurmountable.

One of the most persistent barriers faced by women apostles is theological resistance. Certain interpretations of Scripture have been used to limit women's authority and leadership, particularly in roles involving oversight, church planting, or doctrinal instruction.

Passages like 1 Timothy 2:12 are often cited without context, overshadowing the broader biblical witness of women like Junia, who is named among the apostles in Romans 16:7 (NIV), or Deborah, who led Israel as a prophet and judge. This selective theology restricts the Church from benefiting from the full range of God's gifts through His daughters.

The solution lies in biblical literacy and theological reformation. A careful, Spirit-led study of Scripture, one that considers cultural context, original language, and the totality of the biblical narrative, reveals a God who empowers women for leadership. Churches and leaders who prioritise accurate teaching can help dismantle these theological misunderstandings, restoring the place of women apostles without compromising biblical integrity.

Another challenge is cultural conditioning, where deeply ingrained societal norms dictate what is considered "appropriate" for a woman in a leadership position. In many cultures, women are expected to serve in supportive, not directive, roles. This conditioning not only influences congregations but often shapes women's sense of calling. Many women apostles wrestle privately with feelings of inadequacy, fearing rejection or criticism if they step forward in obedience.

To overcome this, there must be a cultural shift within the Body of Christ, fuelled by testimonies, teaching, and modelling of biblical womanhood that includes strength, vision, and leadership. When communities see women walking in authority with humility, it begins to challenge stereotypes. Pastors, mentors, and male allies play a crucial role in affirming and platforming women apostles, not as exceptions, but as fellow labourers in the Gospel.

A lack of access to mentorship and resources is another significant barrier. Apostolic ministry is weighty and demanding; without guidance, isolation and burnout become real threats. Many women do not have access to experienced apostolic leaders, male or female, who can walk with them through the rigours of spiritual warfare, leadership dynamics, and strategic Kingdom work.

The answer is found in intentional discipleship and community. Apostolic networks and ministry schools should be deliberate about training and equipping women, offering mentorship programs that include theological depth, leadership coaching, and emotional support. Online platforms, ministry cohorts, and interdenominational alliances can also bridge the mentorship gap, especially in regions where female apostolic leadership is rare.

Finally, women apostles often face the subtle yet corrosive barrier of tokenism being included in leadership spaces merely to tick the box of diversity, without being given real authority or influence. This can lead to frustration and disillusionment, as their calling is affirmed in word but not in practice.

The solution lies in structural inclusion, not symbolic presence. Churches and organisations must commit to making space at decision-making tables, offering meaningful leadership roles, and trusting women apostles to lead, teach, and build. Their contributions should not be limited to "women's ministry" alone, but extended across the full spectrum of apostolic influence, planting churches, discipling nations, shaping doctrine, and mentoring both men and women.

When women apostles are fully released, the Church grows in wisdom, breadth, and maturity. These barriers, though real, are not permanent walls but opportunities for prophetic reform.

As Scripture reminds us in Galatians 3:28 (NIV), *"There is neither Jew nor Gentile, neither slave nor free, nor is there male and female, for you are all one in Christ Jesus."* The call to apostolic ministry knows no gender. What matters is obedience to the Sender, not the approval of the crowd.

By confronting these barriers with truth, humility, and courage, the Church becomes a place where all apostles, regardless of gender, can rise and build, ushering in the fullness of God's Kingdom on earth.

Partnering in Apostolic Ministry: Men and Women Together

God's design for ministry is deeply rooted in partnership. From the very beginning, when He created both male and female in His image (Genesis 1:27, NIV), it was with the intention that they would function together in harmony and purpose. This divine pattern is not erased in the context of apostolic ministry; it is reinforced.

The advancement of the Gospel and the edification of the Church require the full expression of both men and women, serving side by side in their God-given assignments, graced with distinct yet complementary gifts.

In the New Testament, we see a compelling model of such collaboration. Priscilla and Aquila, a married couple, played a significant role in discipling Apollos (Acts 18:26, NIV). They hosted a church in their home (1 Corinthians 16:19), supported Paul's ministry, and risked their lives for the sake of the Gospel (Romans 16:3-4).

The order in which their names appear, sometimes with Priscilla first, highlights a mutual respect and shared responsibility in their service to the early Church. Their partnership is a template for what God still desires: co-labourers who advance the apostolic mandate in unity, not rivalry.

The partnership between men and women in apostolic ministry reflects God's heart for wholeness. While roles may differ according to calling, capacity, and season, the authority to lead, teach, plant, and govern is not reserved for one gender. The Holy Spirit distributes gifts according to His will (1 Corinthians 12:11), and the fruit of one's labour is not validated by gender, but by obedience, faithfulness, and the manifestation of Kingdom impact.

Sadly, much of the modern Church has functioned with an imbalanced scale, empowering men while diminishing or dismissing the contributions of women. In some contexts, women are included but not entrusted; they are welcomed in service but excluded from governance. This disunity not only limits the flow of God's anointing but also weakens the Church's ability to reflect the image of Christ fully. The Body suffers when half of its capacity is restrained.

True apostolic partnership requires a mindset of mutual honour. It is not about competing for recognition but completing the work of God together. Men must become affirmers, not gatekeepers, championing the gifts in their sisters in Christ, opening doors for their ministry, and holding them accountable in a spiritual sense. Women, likewise, must step into their callings with humility and boldness, understanding that their authority is God-ordained, not man-granted.

In Philippians 4:3 (NIV), Paul urges the Church to help certain women who "have contended at my side in the cause of the gospel," affirming that they were not background supporters but frontline partners. This acknowledgement is crucial in shaping our understanding of gender in ministry, not as a matter of hierarchy, but of unity in purpose.

When men and women walk together in apostolic ministry, the Church embodies a more complete expression of Christ's character. Men often bring structure, strategy, and spiritual covering; women frequently release nurturing leadership, spiritual discernment, and prophetic sensitivity. These attributes are not exclusive, but when valued equally, they create a robust, Spirit-led synergy that edifies the Church and impacts the nations.

It is time for the Church to rise in maturity, casting off the cultural and religious limitations that divide and embracing the divine model of partnership. As sons and daughters of the Kingdom, our highest loyalty is to the One who calls and sends, not to the traditions that confine.

Let this generation be marked by the visible unity of men and women in apostolic mission, planting churches, equipping leaders, reaching the lost, and building God's house together. For where there is unity, the Lord commands a blessing (Psalm 133:1-3, NIV).

Advancing Women in Apostolic Ministry

The call of God knows no gender restrictions. Throughout Scripture, we see that when God appoints. He also anoints regardless of whether the vessel is male or female. Advancing women in apostolic ministry is not a concession to modern demands but a restoration of biblical truth and divine order. It is a call to honour God's choices and steward the full expression of His gifts in the Body of Christ.

Acts 2:17 (NIV) declares: *"In the last days, God says, I will pour out my Spirit on all people. Your sons and daughters will prophesy..."* This outpouring was not selective.

The same Spirit that empowered Peter to preach at Pentecost is the same Spirit that emboldened women to speak the word of the Lord. To advance women in apostolic ministry is to recognise the fulfilment of this prophetic promise; it is to make room for daughters who are already carrying the fire of heaven.

In advancing women, the Church must move beyond tokenism and begin building structures that genuinely support their growth, leadership, and influence. This begins with recognition, acknowledging the legitimacy of their call and the fruitfulness of their labour.

Women apostles have been overlooked not because they lacked gifts, but because they were constrained by religious culture. Their advancement requires us to break such boxes and restore what was always God's intention: co-labourers in the harvest field.

Training is another essential component. Just as men are discipled, mentored, and positioned for ministry, women must be offered the same spiritual investment. Apostolic ministry requires theological depth, emotional maturity, spiritual authority, and strategic vision. These are not exclusive traits of masculinity; they are developed by intentional equipping. The Church must establish safe and empowering spaces for women to be trained in church planting, governance, teaching, missions, and the prophetic, all integral parts of the apostolic commission.

Advancing women demands that we actively challenge environments where their voices are silenced or diminished. Whether it be pulpit exclusion, lack of ordination pathways, or cultural bias masked as doctrine, we must be courageous in confronting these barriers. The early Church was not afraid to break traditions that restricted the move of the Holy Spirit. It welcomed the prophetic daughters of Philip (Acts 21:9, NIV), the leadership of Junia (Romans 16:7, NIV), and the apostolic labours of women like Priscilla and Phoebe. Their ministry was not marginal; it was foundational.

Advancement also includes public affirmation. The commissioning of women apostles must be visible and intentional. It sends a message to young girls and seasoned women alike that their callings are not imaginary or second-class. As we lay hands on men, so must we lay hands on women. As we release sons, so must we release daughters. Public affirmation is not about applause; it is about alignment with God's will.

Finally, advancing women in apostolic ministry strengthens the entire Body of Christ. It brings balance, nurtures wholeness, and sharpens the Church's spiritual discernment. Women often bring a unique sensitivity to the Holy Spirit, a deep capacity for relational leadership, and a prophetic clarity that strengthens the Church's vision and mission. When this is embraced, not merely tolerated, the apostolic movement flourishes in fullness and fruit.

To advance women in apostolic ministry is to honour the heart of God, respond to the outpouring of His Spirit, and prepare the Bride for Christ's return. It is a call to action that requires courage, humility, and spiritual maturity. May we never be found resisting what God is releasing. Instead, let us be found building altars where His daughters can minister freely, fiercely, and fruitfully.

Women in Missions and Global Outreach

The global expansion of the Gospel has always included faithful, courageous, and Spirit-empowered women. From the early Church to today's remote mission fields, women have carried the message of Christ with boldness and sacrificial obedience. Their contributions have been pivotal in establishing churches, translating Scripture, discipling nations, and transforming communities through acts of compassion, teaching, and evangelism.

The biblical foundation for women in missions is not a modern invention. In Romans 16, Paul mentions several women who laboured alongside him in the work of the Gospel. Phoebe is described as a *deacon* and *benefactor* of many (Romans 16:1-2, NIV), and Priscilla, along with her husband Aquila, is recognised as a teacher and church planter. These women did not merely support mission work; they were central to its execution.

Mary Magdalene, often called the "apostle to the apostles," was the first to proclaim the risen Christ (John 20:17-18, NIV). Her role in declaring the resurrection was not peripheral; it was foundational. The Great Commission, issued by Jesus in Matthew 28:19-20 (NIV), was not gender-specific. It was a charge to all disciples, men and women, to *"go and make disciples of all nations."*

Throughout history, women have answered this call with resolve and resilience. Missionary pioneers like Lottie Moon in China, Mary Slessor in Nigeria, and Amy Carmichael in India broke cultural barriers. They endured great hardship to carry the Gospel's light to unreached people groups. Their legacies continue to inspire countless women worldwide to dedicate their lives to serving God's global mission.

In contemporary times, women continue to serve as missionaries, translators, educators, medical professionals, church planters, and humanitarian workers across every continent. In many regions, particularly in places where men are restricted from ministry, women have become the primary agents of evangelism and discipleship. Their presence often opens doors that remain closed to others, allowing the Gospel to enter families and communities in profound ways.

Women in missions also serve as bridge-builders, often embodying a relational and nurturing approach that fosters trust in resistant cultures. They bring holistic ministry, caring for the physical, emotional, and spiritual needs of individuals while remaining anchored in the truth of the Gospel. Their ability to contextualise the message of Christ to diverse cultural settings makes them indispensable in the global Church's outreach efforts.

However, despite their immense impact, many women in missions still face systemic barriers, including a lack of funding, limited leadership opportunities, and cultural resistance. The Church needs to recognise, affirm, and equip these women with the resources, training, and covering necessary to flourish in their calling. Women are not auxiliary to missions; they are essential to their fulfilment.

The Apostolic Mandate is global in scope, and every believer, regardless of gender, is summoned to play a role. When women respond to the call of missions, the Church expands its reach, deepens its compassion, and quickens its impact. By releasing and supporting women in global outreach, we activate the full capacity of the Body of Christ to disciple nations and demonstrate God's love in tangible, transformative ways.

Let the Church continue to send, support, and celebrate women who say, "Here am I. Send me" (Isaiah 6:8, NIV). In the fields white for harvest, their labour is not only needed, but also divinely ordained.

Celebrating Women's Apostles

The call to apostleship is not confined by gender, and throughout Scripture, history, and modern Church movements, women have arisen in this office with strength, clarity, and divine commissioning. Celebrating women apostles is not merely a matter of recognition; it is a declaration of alignment with God's design for the Body of Christ. Their obedience, leadership, and fruitfulness testify to the Holy Spirit's work and the fullness of Christ's gift to the Church.

In the early Church, we see women moving in apostolic authority, even if the term "apostle" was not always formally assigned to them. Junia, mentioned in Romans 16:7 (NIV), is described as "outstanding among the apostles," a clear affirmation from Paul of her standing and ministry. Her recognition by the apostolic community reveals that women were not only present but prominent in the foundational movement of the Gospel.

To celebrate women apostles is to honour those who have pioneered new works, birthed ministries, discipled leaders, and carried spiritual authority with integrity and fruit. These women have often stepped into uncharted territory, laying foundations where none existed, building structures, training others, and overseeing the growth and health of the Church, hallmarks of the apostolic office.

In many nations and church networks today, women apostles are founding ministries, mobilising mission teams, leading networks of churches, and equipping saints for the work of the Kingdom. Their leadership is marked not by ambition but by surrender. Their authority is not rooted in title, but in the spiritual fruit they bear. They model the apostolic traits of perseverance, humility, divine strategy, and sacrificial love.

To truly celebrate women apostles, the Church must provide platforms for their voices, space for their governance, and covering for their growth. It is a call to affirm them publicly, disciple them deeply, and release them fully. Their wisdom, prophetic clarity, and passion for the Gospel enrich the Body and advance the apostolic mandate in ways that are unique and necessary.

Celebration is not about sentiment; it is about spiritual alignment. When we celebrate what God is doing through women apostles, we bless what He has already ordained. We make room for more to rise, for generations to follow, and for the Church to walk in the fullness of its gifting. As we honour women apostles, we affirm the Spirit's move, the authority of Scripture, and the beauty of a Church where sons and daughters prophesy, lead, and build together.

Let their names not be whispered but celebrated. Let their works not be hidden but supported. Moreover, let the Church be strengthened by the full expression of apostolic leadership that God Himself has set in motion, through both His sons and His daughters.

Conclusion

The calling and commissioning of women in apostolic ministry is not a modern invention or a cultural concession; it is a biblical truth rooted in God's unchanging nature and His inclusive Kingdom purposes. From the pages of Scripture to the pulpits, mission fields, leadership tables, and community frontlines of today, women have always been part of God's divine strategy to advance His Kingdom on earth.

This chapter has brought into focus the reality that women are not secondary participants in ministry but divinely chosen vessels, entrusted with authority, revelation, and spiritual capacity to build, govern, send, and disciple. Whether through teaching, preaching, planting churches, training leaders, or stewarding theological truth, women are doing the work of apostles in every sphere where the Gospel must be established.

Their stories are not rare exceptions; they are prophetic patterns of a Church being restored to its full expression, male and female, old and young, hand in hand, carrying the weight of God's commission with boldness and humility. For every barrier they have faced, God has provided grace. For every opposition, He has given affirmation. For every door that has remained closed, the Holy Spirit is releasing keys in this hour.

As we recognise, affirm, and partner with women apostles, we align ourselves with heaven's rhythm and Christ's vision for a mature Body where every joint supplies, and no gift is ignored. The Apostolic Mandate is too vast to be fulfilled by half the Body. God is raising women not simply to assist, but to lead, establish, and govern in His name.

Let the Church rise in unity. Let every gift be welcomed. Let every calling be confirmed. Let the world witness the glorious beauty of a Church led by the Spirit, shaped by truth, and fuelled by love, where women and men together labour for the Gospel, each one fully called and fully commissioned.

CHAPTER SEVEN

PNEUMATOLOGY: THE HOLY SPIRIT

THE STUDY OF PNEUMATOLOGY, the doctrine of the Holy Spirit, is a vital and transformative aspect of Christian theology. The Holy Spirit, the third person of the Trinity, plays a profound role in the life of believers and the work of the Church. The Holy Spirit is not a distant power or a theological concept to be dissected, but the living presence of God actively working within and among His people. The Spirit reveals the heart of the Father, glorifies the Son, and animates the life of the Church with supernatural clarity, power, and intimacy.

Through the Spirit, the believer moves beyond ritual into relationship, beyond performance into transformation, and beyond form into fire. To understand the Holy Spirit is not merely to understand divine activity; it is to encounter God Himself in a deeply personal, deeply powerful way. Pneumatology calls us to pay attention not just to what the Spirit does, but to who He is.

May our hearts be open to the transformative work of the Holy Spirit. May we deepen our relationship with the Holy Spirit, embracing His guidance, empowerment, and transformation in our lives. Together, through the following pages, let us remember and acknowledge the vital role of the Holy Spirit in fulfilling our apostolic mandate and bringing the Kingdom of God to our spheres of influence.

The Personhood of the Holy Spirit

The Holy Spirit is not an impersonal force or mystical energy. He is a divine person, fully God and fully involved in every aspect of the believer's life and the mission of the Church. Understanding the personhood of the Holy Spirit is foundational to deepening our relationship with Him. He is not simply an agent of God's work; He is God Himself, co-equal with the Father and the Son in the Trinity. His presence is marked not only by power but by personality. He thinks, feels, speaks, teaches, grieves, guides, and intercedes.

Scripture consistently presents the Holy Spirit as a person who engages with humanity in intimate and intelligent ways. In John 14:26 (NIV), Jesus introduces the Spirit as *"the Advocate, the Holy Spirit, whom the Father will send in my name,"* and explains that *"he will teach you all things and will remind you of everything I have said to you."* This verse alone affirms His intellect and teaching role. Similarly, in Romans 8:26 (NIV), we read that *"the Spirit himself intercedes for us through wordless groans."* Only a person can intercede with understanding and compassion. These are not the traits of an abstract power but of a being who knows us and acts with purpose and emotion.

Moreover, the Holy Spirit can be grieved. Ephesians 4:30 (NIV) says, *"And do not grieve the Holy Spirit of God, with whom you were sealed for the day of redemption."* Grief is an emotional response that arises from relational disruption. That the Spirit can be grieved shows He longs for unity and holiness in the hearts of believers. He is not distant or indifferent to how we live; He cares deeply and personally.

The Spirit also has a will. In 1 Corinthians 12:11 (NIV), Paul writes, *"All these are the work of the same Spirit, and he distributes them to each one, just as he determines."* The Holy Spirit chooses, assigns, and empowers believers with gifts according to His divine purpose. This sovereign distribution of gifts underlines His autonomy and role in shaping the Body of Christ.

Acknowledging the personhood of the Holy Spirit transforms our relationship with Him. He is not a power to be summoned, but a person to be known. He is not manipulated by emotion or performance. He leads, corrects, comforts, and empowers as a divine companion and guide.

Many believers engage with the Father in prayer and acknowledge the saving work of the Son, yet live unaware of the daily companionship of the Spirit. To embrace His personhood is to open one's life to communion with God that is moment-by-moment, deeply relational, and profoundly transformational.

The Holy Spirit is God with us present, personal, and purposeful. He walks beside, speaks within, and works through every believer who yields to His voice. He is not distant. He is not silent. He is here.

The Nature, Role, and Work of the Holy Spirit

The Holy Spirit, as the third person of the Trinity, plays a profound and multifaceted role in the life of believers and the work of the Church. Through His divine nature and active presence, the Holy Spirit empowers, guides, and transforms individuals, equipping them to fulfil their God-given callings and participate in the advancement of the Kingdom of God.

The Nature of the Holy Spirit

To understand the Holy Spirit is to come face-to-face with the divine mystery of God's presence among us. The Holy Spirit is not a lesser deity or a supporting member of the Trinity. He is fully God, eternal, omniscient, omnipotent, and omnipresent. His nature reflects the essence of divinity while revealing unique attributes that demonstrate His role within the Godhead and among humanity.

From the beginning of Scripture, we see the Holy Spirit actively involved in creation. Genesis 1:2 (NIV) tells us, *"Now the earth was formless and empty, darkness was over the surface of the deep, and the Spirit of God was hovering over the waters."* This verse introduces us to the creative, life-giving nature of the Spirit, who brings form to chaos and breathes life into what was previously lifeless. He is not a passive observer but a present power, involved in shaping the world according to God's will.

The Spirit is eternal, without beginning or end. In Hebrews 9:14 (NIV), He is referred to as "the eternal Spirit," confirming that He has always existed, just as the Father and the Son have. His work spans from eternity past into the present and continues into the eternal future. Unlike created beings, the Spirit has no origin. He is, and always has been, God.

The Holy Spirit is also omnipresent. He dwells everywhere and fills all things. Psalm 139:7-8 (NIV) declares, *"Where can I go from your Spirit? Where can I flee from your presence? If I go up to the heavens, you are there; if I make my bed in the depths, you are there."* No place is hidden from Him. His presence is not bound by geography or time. Whether in the deepest valley or the highest praise, He is fully present.

Another key aspect of the Spirit's nature is His holiness. As His name suggests, the Holy Spirit is pure, set apart, and completely without sin. His very presence brings conviction of sin and draws believers toward righteousness. John 16:8 (NIV) says, *"When he comes, he will prove the world to be in the wrong about sin and righteousness and judgment."*

This is not merely an act of justice; it is a reflection of His holy character. He leads people into sanctification and makes them partakers of God's holiness.

The Holy Spirit is also a relational entity. He proceeds from the Father and the Son, not as a detached power but as one who reveals, communes, and comforts. *John 15:26 (NIV)* says, "When the Advocate comes, whom I will send to you from the Father, the Spirit of truth who goes out from the Father, he will testify about me." The Spirit draws attention to Christ, not to Himself. His nature is marked by humility, love, and unity.

The Spirit's truthfulness is another vital aspect. He is the Spirit of truth (John 16:13, NIV), leading believers into all truth and glorifying Christ. His nature resists deceit and confusion, offering clarity and wisdom to all who sincerely seek God.

Lastly, the Holy Spirit is powerful. He empowered prophets, kings, and apostles to perform mighty works, and that same power dwells in believers today. Acts 1:8 (NIV) affirms, *"But you will receive power when the Holy Spirit comes on you; and you will be my witnesses..."* His power is not for spectacle but for witness for bold living, holy conduct, and effective ministry.

To grasp the nature of the Holy Spirit is to be drawn into deeper worship, dependence, and awe. He is holy, eternal, present, relational, and powerful. He is God in us and with us, the very breath of the living Church and the One who makes our communion with God alive and transformative.

The Role of the Holy Spirit

The Holy Spirit plays a central and indispensable role in the lives of believers, the Church, and the world. His work is not a secondary aspect of the Christian faith but an active and ongoing ministry that flows directly from the heart of God. To understand the role of the Holy Spirit is to appreciate how God moves in power, speaks with precision, and dwells with intimacy among His people.

At the core of His role is that of a Helper. Jesus introduced the Holy Spirit to His disciples as *"another Advocate"*, one who would remain with them forever. John 14:16-17 (NIV) says, *"And I will ask the Father, and he will give you another advocate to help you and be with you forever, the Spirit of truth."* This means the Spirit stands alongside believers, strengthening, guiding, and defending them. He is not a distant observer but a constant presence.

The Holy Spirit also teaches. Jesus said in John 14:26 (NIV), *"But the Advocate, the Holy Spirit, whom the Father will send in my name, will teach you all things and will remind you of everything I have said to you."* The Spirit brings divine understanding, not merely intellectual knowledge, but revelation that aligns our hearts and minds with God's truth. He ensures that the words of Christ remain living and active in the hearts of believers.

Conviction is another vital role of the Holy Spirit. He convicts the world concerning sin, righteousness, and judgment. John 16:8 (NIV) says, *"When he comes, he will prove the world to be in the wrong about sin and righteousness and judgment."* This convicting work does not condemn, but awakens. It is the Spirit who reveals to us our need for a Saviour, exposes areas of compromise, and draws us into repentance and transformation.

He is also the Spirit of regeneration. Titus 3:5 (NIV) says, *"He saved us through the washing of rebirth and renewal by the Holy Spirit."* Salvation is not a mere moral adjustment; it is a supernatural rebirth, and the Holy Spirit is the divine agent of that transformation. He creates new life in the believer, making them a new creation in Christ.

The Holy Spirit empowers believers for service. In Acts 1:8 (NIV), Jesus promised, *"But you will receive power when the Holy Spirit comes on you; and you will be my witnesses..."* This power enables boldness in witness, authority in preaching, and effectiveness in ministry. The gifts of the Spirit, prophecy, healing, discernment, tongues, and more, are distributed by Him for the edification of the Church and the advancement of the Kingdom.

The Spirit also sanctifies. He sets believers apart and works within them to produce godly character. Galatians 5:22-23 (NIV) lists the fruit of the Spirit: *"love, joy, peace, forbearance, kindness, goodness, faithfulness, gentleness and self-control."* These are not personality traits; they are spiritual evidence of His indwelling presence. Sanctification is an ongoing process, and the Spirit is the One who gently convicts, purifies, and shapes us into Christ's likeness.

The Holy Spirit guides. In a world full of noise and confusion, He leads with divine clarity. Romans 8:14 (NIV) declares, *"For those who are led by the Spirit of God are the children of God."* His leadership is not only reserved for big decisions, but is also available in every moment, whether in choosing a path, responding with love, or discerning truth. The Spirit leads with wisdom, aligning our steps with God's will.

Finally, He seals and assures believers of their eternal inheritance. Ephesians 1:13-14 (NIV) says, *"When you believed, you were marked in him with a seal, the promised Holy Spirit, who is a deposit guaranteeing our inheritance..."* The Spirit's presence is the confirmation that we belong to God. He assures us of our salvation and keeps us secure in Christ until the day of redemption.

In every dimension, spiritual, emotional, communal, and missional, the Holy Spirit is actively involved. He empowers, convicts, teaches, guides, sanctifies, and comforts. The role of the Holy Spirit is not optional; it is essential. Without Him, the Christian life becomes a shell of religious performance. With Him, it becomes a dynamic, Spirit-led walk that bears fruit, glorifies Christ, and fulfils God's purposes in the earth.

The Work of The Holy Spirit

The work of the Holy Spirit is vast, dynamic, and intimately intertwined with every aspect of a believer's life and the mission of the Church. His work begins before salvation, continues through sanctification, and extends into every area of Christian witness and worship.

Unlike a distant force or abstract idea, the Holy Spirit is actively involved in real-time, transforming hearts, revealing truth, and empowering the people of God to live in alignment with His will.

One of the foundational works of the Holy Spirit is conviction. Before a person can respond to the Gospel, it is the Spirit who awakens them to the reality of their need for salvation. John 16:8 (NIV) says, *"When he comes, he will prove the world to be in the wrong about sin and righteousness and judgment."* This conviction is not designed to shame, but to awaken a longing for righteousness and reconciliation with God.

Once a person responds in faith, the Holy Spirit then performs the supernatural work of regeneration, the rebirth of the inner person. This is what Jesus referred to in John 3:5 (NIV): *"Very truly I tell you, no one can enter the kingdom of God unless they are born of water and the Spirit."* At salvation, the Spirit brings dead souls to life, implanting a new nature and making the believer a new creation in Christ. Titus 3:5 affirms that we are saved *"through the washing of rebirth and renewal by the Holy Spirit."*

Following salvation, the Spirit continues His work through sanctification, the ongoing process of making the believer holy and Christlike. This is not self-improvement; it is divine transformation. The Holy Spirit cultivates the character of Christ in us by producing what Scripture calls the fruit of the Spirit: *"love, joy, peace, forbearance, kindness, goodness, faithfulness, gentleness and self-control"* (Galatians 5:22-23, NIV). These qualities are not merely human virtues; they are the evidence of God's presence and power at work within us.

Another vital dimension of the Spirit's work is empowerment. The Holy Spirit equips believers with power for effective service and witness. Acts 1:8 (NIV) states, *"But you will receive power when the Holy Spirit comes on you; and you will be my witnesses..."* This power enables believers to minister boldly, preach the Gospel with authority, and demonstrate the supernatural love of God through signs, wonders, and spiritual gifts.

The work of the Holy Spirit also includes illumination and guidance. He opens the Scriptures to our understanding and brings to remembrance the teachings of Christ. John 14:26 (NIV) declares, *"But the Advocate, the Holy Spirit, whom the Father will send in my name, will teach you all things and will remind you of everything I have said to you."* The Spirit guides our decisions, aligns our conscience with God's truth, and leads us away from deception.

The Spirit also works in the fellowship and unity of believers. He is the bond that unites the Body of Christ. Ephesians 4:3 (NIV) urges believers to *"Make every effort to keep the unity of the Spirit through the bond of peace."* He fosters love, humility, mutual edification, and service among members of the Church. Without His presence, true unity is impossible.

Furthermore, the Holy Spirit is at work in intercession. When we do not know what to pray or are overwhelmed, the Spirit intercedes on our behalf. Romans 8:26 (NIV) says, *"In the same way, the Spirit helps us in our weakness. We do not know what we ought to pray for, but the Spirit himself intercedes for us through wordless groans."* This divine intercession aligns our prayers with the heart and will of God.

In the broader context of the world, the Spirit is actively restraining evil, preparing hearts for revival, and orchestrating the advancement of God's Kingdom. He is not bound by time, space, or human limitations. From Genesis to Revelation, we see His work in creation, empowerment, prophecy, healing, deliverance, and the birthing of divine movements that shape history.

In summary, the work of the Holy Spirit is comprehensive. He convicts, regenerates, sanctifies, empowers, teaches, unifies, intercedes, and guides. His presence is not a supplement to the Christian life; it is the very source of spiritual vitality. To ignore or diminish the work of the Spirit is to rob the Church of its strength and the believer of God's abiding presence.

The Holy Spirit and the Church

The Church of Jesus Christ is a living, Spirit-filled Body whose vitality, unity, and effectiveness wholly depend on the presence and work of the Holy Spirit. From the birth of the Church on the day of Pentecost to the present-day expressions of worship, service, and mission, the Holy Spirit remains central to the Church's identity, function, and destiny.

In Acts 2, we witness the dramatic arrival of the Holy Spirit, fulfilling Jesus's promise to clothe His disciples with power from on high. *"All of them were filled with the Holy Spirit and began to speak in other tongues as the Spirit enabled them"* (Acts 2:4, NIV). This outpouring marked the official birth of the New Testament Church not through political decree or human design, but through divine empowerment. It was the Spirit who gave them boldness to preach, unity to stand, and supernatural signs to confirm the Gospel.

The Holy Spirit remains the lifeblood of the Church, sustaining it through seasons of growth, persecution, and refinement. He is the One who builds the Church by convicting hearts, drawing people to salvation, and baptising them into the Body of Christ.

As Paul writes, *"For we were all baptised by one Spirit so as to form one body whether Jews or Gentiles, slave or free and we were all given the one Spirit to drink"* (1 Corinthians 12:13, NIV). This spiritual baptism unites believers across cultures, backgrounds, and denominations, forming a single, holy, and global fellowship.

The Holy Spirit also equips the Church. He distributes spiritual gifts such as prophecy, healing, teaching, administration, discernment, and tongues to each believer for the common good. *"Now to each one the manifestation of the Spirit is given for the common good"* (1 Corinthians 12:7, NIV). These gifts are not for self-exaltation but for the edification of the entire Body. The Spirit ensures that no part is without purpose, and no gift is without a place. When each member functions under His guidance, the Church thrives in power and effectiveness.

The Holy Spirit is the Teacher and Reminder of all truth. Jesus promised, *"But the Advocate, the Holy Spirit, whom the Father will send in my name, will teach you all things and will remind you of everything I have said to you"* (John 14:26, NIV). It is through the Spirit that Scripture comes alive, that sermons carry divine weight, and that believers grow in wisdom and discernment. Without Him, the Church is left to human reasoning, void of revelation.

In worship, the Holy Spirit draws the Church into deeper communion with God. He enables us to worship "in spirit and in truth" (John 4:24, NIV), aligning our hearts with the heart of the Father. True worship, saturated by the Spirit, transcends songs and rituals, becoming an encounter with God Himself. Through the Spirit, we are convicted, healed, filled, and renewed in the sacred place of worship.

The Holy Spirit is also the sanctifier of the Church. He purifies hearts, reveals sin, and shapes believers into the image of Christ. He does not tolerate complacency but urges the Church toward holiness, humility, and obedience. As Paul writes, *"But if by the Spirit you put to death the misdeeds of the body, you will live"* (Romans 8:13, NIV). This sanctifying work is essential for a Church that seeks to reflect God's character to a watching world.

The Spirit also guides the Church into mission. He is the divine strategist behind the spread of the Gospel. In Acts, it was the Spirit who instructed leaders, redirected missionaries, and opened hearts to believe. *"While they were worshipping the Lord and fasting, the Holy Spirit said, 'Set apart for me Barnabas and Saul for the work to which I have called them'"* (Acts 13:2, NIV). The Church that listens to the Spirit will move in precision and power, reaching the places and people God intends.

Lastly, the Holy Spirit sustains the Church. In times of persecution, confusion, or spiritual drought, He is the Comforter who strengthens and revives. He ignites fresh fire, awakens sleeping hearts, and breathes new life into dry bones. When the Church is weary, it is the Spirit who restores her strength.

In all things, the Holy Spirit is the breath, the wind, the fire, and the oil upon the Church. He animates her worship, empowers her witness, sanctifies her members, and prepares her as a spotless Bride for Christ's return. A Church led by the Spirit cannot be silenced, compromised, or defeated. She will rise, thrive, and endure because she is not operating in her strength but in the power of the One who was sent to dwell within her.

The Promise of the Holy Spirit: Baptism Into The Spirit

From the beginning of Jesus's earthly ministry, the promise of the Holy Spirit stood as a vital aspect of His message and mission. He not only came to redeem humanity from sin through His death and resurrection, but also to prepare them for an empowered life through the indwelling of the Holy Spirit. The baptism into the Spirit, therefore, is not an optional or peripheral matter; it is a divine promise meant to equip believers for holy living, powerful witness, and spiritual fruitfulness.

Before His ascension, Jesus gave clear instructions to His disciples to wait in Jerusalem for the gift the Father had promised. He said, *"For John baptised with water, but in a few days, you will be baptised with the Holy Spirit"* (Acts 1:5, NIV). This was not merely a poetic or metaphorical statement; it was a profound assertion. It was the unveiling of a deeper dimension of the believer's experience with God, one where the Spirit would not only be with them but would dwell in them, empower them, and operate through them.

The promise of the Holy Spirit was fulfilled dramatically on the Day of Pentecost. *"All of them were filled with the Holy Spirit and began to speak in other tongues as the Spirit enabled them"* (Acts 2:4, NIV). This moment was more than an experience of spiritual ecstasy; it marked the birth of the Spirit-empowered Church. It demonstrated that the Holy Spirit was no longer limited to select individuals or occasional moments, as was the case in the Old Covenant. However, it was now available to all believers, regardless of age, gender, status, or background.

Peter, interpreting this outpouring, quoted the prophecy from Joel: *"In the last days, God says, I will pour out my Spirit on all people..." (Acts 2:17, NIV).* He then boldly declared, *"The promise is for you and your children and for all who are far off, for all whom the Lord our God will call" (Acts 2:39, NIV).* The baptism into the Spirit was not confined to the apostles or the early Church. It is a multi-generational promise, stretching into our time and beyond.

To be baptised in the Holy Spirit is to be immersed in His power, presence, and purpose. It is not the same as salvation, though it often accompanies or follows it closely. While salvation deals with regeneration, being made alive in Christ, the baptism into the Spirit deals with empowerment. Jesus clarified this distinction when He told His already-believing disciples, *"You will receive power when the Holy Spirit comes on you; and you will be my witnesses..." (Acts 1:8, NIV).* Baptism brings a supernatural capacity: the power to live boldly, love deeply, and witness effectively.

Throughout the book of Acts, we see this baptism followed by manifestations such as speaking in tongues, prophecy, bold preaching, and signs and wonders. While the outward manifestations may vary, the inward reality remains the same: those baptised in the Spirit are marked by divine boldness, deeper intimacy with God, spiritual gifts, and a compelling passion for advancing the Kingdom.

It is essential to recognise that this baptism is not a reward for spiritual maturity or reserved for a select group of spiritually mature individuals. It is a gift freely given by God to those who believe and ask for it. Jesus assured us, *"If you then... know how to give good gifts to your children, how much more will your Father in heaven give the Holy Spirit to those who ask him!"* (Luke 11:13, NIV). The posture is one of hunger, surrender, and expectation.

The baptism into the Spirit also brings a fresh awareness of God's holiness and an intensified longing for purity. As the Spirit fills the believer, He begins to sanctify, refine, and lead. This internal transformation becomes the foundation for external fruit. Love, joy, peace, patience, kindness, goodness, faithfulness, gentleness, and self-control, the fruit of the Spirit, are cultivated in hearts that are fully yielded to Him.

Today, the Church must rediscover and reclaim the power and promise of the Holy Spirit's baptism. It is not merely a denominational emphasis or theological niche; it is the very engine of a victorious Church. A Spirit-baptised Church cannot remain passive, powerless, or silent. She must rise with prophetic authority, supernatural love, and unwavering courage to fulfil the Great Commission.

To those who have not yet received the invitation, it still stands. The promise has not expired. The heavens remain open. The Spirit still descends upon those who wait, those who hunger, and those who are willing to carry the flame.

Primary Indicators of the Holy Spirit Infilling

Pentecostal and Charismatic perspectives often view the baptism in the Spirit as a distinct experience that follows conversion. However, what are the primary indicators that a believer has received the baptism in the Holy Spirit post-conversion, drawing upon biblical texts, theological interpretations, and ecclesial experience?

Speaking in Tongues as Initial Evidence

One of the most prominent signs cited in Pentecostal theology is the manifestation of glossolalia, or speaking in tongues. This practice is rooted in key New Testament passages, such as Acts 2:4, where the apostles, following the descent of the Holy Spirit at Pentecost, "began to speak in other tongues as the Spirit enabled them."

Similarly, Acts 10:44-46 and Acts 19:6 describe the reception of the Holy Spirit as being accompanied by the gift of tongues and prophecy. The Assemblies of God, among others, have formalised the doctrine that speaking in tongues constitutes the "initial physical evidence" of the baptism in the Holy Spirit.

Boldness in Witness and Evangelism

Another widely reported sign is a newfound boldness in proclaiming the gospel. In Acts 1:8, Jesus tells the disciples, "You will receive power when the Holy Spirit comes on you, and you will be my witnesses." Following the Pentecost event, Peter, who had previously denied Jesus, publicly preaches with courage and clarity (Acts 2:14-41). This transformation is often cited as indicative of Spirit empowerment for evangelistic mission.

Enhanced Prayer Life and Spiritual Devotion

Believers frequently report a deepening of their prayer life following Spirit baptism. Romans 8:26 notes, "the Spirit himself intercedes for us with groanings too deep for words," suggesting a Spirit-aided mode of prayer. In Charismatic practice, this may include praying in tongues or a more intimate communion with God. The experiential dimension of prayer becomes more vibrant, spontaneous, and Spirit-led.

Increased Spiritual Sensitivity and Discernment

A heightened awareness of spiritual realities, including the conviction of sin, spiritual warfare, and the presence of God, often accompanies Spirit baptism. This is interpreted as a result of the Spirit's role in guiding and illuminating the believer (John 16:13; 1 Corinthians 2:10-15). Such sensitivity may manifest as discernment of spirits, prophetic insight, or increased responsiveness to the Word of God.

Empowerment through Spiritual Gifts

The baptism in the Holy Spirit is closely associated with the operation of spiritual gifts (charismata), such as healing, prophecy, interpretation of tongues, and miracles. These are outlined in 1 Corinthians 12:8-10 and are considered manifestations of the Spirit's power for the edification of the Church. Believers may begin to operate in these gifts following their Spirit baptism, affirming the experiential dimension of divine empowerment.

Evidence of the Fruit of the Spirit

Although the fruit of the Spirit (Galatians 5:22-23) is more commonly associated with sanctification and spiritual maturity, it is often observed that individuals who have undergone baptism exhibit accelerated growth in love, joy, peace, and other virtues.

This long-term transformation is viewed as evidence of the Spirit's ongoing work in conforming believers to the image of Christ (2 Corinthians 3:18).

Overflowing Joy and Worship

Accounts of Spirit baptism frequently include an overwhelming sense of joy, worship, and emotional release. This is consistent with descriptions in Scripture, such as Luke 10:21, where Jesus rejoiced "in the Holy Spirit." Worship may become more expressive, spontaneous, and characterised by a deep emotional and spiritual engagement with God.

The Holy Spirit and Spiritual Transformation

The work of the Holy Spirit is not confined to external manifestations or powerful demonstrations; it is profoundly rooted in the inner transformation of the human heart. Spiritual transformation is the evidence of the Spirit's indwelling presence, changing believers from the inside out and shaping them into the likeness of Christ. It is this inward change that authenticates the believer's life and witness in the world.

From the moment a person receives salvation, the Holy Spirit begins the work of renewal. As Paul writes, *"He saved us through the washing of rebirth and renewal by the Holy Spirit"* (Titus 3:5, NIV). This renewal is not a one-time event but a continual process of sanctification, where the believer is progressively made holy, set apart for God's purposes, and refined in character and conduct.

The Holy Spirit exposes sin, convicts the heart, and draws the believer into repentance, not through condemnation, but through the kindness of God that leads to change (Romans 2:4). He operates as both the mirror and the cleansing stream. The mirror reveals the blemishes; the stream washes them away. Transformation begins with this sacred confrontation and continues through ongoing submission to the Spirit's leading.

Paul's words in 2 Corinthians 3:18 (NIV) provide a vivid picture of this process: *"And we all, who with unveiled faces contemplate the Lord's glory, are being transformed into his image with ever-increasing glory, which comes from the Lord, who is the Spirit."* The Spirit's role is to reveal Christ to us and then mould us into His image. This transformation is not based on human effort, but on divine work, as the Spirit reshapes thoughts, desires, habits, and identities.

One of the most tangible outcomes of this transformation is the fruit of the Spirit. As outlined in Galatians 5:22-23 (NIV), *"The fruit of the Spirit is love, joy, peace, forbearance, kindness, goodness, faithfulness, gentleness and self-control."* These virtues are not personality traits or moral achievements; they are the character of Christ reproduced in the life of the believer. The Spirit does not simply inspire us to behave better; He empowers us to become new creations who naturally bear good fruit in season.

This inner transformation also brings freedom. Paul affirms this truth, saying, *"Where the Spirit of the Lord is, there is freedom"* (2 Corinthians 3:17, NIV). The Spirit breaks chains of addiction, fear, shame, and religious striving. He replaces anxiety with peace, anger with gentleness, and self-centeredness with love. The transformation is both liberating and empowering, enabling believers to live authentically and in spiritual maturity.

Moreover, spiritual transformation reorients the believer's mind. The Holy Spirit teaches, reminds, and brings divine revelation (John 14:26). He renews our thinking so that we no longer conform to the patterns of this world but are instead *"transformed by the renewing of [our] mind"* (Romans 12:2, NIV). This mental renewal is essential for discerning God's will and walking in alignment with His purposes.

Transformation also affects the believer's relational life. As the Spirit transforms the inner man, it inevitably influences how one relates to others, bringing about humility, forgiveness, patience, and a burden for reconciliation. The Spirit calls believers into unity with one another, promoting peace in the Body of Christ and breaking down walls of division and hostility.

The goal of the Holy Spirit is not to produce religious people, but to form Christlike disciples who reflect God's glory in everyday life. True spiritual transformation is not just measured by how loudly we can shout or how long we can pray, but by how deeply we love, how consistently we obey, and how faithfully we represent Christ in both private and public settings.

In a world driven by performance and appearance, the Spirit invites us to pursue inner depth. He calls us into quiet spaces where His voice refines and reshapes us. He is not only the fire that falls, but the fire that stays burning away impurities, illuminating truth, and warming the soul to respond with obedience.

The invitation is clear: allow the Spirit of God to do His deep, transforming work within. Yield to His whispers, trust His processes, and embrace the change that brings you closer to Christ. Transformation by the Holy Spirit is the evidence of true discipleship and the foundation for lasting impact in the world.

Worship And Prayer in the Holy Spirit

Worship and prayer are sacred expressions of communion with God, and the Holy Spirit is at the heart of this divine relationship. He draws us beyond the surface of words and melodies into the depths of spiritual intimacy, enabling believers to worship and pray in spirit and truth.

Jesus declared in John 4:23-24 (NIV), *"Yet a time is coming and has now come when the true worshipers will worship the Father in the Spirit and in truth, for they are the kind of worshipers the Father seeks. God is spirit, and his worshipers must worship in the Spirit and in truth."* This was not a suggestion but a revelation of the kind of worship that God desires, worship that is animated, guided, and purified by the Holy Spirit.

To worship in the Spirit means allowing the Holy Spirit to lead us beyond performance or routine into genuine adoration and reverence. It is a posture of the heart, not a production of the lips. Whether in song, silence, weeping, or dancing, Spirit-led worship flows from a place of deep awareness of who God is. It responds to His holiness, love, majesty, and mercy, not out of obligation, but out of awe.

The Holy Spirit unveils the beauty of Christ to the worshiper. He magnifies the Son, stirring the soul to respond in love and surrender. This is why Spirit-filled worship is transformative; it does not simply entertain or console, it changes hearts. Through worship in the Spirit, believers are drawn into a divine exchange: our heaviness for His peace, our ashes for His beauty, our confusion for His clarity.

Likewise, prayer in the Holy Spirit is not limited to human understanding or language. Paul writes in Romans

8:26-27 (NIV), *"In the same way, the Spirit helps us in our weakness. We do not know what we ought to pray for, but the Spirit himself intercedes for us through wordless groans. He who searches our hearts knows the mind of the Spirit, because the Spirit intercedes for God's people per the will of God."* This passage reveals one of the most comforting truths about prayer: the Holy Spirit not only helps us pray, but He prays through us.

There are moments in life when our words fall short, when grief, uncertainty, or spiritual warfare silences our ability to speak. In those sacred moments, the Holy Spirit intercedes from within, aligning our hearts with heaven's will. His prayers are precise, untainted by doubt or flesh. They reach the Father with purity, carrying what we could not express on our own.

Spirit-led prayer also deepens our discernment. As we pray in the Spirit, we become more attuned to God's voice, more sensitive to His leading, and more effective in spiritual warfare. Ephesians 6:18 (NIV) exhorts us, *"And pray in the Spirit on all occasions with all kinds of prayers and requests. With this in mind, be alert and always keep on praying for all the Lord's people."* Here, prayer in the Spirit is presented as a strategy for vigilance and victory, a way to stay spiritually awake and connected to divine insight.

One of the greatest privileges of the Spirit-filled believer is praying in tongues, a spiritual gift that builds up the inner man and allows the Spirit to pray mysteries beyond human comprehension (1 Corinthians 14:2, 4). While not every believer operates in this gift, those who do are encouraged to do so with reverence and understanding, allowing the Spirit to edify their spirit and glorify God in a language not learned but given.

Whether in personal devotion or corporate gatherings, when the Holy Spirit leads worship and prayer, they create atmospheres of freedom, healing, deliverance, and revelation. They usher in the tangible presence of God and make space for His power to move among His people. Chains are broken, hearts are restored, and direction is released when God's people align themselves with the Spirit in worship and intercession.

Worship and prayer in the Holy Spirit are not duties to be performed but privileges to be embraced. They are divine invitations to encounter the living God. The Spirit does not simply teach us how to worship or pray; it also guides us in our spiritual journey. He becomes the breath behind every word, the wind behind every song, and the fire behind every cry. He does not lead us to perform before God; He leads us to pour ourselves out before Him.

Today, there is a filling of noise, distractions, and spiritual dryness. Let us focus on Spirit-filled worship and prayer, which restores our hearts to the centre of our faith: communion with God. The more we yield to the Spirit, the deeper our intimacy with the Father becomes, and the more our lives reflect His glory.

Gifts and Fruit of the Spirit

The Holy Spirit not only empowers believers but also shapes them. His presence in a believer's life is marked by both supernatural enablement and spiritual maturity. These are expressed through the *gifts* and the *fruit* of the Spirit. The gifts are divine tools for ministry manifestations of God's power and grace that equip the Church to serve effectively, heal, teach, lead, and discern.

The fruit, on the other hand, reflects the inner transformation that comes from walking daily with God, as one develops the character and virtues that mirror Christ.

Together, the gifts and the fruit of the Spirit illustrate the complete work of the Holy Spirit in the believer: to build up the Church and to shape individuals into the likeness of Christ. One without the other leads to imbalance. Gifts without fruit can foster pride and abuse, while fruit without gifts can result in passivity and ineffectiveness. Therefore, both are essential not only for personal growth but for the maturity, credibility, and impact of the Church in the world.

The Gifts of the Spirit

The gifts of the Holy Spirit are divine endowments given to believers to build up the Body of Christ and advance God's purposes on the earth. These gifts are not earned, nor are they a mark of spiritual superiority; they are graciously distributed by the Spirit according to His will (1 Corinthians 12:11, NIV: *"All these are the work of one and the same Spirit, and he distributes them to each one, just as he determines."*)

The Apostle Paul provides key lists of these spiritual gifts in 1 Corinthians 12, Romans 12, and Ephesians 4, each highlighting a dimension of the Spirit's work through individuals. These include gifts of revelation, such as the word of wisdom and the word of knowledge; gifts of power, such as faith, healing, and miracles; and gifts of utterance, like prophecy, tongues, and the interpretation of tongues. Administrative and service-oriented gifts such as leadership, teaching, exhortation, giving, mercy, and helps are also vital expressions of the Spirit's grace.

These gifts are not restricted to church services or pulpit ministries. They manifest in homes, workplaces, mission fields, schools, hospitals, and anywhere God's people are present. A believer operating in the gift of healing may bring wholeness in a hospital corridor. One with the gift of wisdom may steer a boardroom decision in righteousness. Prophetic words can encourage a friend wrestling with doubt. The Holy Spirit equips the Church to be both supernatural and practical, holy and effective.

Importantly, the gifts are meant to operate in love. Without love, spiritual gifts can become noisy and fruitless. Paul's exhortation in 1 Corinthians 13 reminds us that gifts are tools, not trophies. They are to edify, not to elevate. The goal is not the display of power, but the building up of the saints and the glorification of Christ.

In receiving and using spiritual gifts, believers must remain accountable, grounded in the Word, and led by the Spirit. Gifts flourish in communities that honour the Spirit's work while testing all things by Scripture. When properly stewarded, the gifts of the Spirit bring depth, direction, healing, conviction, and transformation to the life of the Church.

The world is in need of a Church that is not just informed, but empowered, where every believer walks in their God-given gift with humility, boldness, and clarity. The Holy Spirit gives gifts not for spectacle, but for service. They are Heaven's provision for Earth's need, distributed not to the worthy, but to the willing.

The Fruit of the Spirit

While the gifts of the Spirit empower the believer for ministry, the fruit of the Spirit reveals the character and maturity of a life truly surrendered to God. The fruit is not about performance; it is about transformation. It is not what we do for God, but what He cultivates within us through ongoing fellowship with the Holy Spirit.

Galatians 5:22-23 (NIV) outlines the fruit of the Spirit as: *"love, joy, peace, forbearance, kindness, goodness, faithfulness, gentleness and self-control. Against such things, there is no law."* These nine virtues are not individual fruits from which we pick and choose; they are one fruit, produced in harmony by the Spirit as we abide in Christ.

Unlike the gifts, which may manifest suddenly and powerfully, the fruit of the Spirit grows over time. It requires spiritual surrender, pruning, patience, and a life rooted in God's Word. The fruit is the evidence that the Spirit of God is actively shaping our desires, choices, and relationships. It is the character of Christ formed in us, not just in public ministry, but in private obedience.

Love, the first attribute mentioned, is the anchor. Without love, every other virtue becomes hollow. Joy and peace mark the inner contentment that flows from trust in God. Forbearance (or patience) reflects God's long-suffering nature in us. Kindness and goodness are seen in our treatment of others, especially when it is inconvenient. Faithfulness points to consistency in commitment and integrity. Gentleness displays humility and restraint, and self-control is the Spirit-enabled discipline over our thoughts, words, and actions.

As the world celebrates charisma over character, the fruit of the Spirit reminds us that the measure of spiritual maturity is not how loud we speak, but how well we live. It is not just about operating in power, but walking in purity. People may admire our gifts, but they trust our fruit.

Moreover, the fruit of the Spirit becomes the soil in which the gifts can flourish without corruption. A person with the gift of prophecy but no gentleness may wound instead of healing. One with faith but no self-control can fall into pride. That is why fruit and gifts must go hand in hand.

The fruit of the Spirit is not a checklist for perfection but a mirror of progress. As we walk with the Holy Spirit daily, we begin to look more like Jesus, not just in what we say or do, but in who we are becoming. The fruit is the aroma of Christ that the world longs to smell in the Church: real, humble, holy love expressed in every season and situation.

Global Perspectives on the Work of the Holy Spirit

The work of the Holy Spirit is not confined to a single culture, denomination, or geographical location. From continent to continent, the Spirit continues to move with power, creativity, and diversity, affirming the promise that God will pour out His Spirit on all people (Joel 2:28; Acts 2:17, NIV). Across the globe, believers are witnessing a beautiful tapestry of the Spirit's ministry, each thread woven uniquely through the context of culture, language, history, and spiritual hunger.

In Africa, the work of the Holy Spirit is often expressed through dynamic worship, prophetic movements, deliverance ministries, and community revivals. Churches in both rural and urban settings are marked by vibrant faith, where the Spirit's power is expected and often encountered. Healings, dreams, and prophetic utterances are not rare but seen as integral to the Church's expression of faith. The Spirit empowers believers to stand strong in the face of adversity, calling forth prophetic voices to speak into governance, justice, and community transformation.

In Latin America, the Spirit's activity has fuelled the growth of evangelical and Pentecostal movements at unprecedented rates. Known for passionate expressions of worship and a strong emphasis on signs, wonders, and social justice, the Holy Spirit has moved among the masses, healing the broken, liberating the oppressed, and igniting a deep hunger for the Word. The Spirit has also played a central role in empowering indigenous voices, challenging colonial narratives, and restoring spiritual identity.

In Asia, despite religious persecution in some regions, the work of the Holy Spirit is often characterised by supernatural endurance, house church movements, and miraculous encounters. In countries where public Christian gatherings are restricted, the Spirit quietly but powerfully sustains underground believers with boldness and discernment. Stories abound of dreams leading people to Christ, of miraculous protection, and of hidden revivals sweeping across areas previously deemed unreachable. Governments or borders do not limit the Holy Spirit. He moves wherever hearts are open.

In the Western world, the work of the Holy Spirit is taking on new forms, often revitalising tired structures with fresh breath. In Europe, where church attendance has declined in many places, new communities are forming around Spirit-led discipleship, contemplative worship, and spiritual renewal. In North America, the Spirit is awakening a generation to hunger for more than religious performance. Movements of inner healing, racial reconciliation, and missional living are rising, all energised by the Spirit's convicting, comforting, and commissioning work.

Among diaspora communities worldwide, the Spirit has become a unifying force that transcends language and tradition. As believers relocate, they carry their fire with them, planting churches in new lands and introducing others to the power of the Holy Spirit. Multicultural congregations around the world now bear witness to a shared spiritual DNA, the mark of the same Spirit who baptises all into one Body (1 Corinthians 12:13, NIV).

Globally, the Spirit is raising leaders from every background: women and men, young and old, educated and uneducated, from urban and rural areas. He is equipping the Church with gifts that serve both the pulpit and the marketplace, both the sanctuary and the streets. The Spirit is speaking through dreams in Muslim nations, stirring revival among university students, and convicting hearts in boardrooms and slums alike. His ministry is both intensely personal and broadly communal, deeply rooted in Scripture and powerfully present in experience.

Despite theological differences across traditions, whether Pentecostal, evangelical, liturgical, or charismatic, the undeniable evidence of the Spirit's activity continues to draw the Church into a deeper awareness of His unity and purpose. The Spirit is not a mere doctrinal topic; He is the living Breath of God, animating the global Church into worship, witness, and wisdom.

From the fires of revival in Nigeria to the quiet renewal in Scandinavian prayer rooms, from the spontaneous praise in South American gatherings to the contemplative chants of Asian house churches, the Spirit is at work. He is fulfilling Christ's promise to be with us always, guiding, teaching, convicting, and empowering until the ends of the earth are filled with the knowledge of the glory of the Lord.

Understanding the global perspectives on the Holy Spirit reminds us that we are part of a Spirit-filled movement far greater than ourselves. It challenges narrow thinking, honours diversity in expression, and invites us to celebrate the beautiful breadth of God's presence across the earth. The Church is alive because the Spirit is alive, and His work is not finished.

Conclusion

The Holy Spirit is not a passive presence nor a distant force but the living, active, personal expression of God at work in and through His Church. From creation to redemption, from the early Church to today's global landscape, the Spirit continues to reveal the will of the Father, testify of Christ, and empower believers to live transformed lives.

Across nations, denominations, and cultures, the Spirit is moving with precision and passion, birthing revivals, raising leaders, and revealing God's heart in languages the soul understands. Whether in the solitude of intercession or the fire of corporate worship, the Holy Spirit is breathing life into the Church and drawing her into maturity.

When believers fully embrace the gifts and cultivate the fruit of the Spirit, the Church becomes a vibrant and compelling expression of God's presence on earth. The gifts activate ministry, but the fruit sustains it. The gifts bring a breakthrough, but the fruit builds trust. It is in the harmony of both that the beauty of the Christian life is revealed, a life empowered and refined by the Holy Spirit.

This balance reminds us that ministry is not just about what we do, but who we are while doing it. The Spirit gives gifts to function in our calling, and He bears fruit to form our character. As believers pursue both with humility, surrender, and consistency, the Church is strengthened, the

Gospel advances, and God is glorified in every dimension of our lives.

Let us not relegate the Holy Spirit to a doctrinal category or limit Him to emotional experiences. Let us receive Him as the promise fulfilled, the presence within, and the power upon us to accomplish all that Christ commissioned us to do. To walk with the Spirit is to align our steps with Heaven's rhythm. It is to bear witness, with boldness and humility, to the work of a God who is alive and present.

CHAPTER EIGHT

PRACTICAL THEOLOGY

THEOLOGY BECOMES TRULY alive when it moves from mere concept to practical application in the real world. Practical theology bridges the gap between belief and behaviour, grounding doctrine in the everyday experiences of faith communities. It challenges us not only to affirm what we believe but also to examine how those beliefs shape our actions, decisions, and relationships.

In every context, whether within the Church, in the workplace, or among family, faith must be lived, not just professed. Practical theology is where Scripture intersects with society, where spiritual conviction shapes moral response, and where divine truth meets daily life. It is a call to embody the gospel in word, deed, and presence.

Laying On of Hands

The laying on of hands is a biblically rooted and spiritually significant practice that transcends mere ritual. It is an outward act with profound theological significance, demonstrating the impartation of blessings, authority, healing, or spiritual gifts. This act, though simple in form, reflects profound truths about God's presence, human agency, and the continuity of spiritual power within the Body of Christ.

In Scripture, the laying on of hands appears across both the Old and New Testaments, often marking moments of transition, consecration, or divine encounter. In the Old Testament, we see Moses laying his hands on Joshua to commission him as his successor (Numbers 27:18-23, NIV), symbolising the transfer of authority and spiritual leadership. This pattern of laying on of hands to set apart individuals for service would become a foundational principle in the life of Israel and later, in the early Church.

In the New Testament, Jesus Himself laid hands on the sick and they recovered (Mark 6:5, NIV), a model that demonstrated not only His divine compassion but also the channelling of healing power through physical touch. The apostles continued this practice, as seen in Acts 6:6 (NIV) when seven men were set apart to serve, and again in Acts 8:17 when believers in Samaria received the Holy Spirit through the laying on of hands by Peter and John.

Theologically, the laying on of hands signifies several spiritual realities. It is used in the commissioning of ministry leaders (1 Timothy 4:14, NIV), in the impartation of spiritual gifts, and the confirmation of calling. It reflects not only an affirmation by the Church but also a recognition of what God has already ordained. When performed with faith and discernment, it becomes a means of grace where God's Spirit works through human vessels to release empowerment, healing, or divine direction.

Pastorally, this practice teaches us the power of presence. It is a moment of spiritual solidarity, where one believer ministers to another through touch and prayer, standing as a vessel through whom the Holy Spirit works.

It requires humility, holiness, and sensitivity to the Spirit's prompting. While the act itself may be brief, the effects can be long-lasting, setting in motion spiritual breakthroughs, healings, or divine commissioning that align a person more closely with their calling in Christ.

In today's Church, this practice must be reclaimed with reverence and theological clarity. It is not to be reduced to a routine or theatrical display. Instead, it should be stewarded as a sacred act anchored in Scripture, led by the Holy Spirit, and saturated with prayer. Whether for healing, blessing, ordination, or spiritual impartation, the laying on of hands reminds us that God chooses to work through His people, joining the visible with the invisible to carry out His divine purposes.

Ordination and Commission

One of the most sacred and enduring applications of the laying on of hands is in the context of ordination and commission. This act signifies a public acknowledgement and spiritual empowerment for a specific role or assignment in the ministry of the Church. It is not merely ceremonial— it carries spiritual weight, affirming God's call and transmitting grace, authority, and responsibility for the work of the Gospel.

In the Bible, ordination through the laying on of hands is seen as both a divine affirmation and a communal endorsement. When Moses laid hands on Joshua (Numbers 27:18-23, NIV), it marked a transfer of spiritual leadership and authority. God told Moses, *"Have him stand before Eleazar the priest and the entire assembly and commission him in their presence."* This moment was both public and prophetic, as Joshua was empowered to lead Israel into their next season under God's direction.

In the New Testament, the practice was embraced by the early Church. Acts 13:2-3 (NIV) records the commissioning of Barnabas and Saul: *"While they were worshipping the Lord and fasting, the Holy Spirit said, 'Set apart for me Barnabas and Saul for the work to which I have called them.' So, after they had fasted and prayed, they placed their hands on them and sent them off."*

Here, we see the Church acting in obedience to the Holy Spirit by setting individuals apart and releasing them into apostolic ministry. The laying on of hands in this context was both a response to divine instruction and a visible sign of unity, blessing, and impartation.

Paul also instructed Timothy concerning the gravity of this act. In 1 Timothy 4:14 (NIV), he writes, *"Do not neglect your gift, which was given you through prophecy when the body of elders laid their hands on you."* This reveals that ordination is often accompanied by prophetic insight and the activation of spiritual gifts. The moment of commissioning is not just about appointment to a role; it is a moment when heaven aligns with earth to establish purpose, power, and protection for the calling at hand.

Theologically, ordination through the laying on of hands reinforces the idea that ministry is not self-appointed; rather, it is a divine call. It affirms that those called to lead must also be affirmed, equipped, and covered by the wider body of believers. The hands laid on the individual represent not just people, but the weight of spiritual accountability and the endorsement of the Church under Christ's headship.

In practice, ordination and commission ceremonies should be grounded in Scripture, prayer, and the presence of the Holy Spirit. These moments serve as both a spiritual milestone and a prophetic activation, calling forth the leader's gifts while also reminding the Church of the sacred trust being placed in their hands.

This practice reminds us that leadership in the Kingdom of God is not about status or position; it is about service, stewardship, and submission to God's will. The laying on of hands in ordination is a declaration that the one being commissioned is being set apart not only to lead, but also to love, to serve, and to shepherd under the guidance of the Chief Shepherd, Jesus Christ.

Healing and Prayer Ministry

The laying on of hands in the context of healing and prayer is one of the most visible and powerful expressions of divine compassion and supernatural intervention in the Church. Rooted deeply in the ministry of Jesus Christ and carried on by His apostles, this act serves as a channel through which faith is released, the sick are restored, and burdens are lifted.

Throughout the Gospels, we see Jesus consistently laying hands on the sick as a means of healing. Mark 6:5 (NIV) tells us, *"He could not do any miracles there, except lay his hands on a few sick people and heal them."* This verse reveals both the ordinary nature of this practice in Jesus's ministry and its miraculous outcomes. Laying hands on the sick was not a ritual—it was an intentional act of compassion, authority, and divine power.

In Luke 4:40 (NIV), the Scriptures describe a mass healing event: *"At sunset, the people brought to Jesus all who had various kinds of sickness, and laying his hands on each one, he healed them."* Jesus did not simply speak healing; He often touched the individuals, affirming both their dignity and the nearness of God's presence in their suffering. This physical contact became a tangible extension of God's mercy, releasing healing and wholeness into broken bodies.

The early Church embraced and practised this model. In Acts 28:8 (NIV), when Paul encountered the father of Publius suffering from fever and dysentery, the Scripture records: *"Paul went in to see him and, after prayer, placed his hands on him and healed him."* The laying on of hands here was not mechanical; it was preceded by prayer and motivated by the Spirit's leading. This example reminds us that the act must be grounded in faith, humility, and the desire to see God glorified.

James 5:14-15 (NIV) also provides instruction to the Church on healing ministry: *"Is anyone among you sick? Let them call the elders of the church to pray over them and anoint them with oil in the name of the Lord. And the prayer offered in faith will make the sick person well."*

While the anointing with oil is mentioned, the practice of laying hands is often implied in the act of intercession and blessing. It becomes a sacred moment of agreement, where spiritual leaders partner with the sick in believing for divine intervention.

In healing and prayer ministry today, laying on of hands continues to be a prophetic act, a sign of God's intention to heal, comfort, restore, and renew. It brings the afflicted into a space where faith can be stirred, the presence of God can be experienced, and miracles can be received. Whether it is for physical illness, emotional distress, or spiritual torment, the laying on of hands provides a means by which the Church can embody the love and power of Christ.

However, this act is not to be used carelessly. It must be approached with discernment, purity of heart, and spiritual readiness. It is not the hands themselves that heal; it is the presence and power of the Holy Spirit flowing through obedient vessels. Those engaging in healing and prayer ministry must be people of prayer, deeply submitted to God, and sensitive to the promptings of the Holy Spirit.

The laying on of hands in healing and prayer ministry serves as both a physical expression of faith and a spiritual channel through which God's power is channelled. It reaffirms the Church's call to be a healing community where the hurting are not ignored, but invited into encounters with the Great Physician who still heals today. This ministry keeps alive the tangible presence of Jesus among His people, reminding the world that the Gospel is not only preached, but also felt, experienced, and lived.

Impartation of Spiritual Gifts

This sacred act, often conducted in moments of prophetic significance, serves as a channel through which the Holy Spirit distributes gifts that empower believers for ministry and service within the Body of Christ.

One of the clearest scriptural foundations for this practice is found in 2 Timothy 1:6 (NIV), where Paul exhorts Timothy: *"For this reason I remind you to fan into flame the gift of God, which is in you through the laying on of my hands."* This verse affirms that Timothy received a spiritual gift—not merely through instruction or proximity—but through a specific moment of impartation, where Paul, led by the

Holy Spirit, laid hands on him and released divine empowerment.

Similarly, Acts 8:17 (NIV) reveals an apostolic practice in Samaria: *"Then Peter and John placed their hands on them, and they received the Holy Spirit."* While this passage primarily demonstrates the reception of the Holy Spirit, it also represents the moment where spiritual empowerment was visibly released upon new believers. The laying on of hands in such contexts becomes a point of contact between heaven and earth, where God's gifts are activated in the lives of the faithful.

This practice is not confined to the apostles alone. Romans 1:11 (NIV) captures Paul's deep desire: *"I long to see you so that I may impart to you some spiritual gift to make you strong."* Although this verse does not explicitly mention the laying on of hands, it reflects the apostolic yearning to strengthen the Church through spiritual transmission, often accomplished through prayer, prophecy, and touch.

The laying on of hands for impartation is typically accompanied by prophetic insight, worship, and intercession. It is not a random act, nor a guarantee of instant manifestation, but rather a faith-filled transaction initiated by God and stewarded by spiritually mature leaders. The gift imparted may vary, ranging from teaching, prophecy, and healing to wisdom, leadership, and supernatural insight, depending on what the Spirit desires to bestow at that moment.

Acts 13:2-3 (NIV) provides a vivid example of this in action: *"While they were worshipping the Lord and fasting, the Holy Spirit said, 'Set apart for me Barnabas and Saul for the work to which I have called them.' So, after they had fasted and prayed, they placed their hands on them and sent them off."* In this setting, laying on of hands not only marked their commissioning but affirmed the spiritual gifts and calling necessary for the mission ahead.

In the Church today, impartation through the laying on of hands remains a powerful practice, especially in leadership training, prophetic activation, ministry equipping, and mentoring. When done prayerfully and in accordance with the Spirit's prompting, it can ignite dormant gifts, awaken spiritual callings, and stir the believer's faith to new levels of effectiveness and obedience.

However, this ministry must be exercised with discernment. 1 Timothy 5:22 (NIV) warns: *"Do not be hasty in the laying on of hands, and do not share in the sins of others. Keep yourself pure."* This caution emphasises that the act should never be casual or rushed. Leaders must ensure that impartation is done under the guidance of the Holy Spirit and within the context of integrity, accountability, and holy living.

In conclusion, the laying on of hands for the impartation of spiritual gifts underscores God's ongoing involvement in equipping His people. It is a sacred means by which the Church becomes strengthened and mobilised, not by human effort, but by divine empowerment. This practice testifies that the same Spirit who raised Christ from the dead is still at work calling, gifting, and empowering believers for service in every generation.

Worship and Community through the Laying on of Hands

In the life of the Church, the laying on of hands is not only a sacred gesture of impartation but also a profound expression of worship and community. Rooted in biblical tradition and empowered by the Holy Spirit, this act becomes a bridge between heaven and earth, uniting believers in both reverence for God and loving responsibility toward one another.

Worship is more than songs or sermons; it is a total offering of the heart, a posture of submission and awe before God. The laying on of hands, when practised in worshipful contexts, reflects a physical and spiritual act of surrender to God's presence and authority. Whether in times of corporate prayer, healing, ordination, or intercession, it invites the entire congregation into a moment of holy agreement. As Paul exhorted in 1 Timothy 2:8 (NIV), *"Therefore I want the men everywhere to pray, lifting up holy hands without anger or disputing,"* this lifting of hands, symbolic of our dependence and unity, often accompanies the act of laying hands on others, especially during worship.

In the community, laying on of hands becomes an embodiment of shared life. It signifies spiritual solidarity, love, and accountability. When one member is commissioned, the community affirms their calling through a touch of blessing. When one is sick or struggling, the Church surrounds them in prayer, affirming their value and God's healing power. As seen in James 5:14 (NIV): *"Is anyone among you sick? Let them call the elders of the church to pray over them and anoint them with oil in the name of the Lord."* The prayer is not distant, it is near, personal, and often accompanied by the laying on of hands, reinforcing the communal nature of Christian care.

This practice also deepens our fellowship. It reminds the Church that we are not isolated worshippers but a body, interconnected and interdependent. As hands are laid in ordination, healing, or encouragement, spiritual gifts are stirred, faith is activated, and hearts are knit together in the Spirit. In the early Church, leaders were set apart not just with words, but with the laying on of hands in the presence of the gathered believers, creating a sacred moment of corporate witness and unity (Acts 13:2-3 NIV).

Moreover, laying on of hands serves as a visible act of intercession. It says, *"You are not alone."* It declares the power of God to restore, empower, or send, all within the context of community worship. These moments draw the Church closer into intimacy with God and deeper compassion for one another.

When practised with reverence and scriptural integrity, the laying on of hands enriches both our worship and our fellowship. It moves us from being passive observers to active participants in the work of the Spirit. It calls us to uphold one another in love, affirm one another in calling, and touch one another with the healing hands of Christ.

In this way, the laying on of hands becomes a sacred thread that weaves worship and community into one living tapestry, a Church both gathered in adoration and united in mission.

Ethical Considerations and Pastoral Guidelines in the Laying on of Hands

The laying on of hands is a sacred act that carries significant spiritual, emotional, and symbolic weight. While its roots are deeply biblical, its practice within the Church must be governed by wisdom, discernment, and ethical integrity. The act is not merely ceremonial; it represents spiritual authority, divine endorsement, communal recognition, and personal consecration. Because of its power and public nature, those involved in ministering through the laying on of hands must adhere to clear pastoral guidelines and uphold the highest standards of conduct.

Discernment and Timing

Scripture warns against hastiness in this practice. Paul's instruction to Timothy is clear: *"Do not be hasty in the laying on of hands, and do not share in the sins of others. Keep yourself pure"* (1 Timothy 5:22, NIV). This caution speaks not only to spiritual transfer but to public endorsement.

Laying hands on someone in ministry or leadership without due discernment may imply approval of their character and doctrine, which can mislead others if the person is not spiritually ready. Pastors and leaders must seek God's direction and ensure that the candidate has undergone proper mentorship, testing, and demonstration of faithfulness.

Consent and Personal Boundaries

The act of touch, even within spiritual contexts, must always be conducted with respect and consent. Regardless of intention, laying hands on someone without their permission can result in discomfort, misunderstanding, or harm. This is especially important in cases involving minors, vulnerable adults, or those with trauma backgrounds.

Pastoral guidelines should emphasise consent and maintain appropriate physical boundaries, ensuring that the practice reflects both reverence and care. The pastoral team should educate their congregations on the significance of the laying on of hands, so that it is received with understanding rather than confusion or pressure.

Gender Sensitivity and Accountability

In today's ministry contexts, special attention must be given to the dynamics of gender in ministry interactions. To prevent accusations or inappropriate encounters, many churches have adopted accountability practices, such as team-based prayer ministries, having both male and female ministers available, and avoiding private settings for the laying on of hands.

The laying on of hands should never become a platform for manipulation or hidden misconduct. Ministers must model purity, humility, and transparency in every ministry moment, reinforcing that this sacred act is an expression of God's touch, not human control.

Doctrinal Integrity

Laying on of hands must always align with sound doctrine. It is not a magical rite or a manipulative tool to produce desired outcomes. The Holy Spirit is sovereign, and though He often moves through touch, He is not bound by it. Ministers must guard against sensationalism or unbiblical practices that misrepresent the work of the Spirit. Teaching and practising the laying on of hands should always be grounded in Scripture, allowing believers to engage with both faith and understanding.

Follow-up and Discipleship

The spiritual implications of the laying on of hands often call for follow-up. Whether it is for healing, impartation, or ordination, those who receive ministry may need continued pastoral support. Laying on of hands is often the beginning of something new, an activation, a calling, or a shift in spiritual responsibility. Ethical practice includes shepherding the person in the aftermath: providing guidance, prayer, encouragement, and discipleship. This ensures the act does not become an isolated event, but part of a larger framework of spiritual growth.

A Sacred Practice Worthy of Reverence

When conducted with ethical clarity and pastoral care, the laying on of hands can bring healing, encouragement, commissioning, and divine encounter. It should never be rushed, carelessly performed, or stripped of its spiritual meaning.

Leaders are stewards of this holy act, and as such, must ensure it is approached with reverence, accountability, and love. As the Church continues to grow in spiritual authority and engagement, returning to biblically grounded, ethically sound practices ensures that the laying on of hands remains a channel of God's power and presence—never a cause of confusion, harm, or misuse.

Driving Out Demons

The practice of driving out demons, also known as deliverance ministry, is a significant aspect of the Apostolic Mandate. It involves the authority and power given to believers to confront and expel demonic forces in the name of Jesus Christ. This chapter examines the biblical foundations, theological implications, and practical considerations related to the ministry of casting out demons.

Throughout the pages of Scripture, we encounter numerous accounts of Jesus and His disciples engaging in spiritual warfare, confronting, and driving out demonic forces. Jesus demonstrated His authority over demons through His words and actions, setting captives free and releasing individuals from the grip of darkness. The disciples, empowered by the Holy Spirit, continued this ministry, affirming the reality of spiritual warfare and the power of Christ's name.

Exorcism is a phenomenon that persists to this day. It remains relevant and necessary today as believers encounter the spiritual battles and forces of darkness in their lives and communities. The Apostle Paul reminds us in Ephesians 6:12 that "our struggle is not against flesh and blood, but against the rulers, against the authorities, against the powers of this dark world and the spiritual forces of evil in the heavenly realms." Therefore, the ministry of driving out demons becomes an essential aspect of fulfilling the Apostolic Mandate to bring the Kingdom of God and its transformative power to our spheres of influence.

It requires a solid foundation in biblical truth, a firm understanding of spiritual authority, and a dependence on the power of the Holy Spirit. It is not a practice to be taken lightly, but rather one to be approached with reverence, humility, and love for those in need of deliverance. While the ministry of driving out demons is an essential aspect of the Apostolic Mandate, it must always be carried out in alignment with God's Word, with an emphasis on prayer, spiritual discernment, and the guidance of mature and experienced leaders.

Deliverance and Spiritual Warfare

The ministry of driving out demons, also known as deliverance, is a crucial component of engaging in spiritual warfare. It involves confronting and expelling demonic forces in the name and authority of Jesus Christ. This ministry acknowledges the reality of spiritual battles and the need to set individuals free from the oppressive grip of darkness.

Deliverance is rooted in the understanding that spiritual warfare extends beyond the physical realm. It recognises that there are spiritual forces of evil at work, seeking to hinder God's purposes, oppress individuals, and distort the truth. The ministry of driving out demons aligns with the Apostolic Mandate to bring the Kingdom of God into our spheres of influence, as it involves breaking the power of the enemy and releasing individuals from bondage.

Spiritual warfare demands a solid foundation in biblical truth and a profound reliance on the power of Jesus Christ. It is not a battle fought in our strength, but one in which we engage as instruments of God's authority and anointing. The ministry of deliverance flows from the victory won by Jesus on the cross, where He triumphed over the powers of darkness and disarmed them.

As believers, we have been granted the authority and power to drive out demons in the name of Jesus Christ. We are called to exercise spiritual discernment, relying on the Holy Spirit's guidance to identify and confront the influence of demonic forces. Through prayer, fasting, and the power of the Word of God, we engage in spiritual warfare, breaking strongholds and releasing individuals from the bondage of darkness.

It is indispensable to approach the ministry of deliverance with sensitivity, compassion, and a deep dependence on the leading of the Holy Spirit. Each person's journey and spiritual battle are unique, and it is vital to discern the underlying spiritual roots of their struggles.

Deliverance ministry involves more than simply casting out demons; it requires addressing the woundedness, lies, and strongholds that allow the enemy to operate in a person's life.

Besides, deliverance is not a one-time event, but rather a process that often involves ongoing discipleship, healing, and spiritual growth. It requires the support of a caring community and the provision of resources that enable individuals to walk in the freedom and victory that Christ has secured for them.

As we engage in deliverance and spiritual warfare, let us remember that our battle is not against flesh and blood but against spiritual forces of darkness. It is crucial to approach this ministry with humility, love, and a deep reliance on God's wisdom and power. Let us equip ourselves with the armour of God, engaging in prayer and intercession, and standing firm in the truth of God's Word.

May the ministry of driving out demons bring liberation, healing, and restoration to individuals held captive by spiritual strongholds. May it be carried out in the name and authority of Jesus Christ, reflecting His love, grace, and power. As we engage in spiritual warfare, may we rely on the guidance and empowerment of the Holy Spirit, bringing freedom and the manifestation of the Kingdom of God to those in need.

Understanding Demonic Oppression

Demonic oppression refers to the influence, control, or harassment exerted by demonic forces over individuals, including Christians, affecting various aspects of their lives. It is essential to have a clear understanding of this concept in the context of driving out demons and engaging in deliverance ministry.

The manifestation of demonic oppression is in different ways, such as spiritual bondage, torment, fear, addiction, sickness, and destructive patterns of behaviour. It seeks to hinder individuals from experiencing the fullness of God's love, freedom, and purpose in their lives. Understanding the nature of demonic oppression helps us to recognise its effects and discern the need for deliverance.

It is important to note that demonic oppression can occur in the lives of both believers and non-believers. While believers have the indwelling presence of the Holy Spirit, they can still experience varying degrees of demonic influence. Oppression is not an indication of a lack of faith but rather a spiritual battle that needs to be addressed through the ministry of deliverance.

The root cause of demonic oppression can vary, including generational sin, personal sin, open doors to the enemy through occult involvement, unresolved trauma, or other vulnerabilities. It is crucial to approach each situation with sensitivity and discernment, seeking the leading of the Holy Spirit to identify the underlying spiritual issues that need to be addressed.

In the ministry of deliverance, our goal is not only to cast out demons but also to bring healing and restoration to individuals affected by demonic oppression. This involves addressing the lies, wounds, and strongholds that have allowed the enemy to gain a foothold. It requires a holistic approach that combines spiritual warfare, prayer, biblical counselling, and discipleship to facilitate lasting transformation.

Understanding demonic oppression enables us to approach deliverance ministry with empathy, compassion, and a profound reliance on the power and authority of Jesus Christ. It reminds us that our battle is not against people but against the spiritual forces of darkness. It calls us to stand firm in the truth of God's Word, recognising our authority in Christ to overcome the works of the enemy.

As we engage in deliverance ministry and address demonic oppression, it is essential to do so in alignment with biblical principles and under the guidance of experienced and mature leaders. We must approach each situation with sensitivity, respecting the dignity and privacy of the individuals involved. Confidentiality, love, and discernment should guide our actions as we seek to bring liberation and restoration to those under the grip of demonic oppression.

May our understanding of demonic oppression deepen our compassion for those affected by its influence. May we engage in deliverance ministry with wisdom, humility, and a deep dependence on the Holy Spirit? Let us be agents of freedom and healing, bringing the light of Christ into the darkness and setting captives free through the power and authority bestowed upon us in the name of Jesus Christ.

In Christianity, the Bible offers several insights into the origin and nature of demons, but it does not give a single, systematic explanation. Instead, clues are scattered across various books. Demons Are Fallen Angels? This is the most widely accepted Christian belief, based on scriptural hints.

Revelation 12:7–9 (ESV): "Now war arose in heaven, Michael and his angels fighting against the dragon... and the great dragon was thrown down, that ancient serpent, who is called the devil and Satan... and his angels were thrown down with him." Satan (the devil) and a third of the angels rebelled against God and were cast out of heaven. These fallen angels are understood to be demons.

Jude 1:6: also mentions angels *who "did not stay within their position of authority."* Some fallen angels are already imprisoned, while others (like those Jesus cast out) still roam the earth.

Modern demonology claims that demons are real, malicious spirits. Sometimes, demons team up or *amplify their work* through cooperation. The Gospels show demons actively tormenting people, causing illness, and recognising Jesus as the Son of God. Luke 4:41 (ESV): *"And demons also came out of many, crying, 'You are the Son of God!'"*

The Authority of Jesus

This authority of Jesus is foundational to the ministry of driving out demons and engaging in deliverance. Understanding His authority is crucial for believers as they confront and overcome the forces of darkness in the name of Jesus Christ.

Throughout the Gospels, we witness the authority of Jesus being demonstrated in various ways. He taught with authority, performed miraculous signs and wonders, and displayed power over sickness, nature, and even death. Jesus's authority extended beyond the physical realm, encompassing both the spiritual and physical realms.

Jesus's authority over demons was evident in His encounters with them during His earthly ministry. He confronted demonic forces, commanded them to leave, and set individuals free from their influence. The demons recognised His authority and submitted to His command. His authority was not derived from earthly sources or personal power but was inherent in His identity as the Son of God.

The authority of Jesus is rooted in His victory over sin and death through His sacrificial death and resurrection. Through His atoning work on the cross, Jesus disarmed the powers and authorities, triumphing over them openly (Colossians 2:15). He defeated the enemy and reclaimed the authority that was lost due to humanity's fall from grace. As believers, we share in His victory and authority, participating in His ministry of driving out demons.

The authority of Jesus is not limited to the past; it is a present reality that continues to impact believers today. Through His indwelling Holy Spirit, Jesus empowers and equips believers to walk in His authority and engage in spiritual warfare. We have been given the authority to use the name of Jesus, which carries the weight and power of His authority, to confront and drive out demons.

Believers must understand and operate in the authority of Jesus with humility, dependence on the Holy Spirit, and alignment with God's Word. The authority we exercise is not based on our own merits or abilities but on our position in Christ. As we submit to His lordship and yield to the leading of the Holy Spirit, we can confidently exercise the authority of Jesus to drive out demons, break strongholds, and set individuals free.

The authority of Jesus extends beyond deliverance ministry. It encompasses all areas of our lives as we navigate spiritual battles, face challenges, and fulfil the Apostolic Mandate. We can rely on His authority to bring healing, transformation, and victory in every sphere of influence.

May our understanding of Jesus's authority deepen our faith and confidence in His power to overcome the forces of darkness. Let us walk in His authority with reverence and humility, knowing that it is not our own but a delegated authority from the One who reigns supreme. As we engage in deliverance ministry and spiritual warfare, may we do so in the name and authority of Jesus Christ, bringing His light, freedom, and transformation to a world in need.

Discernment and Diagnostic

Discernment and diagnostic abilities play a vital role in the ministry of driving out demons and engaging in deliverance. They enable believers to recognise and understand the spiritual dynamics at work, helping to identify the presence of demonic influence and discern the appropriate course of action.

Discernment is a spiritual gift that the Holy Spirit imparts to believers to perceive and understand the spiritual realm. It involves the ability to distinguish between what is of God and what is of the enemy. Discernment enables us to recognise the subtle tactics of the enemy and identify the presence of demonic influence in individuals' lives.

In the ministry of deliverance, discernment enables us to distinguish between natural struggles and spiritual oppression or bondage. It helps us understand the root causes of a person's struggles, whether they are primarily spiritual, psychological, or physical. Discernment enables us to discern the need for deliverance and the appropriate steps to address the spiritual aspects of an individual's situation.

Diagnostic abilities are closely related to discernment, as they involve the process of gathering information and understanding the spiritual, emotional, and physical aspects of a person's condition. Diagnostic skills help us to assess the spiritual strongholds, wounds, lies, or generational patterns that may be contributing to the oppression or bondage experienced by an individual.

Effective discernment and diagnostic abilities in deliverance ministry require a combination of spiritual sensitivity, biblical knowledge, and experience. They involve seeking the guidance of the Holy Spirit, listening attentively to individuals' testimonies, and observing behavioural patterns or manifestations that may indicate demonic influence. It is essential to exercise discernment and diagnostic abilities with humility, recognising that it is ultimately God who reveals and uncovers the spiritual realities at work.

While discernment and diagnostic abilities are crucial, they should always be accompanied by prayer and reliance on the Holy Spirit. We must avoid relying solely on our own understanding or human wisdom. Instead, we seek the wisdom and guidance of the Holy Spirit to reveal hidden truths, unveil spiritual strongholds, and bring clarity to complex situations.

It is vital to exercise discernment and diagnostic abilities with love, compassion, and sensitivity. We must approach each person and situation with respect, confidentiality, and a deep understanding of the spiritual battle being waged. Discernment and diagnostic abilities should be utilised to bring understanding, healing, and freedom to individuals, guiding them toward the redemptive work of Jesus Christ.

May we cultivate discernment and diagnostic abilities through prayer, the study of God's Word, and a deep relationship with the Holy Spirit? Let us rely on His guidance and wisdom as we engage in deliverance ministry, bringing discernment, clarity, and hope to those in need. Through discernment and diagnostic abilities, may we effectively confront the spiritual forces of darkness, facilitate healing, and bring liberation in the name of Jesus Christ.

Methods and Strategies

When engaging in the ministry of driving out demons and deliverance, it is essential to employ effective methods and strategies. These approaches help facilitate a safe and fruitful environment for individuals seeking freedom and deliverance from demonic influence.

The foundation of any deliverance ministry is prayer. It is essential to cultivate a lifestyle of prayer and seek the guidance of the Holy Spirit throughout the entire process. Engaging in intercessory prayer for individuals in need of deliverance opens the way for God's intervention and prepares the atmosphere for spiritual breakthroughs.

Deliverance ministry involves engaging in spiritual warfare, understanding the authority and power we have in Christ. This includes using the name of Jesus, declaring the Word of God, and standing firm against the enemy's schemes. Spiritual warfare involves using spiritual weapons such as praise, worship, fasting, and the armour of God to effectively engage in the battle against demonic forces.

The ministry of deliverance should be accompanied by discipleship and teaching. It is crucial to provide individuals with a solid foundation in biblical truth, equipping them to live in the freedom that Christ has provided. Teaching on topics such as identity in Christ, the finished work of the cross, and the believer's authority can empower individuals to resist the enemy and walk in victory.

Deliverance ministry often goes hand in hand with inner healing and restoration. It is essential to address the emotional wounds, trauma, and lies that may have given the enemy a foothold. Incorporating inner healing methods, such as prayer ministry, forgiveness, and addressing root issues, can contribute to lasting freedom and wholeness.

After deliverance takes place, it is crucial to provide ongoing support, accountability, and follow-up for individuals. This can include regular check-ins, pastoral care, and encouragement to ensure their spiritual growth and continued freedom. It is essential to provide resources and referrals for professional counselling if needed.

Engaging in deliverance ministry often benefits from a team approach. A team of experienced and mature believers can provide support, discernment, and additional spiritual covering. Working together as a team ensures accountability, wise counsel, and the ability to handle more complex situations with efficiency and effectiveness.

Deliverance ministry requires utmost confidentiality and respect for the privacy of individuals. It is crucial to create a safe and non-judgmental environment where individuals can share their struggles openly without fear of condemnation. Respecting their boundaries, cultural backgrounds, and personal preferences is essential for building trust and facilitating a conducive atmosphere for deliverance.

Remember, the specific methods and strategies employed may vary depending on the situation and the leading of the Holy Spirit. Flexibility and sensitivity to the unique needs of individuals are important throughout the delivery process.

By implementing these methods and strategies, believers can engage in deliverance ministry with wisdom, discernment, and effectiveness. The goal is to bring individuals into a place of freedom, healing, and wholeness, enabling them to live out their God-given purposes and experience the fullness of life in Christ.

Aftercare and Follow-up

Aftercare and follow-up are crucial aspects of the ministry of driving out demons and deliverance. These practices ensure that individuals who have experienced deliverance receive ongoing support, discipleship, and pastoral care to maintain their freedom and continue their spiritual growth.

After deliverance, individuals may need ongoing pastoral support and guidance. It is essential to provide a safe and non-judgmental environment where they can share their experiences, ask questions, and receive spiritual counsel. Pastors and leaders should be available to provide prayer, encouragement, and guidance as individuals navigate their newfound freedom.

Discipleship is essential for individuals who have experienced deliverance from spiritual bondage. It involves teaching and equipping them with biblical principles, helping them understand their identity in Christ, and empowering them to live in the freedom that Christ has provided.

Discipleship can include regular meetings, small group involvement, Bible studies, and mentoring relationships to support their spiritual growth and transformation.

Deliverance often involves breaking strongholds and lies that have influenced individuals' thinking and behaviour patterns. Aftercare should focus on renewing the mind through the power of God's Word. Encourage individuals to immerse themselves in Scripture, meditate on truth, and replace negative thought patterns with God's promises. This ongoing process helps individuals maintain their freedom and resist the enemy's attempts to regain control.

Alongside deliverance, individuals may benefit from ongoing inner healing. Inner healing addresses emotional wounds, trauma, and unresolved issues that may have contributed to the stronghold or demonic influence. Incorporating inner healing practices such as prayer ministry, forgiveness, and emotional healing techniques can facilitate ongoing healing and restoration.

Establishing accountability structures is vital for individuals who have experienced deliverance. This can include regular check-ins, accountability partners, or involvement in small groups. Accountability helps individuals stay grounded, provides support, and helps them navigate challenges that may arise after deliverance. Encourage individuals to be open and transparent about their struggles and victories, fostering an environment of trust and growth.

It is important to be aware of professional resources and referrals for individuals who may need additional support. Some individuals may require counselling, specialised therapy, or other professional assistance to address deeper issues. Pastors and leaders should have a network of trusted professionals to whom they can refer individuals, ensuring they receive the appropriate care and support.

Continued prayer and intercession are vital for those who have experienced deliverance. Encourage individuals to maintain a consistent prayer life and seek God's guidance and protection. Regularly pray for them, covering them in spiritual warfare and interceding for their ongoing spiritual growth and protection.

Remember, everyone's journey is unique, and their aftercare and follow-up needs may vary. It is essential to approach aftercare with sensitivity, love, and discernment, allowing the Holy Spirit to guide the process.

By providing aftercare and follow-up, we ensure that individuals continue to walk in freedom, grow in their relationship with God, and fulfil their God-given purpose. Let us commit to journeying alongside them, offering support, guidance, and discipleship as they experience the ongoing transformation that comes from deliverance in the name of Jesus Christ.

Conclusion

Practical theology reveals various aspects of ministry and leadership. We have discussed the significance of laying on of hands, understanding its definition and importance in commissioning and ordination. We have also examined the vital role of healing and prayer ministry, recognising the power of God to bring restoration and wholeness to individuals. The impartation of spiritual gifts, recognising the importance of equipping and empowering believers for effective service in the Kingdom.

We have also seen that practical theology extends beyond theoretical knowledge. It is about the lived experience of faith and the application of biblical principles in real-life contexts. It encompasses ethical considerations, pastoral guidelines, and the responsible exercise of authority, touching on crucial topics such as driving out demons, understanding spiritual warfare, and the discernment necessary in addressing demonic oppression.

Here is a call to embody the values of servant leadership and to embrace ethical principles that guide our decisions and actions. It invites us to engage with the world, to bring the transformative power of the Gospel to bear on societal issues and challenges. We have witnessed the importance of aftercare and follow-up, recognising the ongoing support and nurture required in the journey of healing and deliverance.

As we conclude this chapter, let us remember that practical theology is not an isolated endeavour but is intimately connected to the Christian faith. It is in the practical outworking of our beliefs that our faith becomes tangible and transformative. May we continually seek the guidance of the Holy Spirit, remaining rooted in God's Word, as we strive to live out our faith in ways that bring honour to God and bring the Kingdom of God to bear on our world?

CHAPTER NINE

LEADERSHIP

LEADERSHIP IS VITAL to fulfilling the Apostolic Mandate and bringing the Kingdom of God to our spheres of influence. Effective leadership plays a crucial role in equipping, empowering, and mobilising believers to live out their God-given calling and impact the world around them. This chapter explores the principles, characteristics, and responsibilities of leadership within the context of the Apostolic Mandate.

Leadership in the Apostolic Mandate is not confined to a hierarchical or positional structure but encompasses the influence and impact that every believer can have in their respective spheres. It is a call to lead with humility, servanthood, and a deep reliance on the guidance of the Holy Spirit. Whether leading in the church, the workplace, or the community, the principles of leadership remain rooted in the character and teachings of Jesus Christ.

Leadership involves shepherding, guiding, and nurturing the people under one's care, helping them discover and fulfil their unique God-given purposes. Leaders are called to be agents of change, catalysts for transformation, and examples of godly character and integrity.

May our hearts be filled with humility, wisdom, and a deep desire to serve others. Let us seek to lead with integrity, guided by the teachings and example of Jesus Christ. May your leadership inspire and empower those around you to embrace their unique roles and gifts, as together we fulfil the call to bring the Kingdom of God to our spheres of influence.

The Reverse Hierarchy. A Challenge to All Leaders.

The traditional top-down approach, found in many churches and congregations, is challenged by Jesus through the application of a reverse hierarchy.

Christian traditions may suggest functional church structures and organisational charts, where the most powerful members of the congregation sit at the top, while those with the least amount of power are at the bottom.

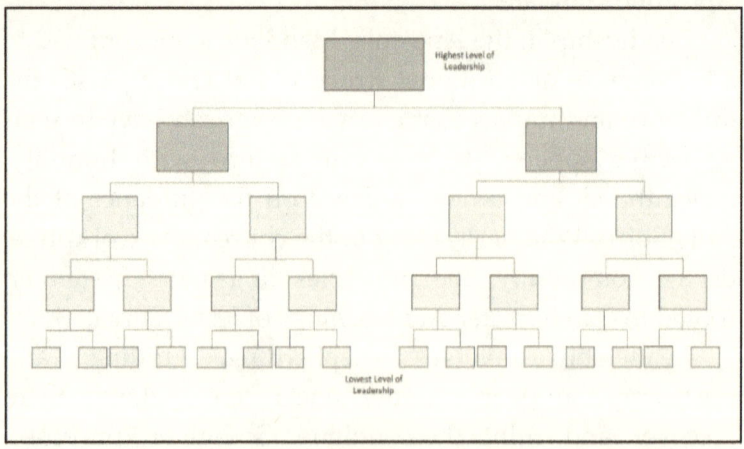

Figure 02: The Top-Down Leadership Hierarchy Approach

In contrast to this top-down hierarchy, which grants the persons at the top of the church organisation significantly more control over key decisions than those lower in the hierarchy, it becomes apparent that the understanding of the New Testament follows a different pattern: an apostle moves within a completely voluntary network, and this role does not have any institutionalised authority. An apostle (and the other four functions) is expected to have an extraordinary character and a very humble attitude.

The passage in Eph. 4:11-12 contains exciting theological principles: "People with leadership gifts are to train others so that every member can contribute to the overall growth of the whole body. The primary purpose of the passage is to demonstrate that gifted leadership was given to the ecclesia in order that it might progress toward a unified spiritual maturity. These leadership gifts are part of an interdependent exercise of gifts of all members of the church. The church as a whole will not reach a unified maturity unless each of its members exercises their gift in concert with other members. The proper interdependent exercise of gifts brings about maturity of oneness in believers and strengthens the ecclesia's eschatological journey towards Christ-likeness." (Thomas Kelebogile Resane)

The aim of the five-fold ministry is not to exercise power, but for Christians to flourish. As a consequence, a different chart is suggested:

A bottom-up hierarchy signals and elucidates the inner heart attitude of an apostolic team:

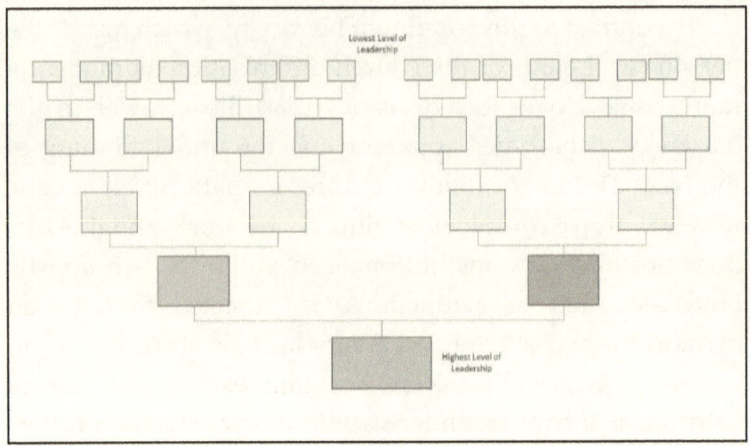

Figure 03: The Reverse Leadership Hierarchy Approach

Such a reverse hierarchy chart is a conceptual organisational structure that attempts to invert the traditional understanding of executive authority, which is traditionally displayed by a top-down pyramid of hierarchical organisations. The functions of the five-fold ministry rather provide support to the local congregations. They adjust, equip, perfect, and build up the body of Christ. A bottom-up chart expresses this serving-focused, humbled attitude.

Pastoral Leadership

Pastoral leadership is a significant aspect of leadership within the Apostolic Mandate. It involves shepherding, guiding, and nurturing God's people with love, compassion, and a deep commitment to their spiritual growth and well-being. Pastoral leaders play a crucial role in equipping believers, providing spiritual care, and leading them into a deeper relationship with God.

In the framework of the Apostolic Mandate, pastoral leadership goes beyond the traditional role of overseeing a church congregation. It extends to leading and shepherding believers in various spheres of influence, including the workplace, community, and family. Pastoral leaders are called to be servant-leaders, modelling Christ-like character and influencing others through their words, actions, and genuine care.

Pastoral leadership is rooted in the example of Jesus, who referred to Himself as the Good Shepherd. He lovingly cared for His disciples, sought the lost, and laid down His life for the sheep. Pastoral leaders are called to emulate His selfless and sacrificial leadership, prioritising the spiritual welfare and growth of those entrusted to their care.

Characteristics such as humility, integrity, compassion, and empathy are foundational to effective pastoral leadership. Pastoral leaders are called to shepherd with authenticity, cultivating genuine relationships with their flock, and being sensitive to their needs. They listen attentively, offer guidance, support, and provide a safe space for individuals to share their struggles and joys.

Pastoral leaders are responsible for teaching and equipping believers with biblical truth, helping them apply God's Word to their lives, and guiding them in their spiritual journeys. They lead by example, demonstrating a life of faith, prayer, and obedience to God's leading. Pastoral leaders also facilitate opportunities for worship, discipleship, fellowship, and ministry, fostering a sense of belonging and spiritual growth within the community.

It requires discernment, as leaders must navigate the unique challenges, complexities, and diverse needs of those under their care. They provide pastoral care, counselling, and prayer support to individuals facing various life circumstances, helping them find healing, restoration, and hope in Christ.

Collaboration and teamwork are crucial in pastoral leadership. It involves working alongside other leaders, both within the church and in the wider community, to fulfil the Apostolic Mandate. Pastoral leaders build strong leadership teams, delegate responsibilities effectively, and empower others to utilise their gifts and talents for God's purposes. They create a culture of unity, trust, and shared vision, fostering an environment where each member of the body of Christ can contribute to the overall mission.

As pastoral leaders hold their calling within the Apostolic Mandate, they play a crucial role in mobilising believers to impact their spheres of influence. They encourage individuals to discover and utilise their spiritual gifts, empowering them to serve others and become agents of transformation in their communities.

When pastoral leaders embrace their role with humility, love, and a deep dependence on the Holy Spirit, they shepherd God's people with care and compassion, leading them into a deeper relationship with Him. May they faithfully fulfil their responsibilities, equipping and empowering believers to live out the Apostolic Mandate, bringing the Kingdom of God to their spheres of influence.

Servant Leadership

Servant leadership is a vital approach within the context of the Apostolic Mandate. It embodies the humility, selflessness, and sacrificial love demonstrated by Jesus Christ during His earthly ministry. Servant leaders prioritise the well-being and growth of others, seeking to empower and serve them rather than seeking personal gain or recognition.

At the core of servant leadership is the understanding that leaders are called to be servants first. They adopt a mindset of humility, willingly placing the needs and interests of others above their own. Instead of exerting authority or control, servant leaders lead through influence, modelling servant-heartedness and inspiring others to do the same.

Servant leadership finds its foundation in Jesus's teaching and example. He washed His disciples' feet, demonstrating humility and servitude. Jesus stated that He came not to be served, but to serve, and to give His life as a ransom for many. As leaders within the Apostolic Mandate, we are called to emulate His servant leadership, reflecting His character and love in our interactions with others.

It prioritises the growth and well-being of those they lead. They aim to empower individuals, helping them discover and develop their unique talents and abilities. Instead of hoarding power or authority, they delegate responsibilities, provide support, and create opportunities for others to flourish. Servant leaders understand that their role is to equip and release individuals to fulfil their God-given potential.

Humility is a hallmark of servant leadership. Servant leaders acknowledge their limitations, strengths, and weaknesses, recognising that they are part of a larger team working towards a common goal. They actively listen to others, value diverse perspectives, and encourage collaboration. By creating an environment of trust and mutual respect, servant leaders foster a sense of belonging and encourage the full participation and contribution of everyone.

Servant leadership entails a profound concern for the holistic well-being of those in one's care. It encompasses the physical, emotional, and spiritual needs of individuals. Servant leaders provide pastoral care, support, and guidance, nurturing the spiritual growth and maturity of those they lead. They create space for individuals to express their joys, sorrows, and struggles, offering a listening ear, prayer, and practical assistance.

Servant leaders are not immune to making difficult decisions or addressing conflict. However, they approach these situations with grace, seeking reconciliation and demonstrating a commitment to the best interests of those involved. They prioritise the unity and harmony of the community, working towards resolution and fostering an environment of forgiveness and restoration.

By implementing servant leadership within the Apostolic Mandate, leaders become agents of transformation and catalysts for change. They model Christ-like character, inspiring others to follow their example of servant-heartedness. Servant leaders play a crucial role in fulfilling the Apostolic Mandate, bringing the Kingdom of God to their spheres of influence through their selfless service and love.

Organizational Leadership

Organisational leadership is an essential component within the context of the Apostolic Mandate. It involves guiding, directing, and overseeing the operations, vision, and strategic initiatives of an organisation or ministry. Effective organisational leadership enables the implementation of the

Apostolic Mandate, ensuring alignment with the organisation's mission, values, and goals.

Organisational leaders within the Apostolic Mandate are responsible for establishing a clear vision and direction for the organisation. They articulate the mission and purpose, setting goals and objectives that align with the Apostolic Mandate's call to bring the Kingdom of God to every sphere of influence. Organisational leaders cast a compelling vision that inspires and mobilises individuals to join in the mission.

The Apostolic Mandate is not confined to the walls of the church but extends to various spheres, including education, business, government, and the arts. Organisational leaders play a crucial role in identifying and stewarding the resources, talents, and opportunities within their specific organisational context. They ensure that all aspects of the organisation, from governance and administration to programming and operations, align with the principles and values of the Apostolic Mandate.

Active organisational leaders exhibit key qualities such as strategic thinking, adaptability, and innovation. They possess the ability to anticipate and respond to changes in the external environment, guiding the organisation in navigating challenges and seizing opportunities. Organisational leaders are forward-thinking, continually seeking ways to enhance and advance the organisation's impact and effectiveness.

Collaboration and teamwork are integral to organisational leadership within the Apostolic Mandate. Leaders foster a culture of collaboration, encouraging the input and involvement of team members and stakeholders. They build strong leadership teams by delegating responsibilities and leveraging the diverse strengths and expertise of team members. Organisational leaders recognise that collective effort and a shared vision are essential for fulfilling the Apostolic Mandate.

Integrity and ethical conduct are fundamental to effective organisational leadership. Leaders exemplify honesty, transparency, and accountability in their decision-making and interactions. They cultivate a culture of trust, where individuals feel safe speaking up, expressing their ideas, and contributing to the organisation's growth and success. Organisational leaders lead by example, modelling godly character and servant leadership within the organisational context.

Leaders within the Apostolic Mandate are responsible for cultivating a culture of continuous learning and growth. They prioritise leadership development, equipping and empowering individuals within the organisation to embrace their leadership potential. Organisational leaders provide mentorship, coaching, and opportunities for professional and spiritual development, fostering a culture of excellence and effectiveness.

Organisational leadership within the Apostolic Mandate requires discernment, wisdom, and a deep reliance on the guidance of the Holy Spirit. Leaders seek divine guidance and engage in prayerful decision-making, acknowledging God as the ultimate source of wisdom and direction for their organisation. They cultivate a spirit of dependence on God, recognising that the success and impact of the organisation are ultimately in His hands.

As leaders encircle organisational leadership within the Apostolic Mandate, they become agents of transformation within their spheres of influence. Through strategic vision, collaboration, and integrity, they guide organisations to fulfil their God-given purpose and impact the world for the glory of God. Organisational leaders align their leadership with the values and principles of the Apostolic Mandate, thereby bringing the Kingdom of God into the fabric of the organisation's operations, culture, and impact.

Women in Leadership and Church Governance

Various biblical passages inform the discussion on women's roles in leadership. Supporters of women in leadership point to examples of women like Deborah, who served as a judge and prophetess in the Old Testament (Judges chapters 4 & 5).

In the New Testament, women such as Phoebe, Priscilla, and Junia are recognised for their leadership and influential roles within the early Christian community. These examples, along with Paul's affirmations of women's participation in ministry (e.g., Romans 16:1-7), are cited in support of women's leadership and governance roles.

The theological debate on women's roles in leadership often centres around the complementarian and egalitarian perspectives. Complementarian theology teaches that men and women have distinct, complementary roles in the family and the Church. Some argue that God ordains male leadership, while women are called to serve in supporting roles. On the other hand, egalitarian theology emphasises the equal value, gifting, and calling of men and women, advocating for equal opportunities for both genders in leadership positions.

Different Christian traditions and denominations hold varying views on women in leadership and church governance. Some traditions have been more open to women's involvement in leadership positions, while others have maintained more restrictive policies. Understanding the historical context and denominational perspectives provides insight into the diversity of practices and interpretations regarding women in leadership roles.

Beyond theological and biblical perspectives, practical considerations play a role in discussions on women's leadership. These considerations may include cultural norms, societal expectations, and the impact of women's leadership on the dynamics of congregations. Understanding the practical aspects and challenges surrounding women in leadership helps shape the conversation and discern the best approaches for promoting gender equality and effective governance within the Church.

Over the years, there has been progress in embracing women's leadership and governance roles within many Christian communities. Churches and denominations have recognised the gifts, talents, and callings of women, allowing them to serve in various leadership capacities. However, challenges and obstacles persist, including persistent gender biases, limited access to leadership positions, and the ongoing need for advocacy to achieve equal representation and opportunities for women.

As Christians engage in discussions on women in leadership and church governance, it is crucial to approach the topic with humility, biblical integrity, and respect for diverse viewpoints. Recognising the diversity of perspectives and theological convictions fosters a spirit of unity and mutual understanding. It is essential to create spaces for dialogue, listening to the experiences and insights of women in leadership, and seeking the guidance of the Holy Spirit in discerning the best path forward.

The goal should be to ensure that the gifts and callings of both men and women are fully recognised, affirmed, and utilised in the service of God's Kingdom. Embracing women's leadership and governance roles enriches the Church, promoting equality, diversity, and effective ministry in the body of Christ.

Spiritual Leadership

Spiritual leadership is a vital component within the context of the Apostolic Mandate. It encompasses leading others with a strong focus on spiritual growth, fostering an environment of spiritual maturity, and guiding individuals in their relationship with God. Spiritual leaders are called to influence and inspire others to pursue a deeper connection with God and fulfil their God-given purpose.

A personal and intimate relationship with God is at the heart of spiritual leadership. Spiritual leaders prioritise their spiritual growth, spending time in prayer, studying God's Word, and seeking the guidance of the Holy Spirit. They model a life of faith, humility, and surrender to God's will, inspiring others to follow their example.

Spiritual leaders lead by serving and exemplifying Christ-like character. They are not driven by personal ambition or a desire for recognition, but are motivated by a love for God and a genuine concern for others. They consider the well-being and spiritual development of those they lead as their primary responsibility.

They facilitate an environment of worship, prayer, and discipleship. They create spaces for individuals to encounter God's presence, worship Him, and seek His guidance. They encourage personal and corporate prayer, fostering an atmosphere of dependence on the Holy Spirit and inviting His leading and empowering.

Discipleship is an integral aspect of spiritual leadership. Spiritual leaders invest in the lives of others, guiding them in their understanding of God's Word, teaching them how to apply biblical principles to their lives, and nurturing their spiritual growth. They equip individuals to become disciples who make disciples, fostering a culture of multiplication and reproducing spiritual leaders.

Spiritual leaders assume the role of shepherds, offering pastoral care and support to those under their care. They listen attentively, offer guidance, and provide encouragement in times of joy and struggle. They shepherd with empathy, compassion, and a genuine desire to see individuals flourish in their faith journey.

Integrity and authenticity are foundational to spiritual leadership. Leaders strive to align their actions, words, and attitudes with their professed beliefs. They recognise that their character has a significant impact on their influence and credibility. Spiritual leaders strive to live lives that honour God, admitting their shortcomings and being transparent about their journey of faith.

Spiritual leaders cultivate a culture of accountability and spiritual discipline, encouraging individuals to develop spiritual practices such as prayer, Bible study, fasting, and meditation on God's Word. They provide guidance and resources for spiritual growth, empowering individuals to take ownership of their faith and pursue an intimate relationship with God.

The power of the Holy Spirit leads spiritual leaders. They rely on His guidance, seeking His wisdom and direction in decision-making and empowering others through His anointing. They create space for the manifestation of spiritual gifts, encouraging individuals to utilise their God-given talents and gifts for the edification of the body of Christ.

As spiritual leaders embrace their calling within the Apostolic Mandate, they become catalysts for spiritual transformation and growth. They guide individuals to live out the Apostolic Mandate, encouraging them to impact their spheres of influence through their spiritual maturity and service. Spiritual leaders cultivate an environment where the presence and power of God are manifested, enabling individuals to experience the fullness of life in Christ.

We pray that spiritual leaders rise, equipped and anointed by the Holy Spirit, to lead with humility, love, and a deep devotion to God. Let us embrace spiritual leadership as a sacred responsibility, guiding others towards a vibrant and transformative relationship with God. Through spiritual leadership, may we fulfil the Apostolic Mandate, bringing the Kingdom of God to our spheres of influence?

The Apostolic Leadership Pattern of Christian Initiation

This section examines the apostolic practices of Christian initiation as described in Acts 8:14-18, Acts 10:44-48, and Acts 19:1-6. These passages consistently reveal a threefold process in which the apostles ensured that converts experienced personal faith in Jesus Christ (being "born again"), received water baptism, and were baptised in the Holy Spirit. We argue that these elements were not viewed as optional or redundant by the early church, but rather as distinct and essential stages in the formation of Christian discipleship.

The Book of Acts serves as a historical and theological account of the birth and expansion of the early Christian church. It also offers a practical record of how the apostles understood and implemented the process of Christian initiation. While contemporary theological traditions often debate the relationship and necessity of water baptism and the baptism in the Holy Spirit, a careful study of Acts reveals that the apostles engaged in a deliberate and consistent practice that emphasised all three: conversion (faith), water baptism, and Spirit baptism.

Acts 8:14-18 – Apostolic Intervention in Samaria

In Acts 8, the evangelist Philip proclaims the gospel in Samaria, resulting in widespread belief and water baptism (v.12). However, when the apostles in Jerusalem hear of this development, they dispatch Peter and John, who upon arrival, lay hands on the converts so that they may receive the Holy Spirit (vv.15–17). The narrative explicitly notes that although they had believed and were baptised, the Holy Spirit had not yet come upon any of them (v.16), suggesting that Spirit baptism was viewed as a distinct event that required apostolic attention.

This passage illustrates that the apostles did not consider the experience of faith and water baptism alone as sufficient for full initiation. Rather, the impartation of the Holy Spirit was seen as a critical third component, one that could not be overlooked in the development of the believer's spiritual life.

Acts 10:44-48 – Gentile Inclusion and the Order of Events

The encounter with Cornelius and his household in Acts 10 presents a unique sequence in which the Holy Spirit falls upon the listeners during Peter's sermon (v. 44), prior to their baptism in water. This spontaneous outpouring, confirmed by the outward manifestation of speaking in tongues (v.46), is interpreted by Peter and his companions as incontrovertible evidence that Gentiles are also recipients of the Holy Spirit.

In response, Peter commands that they be baptised in water (v. 48), thus completing the triadic process of initiation. Although the order is reversed compared to Acts 8, the three elements faith, Spirit baptism, and water baptism are all present and regarded as necessary. The passage highlights that, although the timing may vary, the early church recognised and responded to the necessity of each component in the initiation process.

Acts 19:16 – Doctrinal Clarification and Apostolic Correction

In Ephesus, Paul encounters disciples who had received only John's baptism (v.3). His inquiry *'Did you receive the Holy Spirit when you believed?'* (v.2) suggests that Paul did not assume Spirit baptism to be automatic upon belief.

Upon discovering their limited understanding, Paul re-baptizes them in the name of the Lord Jesus (v.5) and lays hands on them to receive the Holy Spirit, resulting in speaking in tongues and prophecy (v.6). This account reveals the apostolic priority in ensuring that each believer's experience of Christian initiation was complete and aligned with apostolic teaching. Paul's approach reflects a pastoral and doctrinal concern for both orthodoxy and spiritual empowerment.

Each account portrays the apostles as active agents in guiding new believers through all three stages of the faith. Theologically, this triadic pattern may be seen as a reflection of Trinitarian engagement in the life of the believer: the call of the Father through the gospel (conversion), identification with Christ through water baptism, and empowerment by the Holy Spirit.

The accounts in Acts 8, 10, and 19 demonstrate that the apostles upheld a comprehensive model of Christian initiation that involved personal faith, water baptism, and reception of the Holy Spirit. This model was neither mechanical nor legalistic, but intentional and pastoral. It ensured that believers were fully integrated into the life of the church, both in terms of doctrine and spiritual experience. The modern church may benefit from revisiting this apostolic pattern as it seeks to cultivate spiritually mature and fully initiated disciples.

Ethical Leadership

Ethical leadership is a crucial element within the context of the Apostolic Mandate. It involves leading with integrity, honesty, and a strong commitment to ethical principles and moral values. Ethical leaders prioritise doing what is right, both in their personal lives and in their interactions with others, as they seek to align their leadership with the teachings of Jesus Christ.

At the foundation of ethical leadership is a deep understanding of and adherence to ethical principles. Ethical leaders strive to make decisions and take actions that are guided by moral values such as honesty, fairness, respect, and justice. They uphold the sanctity of human life, promote equality, and demonstrate a genuine concern for the well-being and dignity of all individuals.

Ethical leaders demonstrate transparency and accountability in their actions. They are open and honest in their communication, ensuring that information is shared appropriately and responsibly. They take responsibility for their decisions and actions, admitting mistakes when necessary and taking steps to rectify them.

Integrity is a foundational characteristic of ethical leadership. Ethical leaders consistently align their actions with their words and values. They operate with consistency and reliability, earning the trust and respect of those they lead. They prioritise moral courage, standing up for what is right even in the face of opposition or difficult circumstances.

Ethical leaders foster a culture of ethical behaviour within their organisations or communities. They set clear expectations and standards for ethical conduct and hold themselves and others accountable to these standards. They encourage open dialogue and provide channels for individuals to voice ethical concerns or report unethical behaviour without fear of retaliation.

Ethical leaders recognise the importance of empathy and compassion in their leadership. They consider the impact of their decisions and actions on others, taking into account the needs, concerns, and perspectives of those affected. They treat others with dignity and respect, valuing the diversity and inherent worth of every individual.

They prioritise the well-being of their followers over personal gain or ambition. They seek to serve others and promote the common good rather than advancing their interests. They make decisions that consider the long-term consequences and strive to create sustainable and positive outcomes for all stakeholders involved.

In the Apostolic Mandate, ethical leaders lead by example, reflecting the character of Jesus Christ. They embody love, humility, and a servant's heart in their interactions with others. They prioritise the spiritual growth and well-being of those they lead, nurturing a culture of grace, forgiveness, and transformation.

Ethical leaders recognise the significance of ethical decision-making in fulfilling the Apostolic Mandate. They engage in prayerful discernment, seeking the guidance of the Holy Spirit and aligning their decisions with biblical principles. They understand that their leadership carries a profound responsibility to reflect God's character and advance His Kingdom on Earth.

As ethical leaders embrace their role within the Apostolic Mandate, they become beacons of light and hope in a world that often lacks ethical leadership. Their leadership serves as a testament to the transformative power of the Gospel, as they lead with integrity, compassion, and a commitment to upholding ethical principles. Through ethical leadership, they contribute to the advancement of the Apostolic Mandate, bringing the Kingdom of God to their spheres of influence with integrity and righteousness.

Missional Leadership

Missional leadership is a crucial aspect within the context of the Apostolic Mandate. It involves leading with a focus on the mission of God, aligning leadership practices and decisions with the call to bring the Kingdom of God to every sphere of influence. Missional leaders are driven by a deep sense of purpose and a passion to make a transformative impact in the world.

This is a commitment to the Great Commission, which calls believers to go and make disciples of all nations. Missional leaders recognise that their leadership is not confined to the walls of the church but extends to every aspect of life, including the workplace, community, and beyond. They seek to mobilise and equip believers to fulfil the Apostolic Mandate in all spheres of society.

Missional leaders are attentive to the leading of the Holy Spirit. They rely on His guidance and empowerment to discern the needs, opportunities, and strategies necessary to effectively reach and impact their spheres of influence. They foster a culture of listening to and obeying the prompting of the Holy Spirit, allowing Him to lead them into new territories and initiatives for the sake of the Gospel.

Missional leaders cultivate a mindset of servant-heartedness and selflessness. They prioritise the needs of others, demonstrating a genuine concern for the spiritual, emotional, and physical well-being of those they lead. They empower individuals to discover and utilise their gifts and talents for the mission, equipping them to engage with the world around them effectively.

Also, they nurture a culture of evangelism and discipleship. They encourage believers to actively share their faith, engage in meaningful relationships with unbelievers, and demonstrate the love and grace of Christ in their interactions. They equip individuals to articulate and live out their faith in ways that are relevant and impactful within their specific contexts.

Collaboration and partnership are integral to missional leadership. Missional leaders recognise that the Apostolic

Mandate is not an individual endeavour but requires the collective effort of the body of Christ. They actively seek out opportunities to collaborate with other churches, organisations, and individuals who share the same mission and vision. They foster a spirit of unity, recognising that the collective impact of the Church is far greater than individual efforts.

Missional leaders embrace innovation and adaptability. They are willing to explore new approaches, strategies, and technologies to effectively engage with the ever-changing cultural landscape. They encourage creative thinking and problem-solving, enabling individuals to respond contextually to the needs and challenges of their respective spheres of influence.

They prioritise justice, compassion, and the pursuit of societal transformation. They advocate for the marginalised, address systemic issues, and work towards bringing about social, economic, and spiritual change. They engage with the pressing issues of their communities, seeking to bring healing, restoration, and reconciliation.

Through missional leadership, believers are empowered to become agents of transformation, carrying the light of the Gospel into every aspect of society. Missional leaders model a life of purpose, inspire others to live out their faith authentically, and cultivate a culture of missional living within their spheres of influence. They lead with a sense of urgency, recognising the eternal significance of their mission.

Let missional leaders arise, sanctioned by the Holy Spirit, to lead with courage, compassion, and a deep commitment to the mission of God. Let us embrace missional leadership as a sacred calling, bringing the

Kingdom of God to our spheres of influence with intentionality and perseverance. Through missional leadership, may we see lives transformed, communities impacted, and the Gospel proclaimed to the ends of the earth.

Conclusion

From pastoral leadership to servant leadership, from organisational leadership to ethical leadership, and spiritual leadership to missional leadership, we have seen how each form of leadership plays a significant role in fulfilling the call to bring the Kingdom of God to our spheres of influence.

Leadership within the Apostolic Mandate goes beyond positions and titles; it is about influence, service, and empowering others. It is about leading with integrity, humility, and a deep reliance on the guidance of the Holy Spirit. As leaders, we have the privilege and responsibility to shepherd, equip, and empower those entrusted to our care, creating environments where individuals can grow spiritually, discover their purpose, and impact the world around them.

Let us remember that leadership within the Apostolic Mandate is a sacred calling. It is a calling to serve, to guide, and to empower others, reflecting the character and teachings of Jesus Christ. It is a calling to lead with love, humility, and a deep dependence on the Holy Spirit, acknowledging that true transformation and impact come through the power of God.

Together, as leaders within the Apostolic Mandate, let us rise, united in purpose, and make a lasting impact in the lives of those we lead and the world around us.

VOLKER AND DORINE M. KRÜGER

CHAPTER TEN

KINGDOM THEOLOGY IDENTITY

OUR KINGDOM IDENTITY is critical for fulfilling our purpose in bringing the Kingdom of God to our spheres of influence. It is the recognition that, as followers of Christ, we are citizens of the Kingdom of God. We are called to live out our identity as children of God, ambassadors of His Kingdom, and agents of transformation in the world. This chapter explores the biblical teachings and theological foundations that inform our understanding of Kingdom Theology Identity.

Understanding our Kingdom Theology Identity shapes our worldview, impacting how we perceive ourselves, others, and the world around us. It enables us to see beyond the temporal and earthly, embracing an eternal perspective rooted in God's Kingdom values of love, justice, righteousness, and peace. Our Kingdom identity compels us to pursue holistic transformation in every area of life, including individual hearts, relationships, communities, and societal structures.

This chapter will explain the practical implications of Kingdom Theology Identity in our daily lives. We will examine how our Kingdom identity influences our relationships, work, engagement with culture, and pursuit of justice and compassion. Kingdom Theology Identity empowers us to live with purpose and passion, as we align our lives with God's purposes and partner with Him in bringing His Kingdom on Earth as it is in Heaven.

Together, let us grasp the significance of our identity as citizens of the Kingdom and embrace the responsibility and privilege that come with it. Be transformed by the renewing of our minds, aligning our thoughts, attitudes, and actions with the truth of God's Kingdom, and advancing His Kingdom in every sphere of influence.

Understanding the Kingdom of God

To fully grasp our kingdom theology identity within the apostolic mandate, it is crucial to have a deep understanding of the kingdom of God. The kingdom of God is not merely a physical realm or a political entity, but it encompasses the reign and rule of God in every aspect of creation. It is the manifestation of God's divine sovereignty, authority, and redemptive work in the world.

The kingdom of God is rooted in god's plan for creation and redemption. It is the fulfilment of his covenant promises and the ultimate expression of his love, righteousness, and justice. Through the life, death, and resurrection of Jesus Christ, the kingdom of God was inaugurated, and believers are invited to participate in its advancement.

One essential aspect of the kingdom of God is that it operates on principles different from those of the kingdoms of this world. It transcends political systems, cultural norms, and human ideologies. The kingdom of God is marked by righteousness, love, mercy, and peace. It is a realm where God's will is perfectly done, where brokenness is healed, and where relationships are restored.

The kingdom of God means recognising its already-but-not-yet nature. The kingdom has been inaugurated through Jesus Christ's work, but its full realisation awaits his second coming. In the meantime, believers are called to live as kingdom citizens, bearing witness to its values and working towards its fulfilment.

The kingdom of God is not limited to a physical or geographical realm. It extends to every sphere of influence, including the church, families, education, arts, media, business, and government. As believers, we are called to be salt and light in these spheres, representing the values of the kingdom and seeking to transform them according to god's will.

Our understanding of the kingdom of God shapes our identity as a kingdom theology. It reminds us that we are participants in god's redemptive work, co-labourers with Christ, and ambassadors of his kingdom. It calls us to live in alignment with the principles of the kingdom, seeking justice, loving mercy, and walking humbly with our god.

Kingdom Mission and Purpose

Central to our Kingdom Theology Identity within the Apostolic Mandate is the understanding of the Kingdom Mission and Purpose. As citizens of the Kingdom, we are called to actively participate in God's mission, joining Him in the work of bringing His Kingdom to every sphere of influence. Our purpose is to advance the redemptive purposes of God and participate in the transformation of individuals, communities, and society as a whole.

The mission of God is rooted in His love for humanity and His desire to reconcile all things to Himself. It is a mission of restoration, healing, and redemption. As believers, we are entrusted with the task of proclaiming the good news of the Kingdom, making disciples, and demonstrating the love and power of God in our words and actions.

Our purpose as Kingdom citizens is to reflect the character and values of the Kingdom in every aspect of our lives. We are called to love God with all our heart, soul, mind, and strength, and to love our neighbours as ourselves. Our purpose is to live out the principles of the Kingdom in our relationships, work, and interactions with the world.

Kingdom Mission and Purpose are not limited to specific ministries or roles within the church. They encompass every area of life, encompassing the full spectrum of human existence. Whether we are teachers, healthcare workers, business professionals, artists, parents, or community leaders, we are called to engage with the world around us as ambassadors of the Kingdom.

Our mission and purpose in the Kingdom involve both proclamation and demonstration. We are called to proclaim the gospel of the Kingdom, sharing the message of salvation and hope found in Jesus Christ. At the same time, we are called to demonstrate the power and love of God through acts of compassion, justice, and service to others.

Accepting our Kingdom Mission and Purpose requires an active and intentional approach. It involves discerning the leading of the Holy Spirit, seeking opportunities to share the gospel, and engaging in acts of service and justice. It means being attentive to the needs of others, advocating for the marginalised, and working towards the holistic transformation of individuals and communities.

As we fulfil our Kingdom Mission and Purpose, we participate in the fulfilment of the Apostolic Mandate. We bring the reality of the Kingdom of God into the brokenness of the world, impacting lives, communities, and systems. We recognise that our mission is not accomplished in our strength but through the empowering presence of the Holy Spirit, who equips and enables us for the task at hand.

Kingdom Witness and Evangelism

Kingdom Witness focuses on proclaiming and demonstrating the reality of God's Kingdom on earth. Believers seek to reflect the love, justice, mercy, and transformative power of the Kingdom in their words and actions. Their witness is rooted in their relationship with Jesus and the transformation they have experienced through His grace.

It encompasses both proclamation and demonstration of the Gospel. Believers not only communicate the message of salvation but also engage in acts of compassion, justice, and service. This holistic approach reflects the heart of God, who desires to see all aspects of human life redeemed and restored.

Kingdom witness involves building authentic relationships with others. Believers seek to understand people's stories, listen to their concerns, and demonstrate genuine care and empathy. By cultivating meaningful connections, they create opportunities to share the Gospel and demonstrate the love of Christ in practical ways.

Includes boldly proclaiming the Gospel, sharing the story of Jesus, His life, death, and resurrection. Believers communicate the transformative power of the Gospel, inviting others to experience forgiveness, reconciliation, and abundant life in Christ. They share the hope and joy found in the Kingdom of God and its implications for personal salvation.

It involves demonstrating God's power through signs, wonders, and the manifestation of the Holy Spirit. Believers rely on the Holy Spirit to empower them to minister in the supernatural, praying for healing, deliverance, and spiritual breakthrough. These demonstrations of Kingdom power point to the reality of God's reign and awaken faith in those who witness them.

Kingdom witness incorporates a prophetic voice that challenges societal norms, speaks out against injustice, and advocates for righteousness. Believers engage in cultural critique, addressing systemic issues and advocating for the oppressed and marginalised. They boldly confront the powers and structures that hinder the full realisation of God's Kingdom on earth.

The Identity of Kingdom Citizens

As believers within the Apostolic Mandate, we are called to embrace our identity as citizens of the Kingdom. Understanding and living out our identity as Kingdom citizens is essential for fulfilling the mission of bringing the Kingdom of God to our spheres of influence. Our identity shapes our beliefs, values, and actions as we seek to reflect the character of God and participate in His redemptive work.

As citizens of the Kingdom, our primary identity is found in Christ. Our past no longer defines us, our accomplishments, or our social standing. Our identity is rooted in being children of God, redeemed by the blood of Jesus, and recipients of His grace and mercy. We are called to live in the freedom and fullness of our identity in Christ.

Our identity as citizens of the Kingdom also encompasses our relationship with God. We are His beloved children, chosen and adopted into His family. We have direct access to the Father through Jesus Christ and the empowering presence of the Holy Spirit in our lives. Our identity as Kingdom citizens means that we are intimately connected to God, able to commune with Him, and recipients of His love, guidance, and provision.

As Kingdom citizens, we are called to reflect the character and values of the Kingdom. We are called to live in righteousness, love, justice, and humility. Our identity is marked by qualities such as faith, hope, and perseverance in the face of challenges. We are called to be a light in the darkness, bearing witness to the transformative power of God's Kingdom in our lives.

Our identity as citizens of the Kingdom also implies that we are participants in God's redemptive work. We are called to bring healing, restoration, and reconciliation to a broken world. Our identity equips us to engage in acts of compassion, justice, and mercy. We are called to stand against injustice, to advocate for the marginalised, and to work towards the holistic transformation of individuals and communities.

Agreeing to our identity as citizens of the Kingdom involves a transformation of our minds, hearts, and actions. It means aligning our thoughts, attitudes, and behaviours with the truth of God's Word and the principles of His Kingdom. It means surrendering our desires and ambitions to the lordship of Christ and allowing Him to shape our identity and guide our lives.

Living out our identity as citizens of the Kingdom is not without challenges. We may face opposition, persecution, and the temptations of this world. However, we can draw strength and encouragement from our identity in Christ and the promise of His presence with us. Our identity as citizens of the Kingdom empowers us to overcome obstacles, persevere in faith, and make a lasting impact on the world around us.

We are part of a global and diverse body of believers. Our identity transcends cultural, ethnic, and social boundaries. We are united in our commitment to follow Christ, to love one another, and to advance the Kingdom of God together.

Our identity as citizens of the Kingdom shapes our beliefs, values, and actions. It permits us to live as salt and light in the world, bringing the transformative power of God's Kingdom to our spheres of influence. Understanding the Kingdom of God has a profound impact on our identity, worldview, and engagement with the world. Here is how it can shape these aspects of our lives:

It reminds us that we are children of God, redeemed and loved by Him. Our identity is no longer defined by the world's standards or our achievements, but by our relationship with God. This understanding frees us from seeking validation and significance from worldly sources, empowering us to live confidently as citizens of the Kingdom.

The Kingdom of God provides a lens through which we view the world. It shapes our perspective on reality, purpose, and the meaning of life. We understand that the world is fallen and broken, but we also have hope in God's redemptive work. Our worldview is rooted in God's sovereignty, love, justice, and the ultimate triumph of His Kingdom. This perspective enables us to see beyond the temporal and the superficial, focusing on eternal values and the pursuit of God's purposes in all aspects of life.

It compels us to engage with the world in transformative ways. We recognise that our purpose is not to isolate ourselves from the world, but to bring the reality of God's Kingdom into every sphere of influence. It influences how we interact with others, how we approach our work, and how we navigate societal issues. Our engagement with the world is marked by love, compassion, justice, and the proclamation of the Gospel, as we seek to make a positive impact and bring about Kingdom transformation.

The Kingdom of God shapes our values and priorities. We align our lives with Kingdom principles such as love, righteousness, justice, and mercy. Our values are no longer dictated solely by societal norms or personal preferences but by the standards set by God's Kingdom. This impacts our decision-making, relationships, stewardship of resources, and pursuit of justice. We prioritise what is of eternal significance and seek to honour God in all that we do.

We know that ultimately, God's Kingdom will triumph over all darkness and evil. This perspective gives us the strength to persevere, to stand against injustice, and to overcome obstacles in our pursuit of God's purposes. It reminds us that our efforts are not in vain, as we participate in God's redemptive work.

This Kingdom fosters a spirit of collaboration and unity among believers. We recognise that our identity as Kingdom citizens transcends cultural, ethnic, and social boundaries. We embrace the diversity of the body of Christ and work together to advance the Kingdom. This collaborative mindset enables us to learn from one another, support and encourage each other, and have a greater impact on the world around us.

Kingdom Community and Unity

The Kingdom of God has significant implications for believers in fostering community and unity. It transcends cultural, racial, and social boundaries, calling believers to embrace a shared identity as citizens of the Kingdom.

This Kingdom community celebrates and values the diversity of its members. Believers recognise that all individuals, regardless of their background or social status, are equally valued and loved by God. In the Kingdom community, diverse cultures, ethnicities, and backgrounds are characterised by mutual love, support, and care for one another.

Believers are called to bear one another's burdens, encourage one another, and extend grace and forgiveness. They prioritise the building of healthy relationships and strive to create an environment where individuals feel safe, valued, and affirmed.

Kingdom unity transcends personal preferences and differences. Believers strive to foster unity within the body of Christ by prioritising common values, a shared purpose, and a focus on Christ. They actively work to overcome divisions, promote reconciliation, and pursue a spirit of unity amidst diversity. Kingdom unity reflects the love and grace of God and testifies to the power of the Gospel.

The Kingdom community encourages collaboration and cooperation among believers. Recognising that they are part of a larger body, believers join in pursuing Kingdom initiatives, such as evangelism, discipleship, and acts of justice and mercy. They support and empower one another to use their gifts and talents for the edification of the community and the advancement of the Kingdom.

Kingdom community promotes a culture of servant leadership, where individuals humbly serve one another and the broader community. Leaders within the Kingdom community exemplify Christ's servant-heartedness, leading by example and empowering others to serve. Servant leadership promotes a sense of equality, respect, and shared responsibility among believers.

It extends its impact beyond its boundaries, seeking to influence and transform the wider society. Believers in the Kingdom community are committed to engaging in acts of justice, advocating for the marginalised, and being agents of societal transformation. Their collective witness in the world demonstrates the transformative power of the Kingdom and mirrors the values of love, justice, and compassion.

Kingdom Authority and Power

As citizens of this Kingdom, we have been entrusted with the authority and power of God to advance His Kingdom on Earth. This authority and power are not derived from our abilities or accomplishments but are rooted in our relationship with God and our alignment with His purposes.

Kingdom Authority refers to the delegated power and authority that God has bestowed upon believers to carry out His purposes on Earth. It is the authority to represent and act on behalf of the King, Jesus Christ. This authority is rooted in Jesus's victory over sin, death, and the powers of darkness through His life, death, and resurrection. As citizens of the Kingdom, we have been given the authority to proclaim the Gospel, to heal the sick, to cast out demons, and to bring about spiritual transformation in individuals and communities.

Our Kingdom Authority means recognising that our words, actions, and prayers have power and impact. It means operating in the confidence that comes from knowing the King of kings has given us authority. This authority is not to be taken lightly but exercised with humility, integrity, and in alignment with the will of God.

Kingdom Power refers to the supernatural and transformative power of God that works in and through believers. It is the power of the Holy Spirit, who empowers us to fulfil the Apostolic Mandate. This power enables us to live victoriously, to overcome the forces of darkness, and to manifest the presence and love of God in tangible ways.

Understanding Kingdom Power involves relying on the Holy Spirit and allowing Him to work in and through us. It means seeking the infilling and empowerment of the Holy Spirit to carry out the work of the Kingdom. It is through the power of the Holy Spirit that we can perform miracles, experience spiritual breakthroughs, and demonstrate the transformative nature of God's Kingdom.

Exercising Kingdom Authority and Power requires a posture of surrender and obedience to God. It involves aligning our will with His, seeking His guidance, and operating in accordance with His Word. It requires a life of intimacy with God, cultivating a deep relationship with Him through prayer, study of His Word, and worship.

As we exercise Kingdom Authority and Power, we are called to be vessels through which God's love, grace, and power flow. It is not about exalting us but about magnifying the name of Jesus and bringing glory to God. We are called to use our authority and power to serve others, to bring healing and restoration, and to advance the Kingdom of God in every sphere of influence.

Understanding our Kingdom Authority and Power enables us to stand firm against the enemy's schemes, to break strongholds, and to release captives from bondage. It equips us to confront injustice, to bring about societal transformation, and to manifest the values and principles of God's Kingdom in the world.

As we exercise our Kingdom Authority and Power, let us do so with humility, dependence on the Holy Spirit, and in alignment with the heart and will of God. May our exercise of authority and power always reflect the character and love of Jesus Christ, drawing others to experience the transformative power of the Kingdom. May we fulfil the Apostolic Mandate by boldly and faithfully utilising the authority and power entrusted to us, advancing the Kingdom of God in every sphere of influence?

Living Kingdom Values

Living out Kingdom values is essential to embracing our Kingdom Theology Identity within the Apostolic Mandate. As citizens of the Kingdom, our lives should reflect the values and principles of God's Kingdom in every area. Here are notable Kingdom values and how they shape our lives:

Love is at the heart of God's Kingdom. It is a selfless, sacrificial love that extends to all people, regardless of their background or circumstances. As Kingdom citizens, we are called to love God with all our heart, soul, mind, and strength, and to love our neighbours as ourselves. Love permeates every aspect of our lives, influencing our attitudes, actions, and relationships. It compels us to seek reconciliation, to show compassion, and to work for justice and equality.

Righteousness is an integral value of God's Kingdom. It is the state of being in right relationship with God, characterised by living in obedience to His commands and adhering to His moral standards. As Kingdom citizens, we are called to pursue righteousness in our thoughts, words, and actions. This involves aligning our lives with the truth of God's Word, practising integrity, and seeking justice and righteousness in all areas of life.

Humility is a counter-cultural value in a world that often exalts self-promotion and pride. In God's Kingdom, humility is esteemed. It involves recognising our dependence on God, acknowledging our limitations, and esteeming others above ourselves. Kingdom citizens are called to serve others with humility, using our gifts and resources to bless and uplift others rather than seeking personal gain or recognition.

Forgiveness is a transformative Kingdom value. It involves releasing others from the debt of their offences, just as God has forgiven us through Christ. As Kingdom citizens, we are called to forgive others, even when it is difficult, and to seek reconciliation and restoration. Forgiveness breaks the cycle of bitterness, allowing the healing power of God's love to flow in our relationships and communities.

Compassion is a hallmark of the Kingdom of God. It involves having empathy and concern for the suffering and needs of others. Kingdom citizens are called to demonstrate compassion by caring for the poor, the marginalised, and the oppressed. We are called to be advocates for justice, to stand against injustice and oppression, and to work towards the holistic well-being of individuals and communities.

Faithfulness is a key Kingdom value. It involves steadfastness, loyalty, and commitment to God and His purposes. Kingdom citizens are called to be faithful stewards of the resources, talents, and opportunities entrusted to them. It means remaining true to our commitments, persevering in the face of challenges, and living with integrity and consistency.

Hope is a powerful Kingdom value that sustains us in difficult times. It is the confident expectation that God's promises will be fulfilled. As citizens of the Kingdom, we carry the hope of the Gospel, knowing that God is at work, even in darkness and uncertainty. This hope empowers us to persevere, to bring encouragement to others, and to be a beacon of light in a world longing for hope.

Living out Kingdom values is not always easy, and we may face opposition and challenges. However, through the power of the Holy Spirit, we can align our lives with these values and reflect the character of God's Kingdom. As we do so, we become agents of transformation, impacting lives, communities, and systems.

Let us strive to embody these Kingdom values in our daily lives, within our families, workplaces, and communities. May our lives reflect the love, righteousness, humility, forgiveness, compassion, faithfulness, and hope of God's Kingdom. As we live out these values, we bring the reality of the Kingdom of God to our spheres of influence and fulfil the Apostolic Mandate of advancing the Kingdom in every aspect of life.

Kingdom Ethics and Social Justice

The Kingdom of God is characterised by love, justice, mercy, and compassion. As citizens of the Kingdom, believers are called to embody these values in their attitudes, actions, and relationships. Kingdom ethics shape believers' understanding of justice as seeking to restore right relationships, challenging unjust systems, and advocating for the rights and dignity of all individuals.

Throughout Scripture, God's heart for social justice is evident. The prophets spoke out against oppression and injustice, and Jesus's ministry was characterised by a concern for the marginalised and vulnerable. Understanding the Kingdom of God compels believers to follow this biblical mandate by actively engaging in acts of justice and working towards systemic transformation.

Kingdom ethics go beyond individual acts of charity to address the root causes of systemic injustice. It calls believers to challenge and dismantle structures that perpetuate inequality, discrimination, and oppression. This involves advocating for equitable social policies, engaging in community organising, and supporting initiatives that empower marginalised communities.

Kingdom ethics prompt believers to respond to human suffering with compassion and empathy. It motivates them to alleviate the physical, emotional, and spiritual needs of others through acts of service and mercy. This includes caring for the poor, the marginalised, the sick, and the oppressed, seeking to bring healing, restoration, and hope to individuals and communities.

Kingdom ethics emphasises the importance of reconciliation and peace-making. Believers are called to be agents of reconciliation, promoting unity and seeking to reconcile relationships that have been broken by injustice or conflict. They are also called to be peacemakers, actively working towards peace in their communities and advocating for nonviolent approaches to resolving conflicts.

They empower believers to speak out against injustice and use their voices to advocate for change. It encourages them to stand in solidarity with the marginalised and oppressed, amplifying their voices and advocating for their rights. Believers are called to be prophetic voices in society, challenging unjust systems and calling for transformation.

Kingdom Living in Everyday Life

Understanding the Kingdom of God has a profound impact on how believers live out their faith in their daily lives. It transforms their perspectives, priorities, and interactions, shaping every aspect of their existence. Here are some key aspects to consider when discussing Kingdom living in everyday life:

Begins with a transformed mindset. Believers are called to adopt a Kingdom perspective, seeing the world through the lens of God's reign and rule. This mindset acknowledges God's sovereignty, aligns with His values, and seeks to bring His Kingdom principles into every aspect of life.

Involves seeking God's will in all decisions and actions. It means surrendering personal desires and submitting to God's leading in every area of life. Believers strive to align their thoughts, attitudes, and choices with God's purposes, seeking to bring His Kingdom to bear in their circumstances.

Kingdom living underscores the centrality of a personal and intimate relationship with God. Believers prioritise cultivating a vibrant prayer life, studying Scripture, and seeking the guidance of the Holy Spirit. They rely on God's wisdom, strength, and grace to navigate life's challenges and make decisions that align with His Kingdom values.

It impacts how believers engage in relationships. It promotes love, forgiveness, reconciliation, and the pursuit of unity. Believers strive to exhibit the fruit of the Spirit (Galatians 5:22-23) in their interactions, treating others with kindness, compassion, and respect. They prioritise building healthy, Christ-centred relationships that reflect the love and grace of God's Kingdom.

Comprises a mindset of stewardship, recognising that everything belongs to God. Believers view their time, talents, and resources as gifts to be used for God's purposes. They prioritise generosity, using their blessings to bless others and advance the work of the Kingdom. This includes being good stewards of the environment, advocating for justice, and meeting the needs of those in need.

Kingdom living compels believers to be salt and light in the world (Matthew 5:13-16). They actively engage with their communities, seeking opportunities to share the Gospel, serve others, and bring about positive change. Whether in their workplaces, neighbourhoods, or social circles, believers seek to make a difference by embodying Kingdom values and demonstrating God's love in practical ways.

Kingdom Hope and Future

Hope is an integral part of our Kingdom Theology Identity within the Apostolic Mandate. As citizens of the Kingdom, we have a unique perspective on the future and a steadfast hope in the fulfilment of God's Kingdom. Understanding Kingdom Hope and Future empowers us to navigate life's challenges, pursue God's purposes, and eagerly anticipate the fullness of His Kingdom.

Kingdom Hope is rooted in God's promises. Throughout Scripture, God reveals His plans for the redemption and restoration of all things. He promises to make all things new, to wipe away every tear, and to dwell among His people. This hope in God's promises sustains us in times of uncertainty, reminding us that God is faithful, and His plans will ultimately come to pass.

While we experience the presence of God's Kingdom in part here and now, we eagerly anticipate its complete realisation when Jesus returns. This hope gives us a sense of purpose, knowing that our current efforts in advancing the Kingdom are not in vain. We work confidently, knowing that our labour contributes to the ultimate fulfilment of God's redemptive purposes. Kingdom Hope looks forward to the future fulfilment of God's Kingdom.

It shifts our focus from the temporal to the eternal, from the transient to the everlasting, through granting us an eternal perspective on life. We recognise that the challenges and sufferings of this present age are temporary, while the joy and glory of the Kingdom to come will far surpass them. This perspective enables us to endure hardships, to persevere in faith, and hold fast to our hope in God's Kingdom, knowing that the best is yet to come.

Kingdom Hope inspires us to live transformed lives. We recognise that the power of God's Kingdom is at work within us, shaping us into the image of Christ and equipping us for Kingdom living. This hope compels us to live with intentionality, seeking to reflect the values and character of the Kingdom in all that we do. It motivates us to pursue righteousness, love, and justice, knowing that our actions have eternal significance.

As citizens of the Kingdom, we are called to be carriers of hope, sharing the good news of God's Kingdom with a world in need. We have the privilege of inviting others into the hope and future that God offers through Christ. Through our words and actions, we can bring hope to the hopeless, healing to the broken, and a glimpse of the Kingdom's reality to those who have lost sight of it.

Kingdom Hope fuels our anticipation and preparation for the coming of God's Kingdom. We live with a sense of urgency, knowing that the time is short and that we are called to make the most of every opportunity to advance the Kingdom. This hope prompts us to live holy and obedient lives, pursue spiritual growth, and be actively engaged in Kingdom work until the day of Christ's return.

Kingdom Discipleship

Kingdom discipleship centres on following Jesus as the ultimate model and example. Believers seek to emulate His character, teachings, and ministry. They study His life and teachings, allowing His example to shape their attitudes, values, and actions. Kingdom discipleship entails a lifelong commitment to growing in intimacy with Jesus and reflecting His love and grace to others.

This type of discipleship involves intentional spiritual formation, which includes practices such as prayer, Bible study, worship, meditation, and the cultivation of spiritual disciplines. Believers recognise the importance of nurturing their relationship with God, allowing the Holy Spirit to transform their hearts, minds, and lives. They actively engage in practices that draw them closer to God and deepen their understanding of His Kingdom.

Living out Kingdom values, which include practising love, justice, mercy, forgiveness, and humility. Kingdom values shape their interactions with others, their approach to decision-making, and their pursuit of holiness. Believers strive to align their lives with the teachings of Jesus, recognising that their actions bear witness to the reality of God's Kingdom on earth.

Engaging in the Kingdom mission to reconcile and restore all things to Himself. Believers are called to join God in His redemptive work, sharing the Gospel, making disciples, and bringing the transformative power of the Kingdom to every sphere of society. Kingdom disciples engage in acts of compassion, seek justice, and actively work towards transforming individuals, communities, and systems.

Discipling others is the responsibility to disciple others and multiply the work of the Kingdom. Believers are called to mentor, teach, and empower others in their journey of faith. They seek to nurture and equip others to become Kingdom disciples, helping them grow in their relationship with Jesus, develop Kingdom values, and participate in God's mission.

Perseverance and Growth: Kingdom discipleship is a lifelong journey marked by perseverance and continuous growth. Believers recognise that discipleship is not a one-time event but a process of ongoing transformation. They embrace the challenges, setbacks, and joys that come with following Jesus, knowing that God's grace and presence sustain them along the way.

Conclusion

The practice of laying on of hands is more than a ritual; it is a sacred act that embodies divine partnership. Whether used in commissioning leaders, ministering healing, imparting spiritual gifts, or affirming someone in prayer, this biblical practice serves as a visible expression of invisible grace. It marks moments of spiritual significance and signals a divine endorsement that should not be taken lightly.

For those called to minister in this way, three priorities emerge clearly: discernment, humility, and accountability. Laying on of hands must always be preceded by a heart submitted to the Holy Spirit. Ministers must be led by God's voice, not pressured by emotion or expectation. When done rightly, this act strengthens the Church, reinforces unity, and opens hearts to the transformative work of God.

For those receiving ministry, this act should be approached with faith and a spirit of understanding. The laying on of hands is not a performance, nor is it a shortcut to maturity. It is a means through which God affirms, heals, empowers, and directs. Those who receive must remain anchored in the Word and rooted in discipleship.

As the Church continues to grow in its understanding of spiritual authority and function, we must preserve the sanctity of this practice. Let us train others with wisdom, protect the vulnerable with ethical clarity, and always remember that every hand extended in the name of Christ should reflect the heart of Christ, gentle, powerful, and holy.

In all things, let us endeavour to keep our hands clean, our motives pure, and our ministries marked by love and obedience to the Chief Shepherd, who laid His hands on us first by laying down His life.

VOLKER AND DORINE M. KRÜGER

CHAPTER ELEVEN

IS CHRISTIANITY MOVING TOWARDS A NEW ERA?

HISTORY REVEALS THAT the Christian faith has never been static. From the early church in Jerusalem to the Great Awakenings, from the Reformation to the global rise of Pentecostalism, Christianity has continuously responded to spiritual, cultural, and generational shifts. In every age, the Spirit of God has stirred believers to discern the times, realign with divine purpose, and step into fresh expressions of faith and mission. Today, the Church stands once again at a crossroads facing seismic changes in worldview, technology, social structure, and spiritual hunger.

There is a growing awareness among leaders and believers alike that we may be witnessing the early tremors of a new era of Christianity one that calls for greater authenticity, deeper discipleship, bold innovation, and radical obedience to the Holy Spirit. This chapter opens up a space for discernment, reflection, and prayerful consideration: not simply to predict the future, but to ask how we are being invited to live, lead, and witness in a changing world while holding fast to an unchanging Gospel.

Historical Perspectives

To gain insights into whether Christianity is moving towards a new era, it is valuable to examine historical perspectives. The study of church history offers a rich tapestry of developments, shifts, and transformations that have shaped Christianity throughout the centuries. By reflecting on past eras and their impact on the Church, we can glean valuable lessons and discern potential patterns that may inform our understanding of the present and future.

The early years of Christianity were characterised by rapid growth, fervent devotion, and the widespread dissemination of the Gospel throughout the Roman Empire. This era witnessed the establishment of foundational doctrines, the formation of the New Testament canon, and the emergence of apostolic leadership. Understanding the challenges, triumphs, and theological debates of this era provides a backdrop for evaluating the current state of Christianity.

The medieval period witnessed significant developments within the Church, including the rise of monasticism, the formation of religious orders, and the establishment of the Roman Catholic Church's dominance. This era also saw the emergence of scholasticism, with theologians like Thomas Aquinas seeking to reconcile faith and reason. Examining the historical context of the medieval era allows us to consider the impact of institutional structures and the tension between religious authority and individual spirituality.

The Reformation in the 16th century marked a significant turning point in Christian history. Reformers such as Martin Luther, John Calvin, and others challenged the doctrinal and institutional practices of the Catholic Church, emphasising the authority of Scripture, salvation by faith alone, and the priesthood of all believers. This era gave rise to new theological perspectives, denominational divisions, and shifts in the relationship between the church and the state.

The modern era saw Christianity engaging with the Enlightenment, scientific discoveries, and the rise of secularism. Theological movements, such as the Great Awakenings and the emergence of evangelicalism, influenced the trajectory of Christianity, emphasising personal conversion, evangelism, and social reform. This era witnessed the expansion of Christianity to new regions through missionary efforts and the birth of global Christianity.

Christianity has continually adapted and responded to changing cultural, intellectual, and societal contexts. Each era brought new challenges, theological insights, and expressions of faith. These historical perspectives invite us to consider how Christianity has evolved and how it may continue to do so in the present and future.

Contemporary Cultural Context

The dynamics of our modern world shape the way people perceive and engage with faith. In the cultural context, we can discern the potential shifts and challenges that may influence the future of Christianity.

The advent of globalisation has connected people and cultures like never before. This interconnectedness enables the exchange of ideas, diverse perspectives, and the rapid dissemination of information. Christianity is no longer confined to specific geographical regions but has become a global phenomenon. This cultural context opens new opportunities for cross-cultural dialogue, collaboration, and the sharing of diverse expressions of faith.

Contemporary culture is characterised by religious pluralism, with various worldviews and belief systems coexisting in proximity. This pluralistic context challenges Christians to engage in respectful dialogue and to navigate the complexities of religious diversity. Additionally, a growing trend towards spirituality, apart from traditional religious structures, poses both opportunities and challenges for Christianity.

The digital age has revolutionised communication, transforming the way people connect, access information, and engage with their faith. Social media, online platforms, and digital resources have provided new avenues for worship, teaching, and community building. Technology has also facilitated the global dissemination of Christian teachings, enabling believers to engage with resources and perspectives from around the world.

Postmodern thought has shaped contemporary culture, challenging traditional authorities, metanarratives, and absolute truths. This cultural context calls for Christians to articulate and live out their faith in ways that resonate with a postmodern audience. Additionally, secularism continues to influence the public sphere, posing questions about the role of faith in societal structures and public discourse.

Contemporary culture is marked by a heightened awareness of social justice issues and a growing desire for activism and change. This context calls Christians to address issues of poverty, inequality, racism, gender discrimination, and environmental stewardship. There is an increasing emphasis on integrating faith and action, as believers seek to embody the values of the Kingdom of God in tangible ways.

Emerging Theology and Doctrine

The theological landscape is continually evolving as scholars, theologians, and communities of faith engage with Scripture, cultural contexts, and contemporary issues. Understanding these emerging theological perspectives is crucial in assessing the direction of Christianity's theological development.

Contextual theology emphasises the importance of interpreting and applying theological principles within specific cultural and social contexts. This approach recognises that the message of the Gospel needs to be communicated in ways that resonate with the experiences and realities of different cultures and communities. Contextual theology emphasises the diversity of expressions within Christianity and fosters a deeper understanding of God's work in the world.

Inclusive theology seeks to challenge and overcome exclusivist narratives by embracing a more expansive understanding of God's love and acceptance. It emphasises the inclusion of marginalised groups, such as women, LGBTQ+ individuals, racial and ethnic minorities, and people with disabilities. Inclusive theology recognises the inherent worth and dignity of all individuals and strives to create spaces where everyone can fully participate in the life of the Church.

Liberation theology emerged in response to the social and economic injustices prevalent in Latin America. It emphasises the Christian call to address systemic oppression and advocates for social, political, and economic transformation. Liberation theology views faith as inseparable from the pursuit of justice, emphasising the preferential option for the poor and marginalised.

Ecological theology acknowledges the interconnectedness of creation and the call to be responsible stewards of the Earth. It recognises the environmental crisis and the imperative for Christians to engage actively in environmental sustainability and care for the planet. Ecological theology invites a holistic understanding of redemption that encompasses both human flourishing and the well-being of the natural world.

Postmodern theology responds to the cultural shifts brought about by postmodernism, questioning traditional assumptions about absolute truth and authority. It encourages a more nuanced and dialogical approach to theological discourse, recognising the multiplicity of perspectives and the importance of engaging with diverse voices. Postmodern theology seeks to embrace the complexities and uncertainties of faith while remaining grounded in the centrality of Christ.

Today's Deconstruction theology, for instance, refers to a process of critically examining and dismantling one's existing beliefs and understanding of traditional Christianity, often leading to a re-evaluation or even abandonment of those beliefs. It involves questioning core doctrines, traditions, and practices within the Christian framework, potentially leading to a reconstruction of faith or a shift away from the original belief system.

As emerging theology and doctrine continue to shape the trajectory of Christianity, it is essential to approach these developments with discernment and a commitment to biblical truth. While embracing new perspectives, it is crucial to evaluate their consistency with Scripture, the Church's historic teachings, and the guidance of the Holy Spirit.

Engaging with emerging theology invites us to be open to growth, to critically examine our beliefs, and to seek a deeper understanding of God's purposes in our world. It challenges us to be attentive to the leading of the Holy Spirit and to be humble learners, recognising that God's truth is multifaceted and can be revealed through various theological perspectives.

Worship and Spirituality

When considering whether Christianity is moving towards a new era, an examination of worship and spirituality is crucial. How we worship and cultivate our spiritual lives reflects our understanding of God, our relationship with Him, and our engagement with the world around us. Exploring the shifts and trends in worship and spirituality provides insights into the evolving dynamics within Christianity.

Contemporary worship has gained prominence in many Christian communities, characterised by a more casual and participatory style. This form of worship often incorporates modern music, multimedia elements, and a focus on creating an engaging and accessible environment. Contemporary worship seeks to connect with contemporary culture and provide a space for personal expression and heartfelt worship.

Alongside contemporary worship, there has been a renewed interest in liturgical and sacramental traditions. Many Christians are rediscovering the richness and depth found in ancient liturgies, the sacraments, and liturgical seasons. This return to liturgical practices can provide a sense of historical continuity, a deep connection to tradition, and a stronger bond with the universal Church.

In response to the fast-paced and fragmented nature of modern life, there has been a growing interest in contemplative practices and a spirituality of presence. Christians are seeking opportunities for silence, stillness, and reflection as they cultivate a deeper awareness of God's presence in their lives. Practices such as meditation, centring prayer, and mindfulness have been embraced as means of connecting with God in the present moment.

Christians are increasingly recognising the importance of holistic spirituality, which integrates faith with all aspects of life. This approach emphasises the integration of spiritual practices, social justice, care for creation, and engagement with the wider world. Holistic spirituality acknowledges that following Christ involves not only personal piety but also a commitment to seek justice, love mercy, and walk humbly with God.

Christianity encompasses a rich tapestry of spiritual traditions, reflecting the cultural, historical, and theological diversity of believers worldwide. Different traditions, such as contemplative, charismatic, monastic, or missional, offer unique ways of encountering God and deepening one's spiritual journey. Embracing diverse expressions of spirituality enables a deeper understanding of the richness and breadth of Christian worship and spiritual practices.

Ecumenical and Interfaith Relations

When considering whether Christianity is moving towards a new era, an examination of ecumenical and interfaith relations is essential. The relationships between different Christian denominations and faith traditions play a significant role in shaping the future of Christianity and its engagement with the wider world. Understanding the dynamics and developments in these areas provides insights into the changing landscape of Christian unity and engagement with other faiths.

Ecumenism refers to the movement towards greater unity among Christian churches and traditions. Ecumenical dialogue and cooperation aim to bridge historical divisions, foster mutual understanding, and promote collaborative efforts in areas of shared concern. Ecumenism recognises the shared beliefs, practices, and missions that bind Christians together, regardless of denominational differences. It encourages Christians to work together, respect one another's traditions, and pursue visible unity rooted in the love of Christ.

Interfaith relations involve engaging with people of different religious beliefs in a spirit of respect, understanding, and dialogue. Interfaith dialogue aims to foster cooperation, explore shared values, and address common societal concerns, recognising the importance of mutual learning, empathy, and cooperation among diverse faith communities. Through interfaith relations, Christians can share their faith while also listening to and learning from others, promoting mutual respect and fostering peaceful coexistence.

Ecumenical and interfaith dialogue encourages Christians to engage in meaningful conversations with those who hold different theological perspectives or faith traditions. These dialogues provide opportunities to deepen understanding, challenge stereotypes, and identify areas of common ground. Such dialogue fosters relationships based on respect, enriches theological and spiritual perspectives, and cultivates a spirit of cooperation for the greater good of society.

In a world marked by divisions and conflicts, the search for unity and common ground is vital. Christians are called to be ambassadors of reconciliation, seeking ways to bridge differences and work towards a more harmonious world. Ecumenical and interfaith relations challenge Christians to examine their own beliefs, confront prejudices, and recognise the shared humanity and dignity of all people.

Ecumenical and interfaith relations also present challenges and opportunities. Differences in theological perspectives, cultural practices, and social contexts can create tensions and misunderstandings. However, these challenges provide opportunities for growth, humility, and deeper theological reflection. Engaging with diverse Christian traditions and other faiths allows for mutual learning, the sharing of spiritual insights, and the discovery of shared values that can contribute to building a more compassionate and just world.

Faith and Technology

In today's interconnected world, the relationship between faith and technology is no longer a peripheral conversation; it is central to how we live, worship, and minister. Technological advancements have radically transformed communication, education, commerce, and social life. Amid this digital revolution, Christians are called to thoughtfully integrate faith with innovation, leveraging new tools while maintaining biblical values. Rather than viewing technology as a threat, the Church can embrace it as a meaningful avenue for outreach, discipleship, and cultural engagement if used with discernment.

Technology now makes it possible for the Church to reach people far beyond physical walls. Through live-streamed services, online worship, and virtual small groups, believers who are homebound, geographically distant, or travelling can remain actively involved in fellowship and spiritual growth. Digital platforms enable inclusive access to the Gospel, providing spiritual nourishment even when physical gatherings are not possible.

Beyond corporate worship, technology offers unprecedented channels for evangelism. Social media, podcasts, blogs, and websites serve as modern pulpits, extending the message of salvation to diverse audiences. The digital world eliminates borders, allowing believers to engage in cross-cultural conversations, address contemporary issues, and demonstrate Christ's love in both word and deed.

Education within the Christian context has also flourished online. From digital libraries and Bible study apps to formal theological courses and mentorship programs, technology equips believers for deeper scriptural engagement. This fosters a culture of lifelong learning, enabling Christians to grow in knowledge and wisdom without being limited by geography or schedule.

Online communities such as discussion groups, prayer chains, and digital mentorship platforms also contribute to the strength of the Body of Christ. These virtual spaces allow believers to share testimonies, offer pastoral care, and form meaningful relationships. While not a substitute for in-person fellowship, digital tools can complement traditional church life by offering encouragement and connection throughout the week.

Technology also supports the Church's missional objectives. Believers can participate in virtual mission trips, donate through online giving platforms, and raise awareness for justice initiatives through digital campaigns. These efforts expand the Church's reach and mobilise resources more quickly and effectively than ever before.

Importantly, technology enables Christians to contribute to the moral and spiritual discourse of our times. Faith-filled perspectives on ethics, justice, and current events can be communicated through vlogs, webinars, and blogs offering biblically grounded insights in the marketplace of ideas. However, this also calls for wisdom. The temptation to pursue popularity over truth or to engage in divisive rhetoric must be resisted. Digital engagement should reflect the character of Christ, marked by truth, compassion, and integrity.

One of the growing trends is online discipleship and spiritual mentoring. Virtual platforms allow for consistent accountability, teaching, and encouragement, even across great distances. However, digital discipleship must be approached with intentionality, ensuring depth and authenticity in relationships. Whenever possible, believers should complement virtual engagements with in-person connections to foster holistic growth.

Another area where technology intersects with faith is in advocacy. Christians can utilise digital media to amplify the voices of the voiceless, advocate for justice, and address pressing social concerns. Online petitions, fundraising efforts, and awareness campaigns offer tangible ways to embody Micah 6:8's call to act justly, love mercy, and walk humbly with God. Still, ethical caution is required; virtue-signalling and shallow activism must give way to long-term commitment and Spirit-led action.

However, the ethical challenges of technology are real. Issues such as data privacy, artificial intelligence, and digital addiction demand careful theological reflection. Christians are called to be thoughtful stewards of these tools, asking not just what is possible but what is right. Responsible use involves protecting human dignity, respecting personal boundaries, and promoting the well-being of all.

This discussion must also include theological engagement. As technology reshapes our understanding of time, relationships, and identity, believers must reflect biblically on what it means to be human in the digital age. Questions about embodiment, presence, creativity, and rest are not merely philosophical; they are deeply spiritual. Christian theology provides rich resources for navigating this space, reminding us that while tools may evolve, our calling remains rooted in love, community, and stewardship.

Finally, the Church cannot ignore the digital divide. Many communities, especially in rural or low-income areas, lack access to the very tools that could enhance their spiritual and social well-being. Addressing this inequity is a gospel issue. Supporting digital literacy programs, advocating for inclusive policies, and partnering with tech-enabled missions can ensure that no one is left behind in the digital age.

Conclusion

Christianity is not at a standstill. Across continents and cultures, in digital spaces and sacred sanctuaries, among scholars and everyday believers, there is an unmistakable stirring. The Church is responding to new questions, complex realities, and opportunities that no previous generation could have fully anticipated. From the rapid rise of technology to the reawakening of spiritual hunger, from calls for justice to theological re-examinations, we are witnessing both disruption and divine invitation.

History has shown us that God often breathes new life into the Church during times of great transition in the world. The early Church rose within a pagan empire; the Reformation challenged long-standing structures; and global Pentecostalism emerged amid social and political instability. Similarly, today's Church faces unique pressures: digital saturation, cultural pluralism, institutional scepticism, and widening generational divides. Yet, these are not threats to be feared they are signs to be read, contexts to be interpreted through the eyes of faith.

If this is indeed the threshold of a new era, it is not marked by novelty for novelty's sake, but by a fresh call to deeper alignment with Christ. It is a season that demands courage to question, humility to listen, and faith to obey. It is not the Gospel that must change, but our postures, less defensive, more discerning; less performative, more prayerful; less fixated on what was, more attuned to what God is doing now.

The Church must rise as both student and servant in this emerging age. We must learn again how to carry the unchanging truth of Christ into evolving realities, speaking with relevance without compromising reverence. This means reimagining discipleship, reforming leadership, restoring prophetic voice, and rebuilding community not for survival, but for faithful witness.

The Holy Spirit is not silent. The shifts we sense are not merely social—they are spiritual. Moreover, while we cannot predict the full shape of what is to come, we can choose how we respond. With open hearts, wise minds, and surrendered lives, we are invited to participate in the unfolding work of God in our time.

APOSTOLIC BENEDICTION

THE APOSTOLIC-PROPHETIC Mandate: Bringing the Kingdom of God to Your Sphere of Influence has taken us through the rich dimensions of faith, theology, and practice, inviting every believer to step fully into their role as an ambassador of the Kingdom. From the firm foundation of foundational theology to the dynamic work of the Holy Spirit, from biblical interpretation to practical expressions of leadership and mission, this book aims to equip, challenge, and inspire.

We began by anchoring our faith in the study of church history and theology, recognising their power to shape convictions and sustain spiritual depth. We explored the principles of sound biblical exegesis and hermeneutics, learning how to rightly divide the Word of truth. We examined the person and work of the Holy Spirit, including His presence in worship, empowerment in ministry, and role in our personal and communal transformation.

Our study of practical theology emphasised the hands-on nature of Kingdom living, highlighting leadership, servanthood, and the Church's apostolic mission. We gave attention to the vital role of women in apostolic ministry, affirming their contributions and confronting the challenges they continue to face. We embraced unity in diversity, affirming that the Kingdom advances most powerfully when every part of the Body is honoured and activated.

Throughout, we have considered the forces shaping today's Church technology, cultural transformation, and emerging theological paradigms. Rather than retreat in fear, we are called to engage with wisdom and boldness, allowing the unchanging Gospel to speak into a rapidly evolving world.

The invitation of this book is clear: embrace the Apostolic Mandate. Let your faith extend beyond personal devotion into public transformation. As citizens of the Kingdom, we are called to carry its values into our families, workplaces, ministries, and nations. In prayer, worship, service, and proclamation, may we be led by the Spirit and marked by Christlikeness.

As this book closes, may it continue to stir within you a deepened passion for God's purposes. May it serve as a guide, a source of strength, and a call to action. Go forth unashamed, Spirit-empowered, and Kingdom-minded. Let the love and truth of the Gospel flow through you into every sphere of your influence, and may your life bear lasting fruit for the glory of God.

ABOUT THE AUTHORS

DR. VOLKER AND DORINE M. KRÜGER are co-founders of *The Apostolic-Prophetic Hub*, a ministry dedicated to equipping leaders, reforming Church structures, and aligning the Body of Christ with its end-time mandate. As a married couple called to walk in apostolic and prophetic partnership, they serve together with one voice, one mission, and one Spirit-led purpose: to restore biblical patterns of Kingdom leadership.

Volker Krüger, Ph.D., is a theologian, management scholar, and international speaker known for his work on apostolic reformation and organisational transformation within the Church. With a dual background in theology and management, he offers rare insight into how apostolic hubs and the five-fold ministry can be implemented practically.

His ministry has influenced churches and leaders across Europe, calling them to rediscover their apostolic identity.

Dorine M. Krüger is a prophetic teacher, author, and intercessor whose writings and teachings are rooted in divine revelation and deep scriptural reflection. Having lived in Uganda, Germany, and the United Kingdom, she brings a global perspective to her prophetic voice. Dorine is the author of *Iron Eagle Mum*, *Garden to Gut*, and *Revival Echoes*, and her work consistently calls believers to spiritual awakening, holistic healing, and identity in Christ.

Together, the Krügers serve through *The Apostolic-Prophetic Hub* as a living expression of the biblical synergy between the apostolic and prophetic. Their ministry equips the saints, strengthens leaders, and rebuilds Kingdom foundations one life, one church, one region at a time.

www.ingramcontent.com/pod-product-compliance
Lightning Source LLC
Chambersburg PA
CBHW020053200426
43197CB00050B/506